A Pilgrim's Spiritual Handbook to the Holy Land

Franciscan Custody of the Holy Land
1400 Quincy Street, NE
Washington, DC 20017

A Pilgrim's Spiritual Handbook to the Holy Land

BY DAVID WATHEN, OFM

Franciscan Custody of the Holy Land
Washington, DC 20017

*I humbly dedicate this book
to my pilgrims
— past, present and future —
for sharing our journeys
to the Holy Land.*

TABLE OF CONTENTS

"Five Gospels record the life of Jesus. Four you will find in books and one you will find in the land they call Holy. Read the fifth Gospel and the world of the four will open to you."

— ST. JEROME, FOURTH CENTURY

FOREWORD

Since the early fourth century pilgrims from every walk of life have traveled to the Holy Land to follow in the footsteps of Jesus. Through wars and strife and the storms of life, they have come to see firsthand the sacred places where he lived and worked his ministry and proclaimed the Gospel.

For nearly 25 years, I have led many groups on pilgrimage to Israel, Jordan and Egypt. It has been my privilege and honor to serve as a spiritual director and pilgrimage guide for these followers of Christ who arrive with searching hearts and curious minds. For many, it is their one and only opportunity to visit the holy sites so dear to all true Christians. They want to see for themselves the places of Christ's birth, the towns where he preached and healed, and the city where he suffered, died and was resurrected for our salvation.

To enrich the experience of my pilgrims and to answer their questions, I have relied on many helpful guidebooks through the years. Some focus on biblical history and archeology; some on the prayers and hymns appropriate for visits to the holy sites; others on the rich and fascinating stories of the shrines themselves.

In recent years, there have been occasions when an out-of-date reference has me thumbing through different guides to find the accurate information that I need. Often I've spent precious time trying to address a difficult or controversial question from the various sources at hand which has left me with conflicting versions of an event.

Having to consult my bulky mobile library of dog-eared guides has left me wishing there were a single handy reference book for my groups to enhance our journey together. A book that would weave together the various strands of divine revelation and early-church history and spiritual reflection without ever losing sight of the golden thread of Jesus' life that brought us here.

As a Franciscan, my main purpose is to point the way to Jesus, no matter what particular subject I am trying to illuminate. *A Pilgrim's Spiritual Handbook to the Holy Land* hopes to accomplish the same goal.

First and foremost, it is a practical, easy-to-read guide that celebrates the landscape where Christ lived, where present-day pilgrims can hopefully catch glimpses of the ancient world that can still instruct and delight after two thousand years.

It is called a "handbook" because it can be used as a pocket reference that can be carried and read everywhere, whether walking on a crowded Jerusalem street or riding on a bus through the desert, or standing under the open sky in rough terrain. A handy and durable guide to dip into amid the hustle-and-bustle of a pilgrimage or to delve into more carefully in a quiet moment alone.

Secondly, it is a book that is meant to last long after the pilgrimage is over, a book that can take a worthy place on the shelf to be consulted and meditated on for many years to come. Even perhaps, to serve as an inspiration for a friend or relative or to anyone who's always wondered what it would be like to go to the Holy Land themselves. I can only hope that a chance perusal of this book will lead more pilgrims our way!

To these ends, there are extensive quotations from Scripture woven into the text to illuminate the Gospel narrative at the sites where they occurred. For the quotations, I have used the Revised Standard Version Catholic Edition.

There are also sidebars to enlarge your appreciation of the history of the faithful from centuries past who made their own pilgrimages and recorded what they saw. Hopefully, these sidebars will help you feel an affinity and fellowship with those that came before us and gave witness to their time in the Holy Land.

With this handbook as your guide and prayer companion, I hope that you can better appreciate the sites of the Fifth Gospel with the eyes of a deepened faith. I also pray that it will help you listen ever more attentively to the voice of the Holy Spirit and savor more fully the Glory of the Holy Land.

Chapter One

Nazareth

Nazareth in the Gospels

It has been described as the greatest surprise in human history: God took on flesh and became man. Our God is a God of surprises. Not even the wisest of wise men or the prophets themselves could have dreamed that this greatest of all surprises would come from such humble origins as Nazareth, a Jewish farming village so obscure and insignificant that it does not appear in the Old Testament or rabbinic literature.

For generations, the ancient Jews had been waiting with great anticipation for the coming of the Messiah. Their prophets had prepared them for his arrival, but what remained a mystery was what kind of a Messiah he would turn out to be. It was the subject of debates among their rabbinic scholars as well as the ordinary folk untrained in their sacred writings; but one thing was clear: they believed the chosen one would bring about the redemption of Israel.

Their hope intensified after the conquest of their land by the Romans whose pagan practices and heavy taxes had, for nearly a century, brought oppression and humiliation and a weariness of life. They longed for freedom and for a Messiah who would establish justice and righteousness in the world; for a Messiah who would bring peace to the land of Israel. They would not have to wait much longer as the time for the Prince of peace to enter this world had come ... but would he be the Messiah they expected?

The true light that enlightens every man was coming into the world. He was in the world, and the world knew him not. He came to his own home, and his own people received him not ... And the Word became flesh and dwelt among us, full of grace and truth, glory as of the only Son from the Father (Jn 1:9-11; 14). The Jews could never have imagined the Messiah that God would send would be his only Son, Jesus of Nazareth. It was an unexpected and quite unwelcome revelation. It was simply incomprehensible that God would appear in the form of a man, the humble son of a carpenter. Later, when Jesus begins to reveal his true identity in the course of his public ministry, he finds that many of his own people simply reject him, and some even call him a blasphemer. He was not the kind of Messiah that the Jews were expecting, especially not from a place such as Nazareth, a town with a poor reputation in a remote region of Galilee.

A young Jewish maiden named Mary lived in Nazareth. The Gospels tell us nothing about Mary's early life, but it is fair to assume that she had been nurtured on the sacred writings and traditions of her people. She would have learned about the covenant that God had entered into with the Jews and how God had worked wonders for his chosen people. Mary took the words of their sacred books to her heart and she cherished them. Now she would be asked to accept the eternal Word in her womb.

In the sixth month, the angel Gabriel was sent from God to a city of Galilee named Nazareth, to a virgin betrothed to a man whose name was Joseph, of the house of David; and the virgin's name was Mary. And he came to her and said, "Hail, full of grace, the Lord is with you!" But she was greatly troubled at the saying, and considered in her mind what sort of greeting this might be. And the angel said to her, "Do not be afraid, Mary, for you have found favor with God. And behold, you will conceive in your womb and bear a son, and you shall call his name Jesus. He will be great, and will be called the Son of the Most High; and the Lord God

Annunciation, Henry Ossawa Tanner (1898)

will give to him the throne of his father David, and he will reign over the house of Jacob for ever; and of his kingdom there will be no end."

And Mary said to the angel, "How shall this be, since I have no husband?" And the angel said to her, "The Holy Spirit will come upon you, and the power of the Most High will overshadow you; therefore the child to be born will be called holy, the son of God.

And behold, your kinswoman Elizabeth in her old age has conceived a son; and this is the sixth month with her who was called barren. For with God nothing will be impossible. And Mary said, "Behold, I am the handmaid of the Lord; let it be to me according to your word." And the angel departed from her (Lk 1:26-38).

Upon learning of Elizabeth's pregnancy, Mary goes to be with her cousin to assist her in the final months of her pregnancy, travelling a distance of nearly 100 miles to a village near Jerusalem called Ein Kerem. Luke's Gospel tells us that Mary stayed with Elizabeth for three months, which suggests that Mary was present for the birth of John.

In his narrative of Jesus' birth, Matthew writes that before Joseph and Mary came together Joseph learns that Mary, his betrothed, is pregnant and he *being a just man and unwilling to put her to shame, resolved to send her away quietly* (Mt 1:19). But Joseph was visited by an angel of the Lord in a dream and was told to not be afraid to take Mary as his wife, as she conceived of the child through the power of the Holy Spirit. He did as the angel had commanded and took Mary as his wife. They made their home in Nazareth.

When the Roman ruler Caesar Augustus ordered a world-wide census, a simple tradesman such as Joseph dutifully obeyed the edict. So, even though Mary was in the advanced stages of her pregnancy, she and Joseph made the arduous journey from Nazareth to Bethlehem, the home town of Joseph's ancestor, David. After Jesus' birth in Bethlehem, Joseph is told in a dream by an angel of the Lord to take Mary and the child Jesus and flee to Egypt, because King Herod was planning to kill the newborn King of the Jews. A few years pass, when Joseph is once again visited by an angel of the Lord and is told to return to the land of Israel, *And he went and dwelt in a city called Nazareth* (Mt 2:23).

Jesus was twelve years old when his parents brought him to Jerusalem for the feast of Passover. After the celebration, Joseph and Mary began the journey home to Nazareth assuming that Jesus was among the crowd of fellow travelers but, in fact, he had stayed behind. When they returned to Jerusalem, they found him in the Temple sitting and conversing among the teachers, who were amazed at his understanding

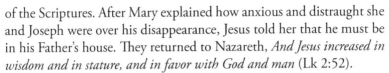
of the Scriptures. After Mary explained how anxious and distraught she and Joseph were over his disappearance, Jesus told her that he must be in his Father's house. They returned to Nazareth, *And Jesus increased in wisdom and in stature, and in favor with God and man* (Lk 2:52).

Jesus' public life began with his baptism in the Jordan River when he was *about thirty years of age* (Lk 3:23). This was followed by forty days of fasting in the desert, during which time he was tempted by the devil. Fortified by prayer and fasting, Jesus was now prepared to begin his task of proclaiming the kingdom of God.

Matthew records Jesus' decision to leave Nazareth and settle in Capernaum, a village on the northwest shore of the Sea of Galilee: *Now when he heard that John had been arrested, he withdrew into Galilee; and leaving Nazareth he went and dwelt in Capernaum by the sea* (Mt 4:12). The evangelist does not give an explanation for Jesus' decision to move to Capernaum. Perhaps it was because of its strategic location on one of the busiest trade routes in the eastern Mediterranean, the Via Maris (Latin for "Way of the Sea"), which would make it possible for his words and reports of his miracles to travel quickly to distant regions.

Once in Capernaum, Jesus began to proclaim: *"The time is fulfilled, and the kingdom of God is at hand; repent, and believe in the gospel"* (Mk 1:15). He heals the sick, he expels demons, and he works many other wonders. His fame spreads rapidly. From Capernaum, Jesus traveled to other cities and villages in the Galilee preaching the Gospel of God.

In the course of his travels, Jesus began to gather his disciples, the twelve apostles who would be entrusted with the task of bringing their Master's message of salvation to the entire world. John writes that Jesus found Philip and said to him *"Follow me"* (Jn 1:43). Without hesitation, Philip became Jesus' disciple. Later Philip found Nathaniel, and said to him *"We have found him of whom Moses in the law and also the prophets wrote, Jesus of Nazareth, the son of Joseph."* Nathaniel said to him, *"Can anything good come out of Nazareth?"* (Jn 1:45-46). Apparently, Nathaniel did not have a high regard for Nazareth, perhaps reflecting the prevailing attitude of the time.

On one occasion Jesus visits his home town of Nazareth, and he preaches a sermon that enrages the local populace for its radical teachings:

And he came to Nazareth, where he had been brought up; and he went to the synagogue, as his custom was, on the Sabbath day. And he stood up to read; and there was given to him the book of the prophet Isaiah. He opened the book and found the place where it was written,

"The Spirit of the Lord is upon me, because he has anointed me to preach good news to the poor. He has sent me to proclaim release to captives and recovery of sight to the blind, to set at liberty those who are oppressed, to proclaim the acceptable year of the Lord."

And he closed the book, and gave it back to the attendant, and sat down; and the eyes of all in the synagogue were fixed on him. And he began to say to them, "Today this scripture has been fulfilled in your hearing." And all spoke well of him, and wondered at the gracious words which proceeded out of his mouth; and they said, "Is not this Joseph's son?" And he said to them, "Doubtless you will quote to me this proverb, 'Physician, heal yourself; what we have heard you did at Capernaum, do here also in your own country.'" And he said, "Truly, I say to you, no prophet is acceptable in his own country. But in truth, I tell you, there were many widows in Israel in the days of Elijah, when the heaven was shut up three years and six months, when there came a great famine over all the land; and Elijah was sent to none of them but only to Zarephath, in the land of Sidon, to a woman who was a widow. And there were many lepers in Israel in the time of the prophet Elisha; and none of them was cleansed, but only Na'aman the Syrian." When they heard this, all in the synagogue were filled with wrath. And they rose up and put him out of the city, and led him to the brow of the hill on which their city was built, that they might throw him down headlong. But passing through the midst of them he went away (Lk 4:16-30).

The passage that Jesus read from the book of the prophet Isaiah refers to the works of the Messiah. Jesus is saying, in effect, I am the Messiah. Because the residents of Nazareth had known Jesus for most of his life this claim was too much to accept. They must have thought to themselves: "We know who he is; he is the son of Joseph, a carpenter. He cannot be the Messiah." To make matters worse, Jesus seemed to be telling his audience, in his references to the prophets Elijah and Elisha and their ministry to Gentiles (non-Jews), that because they did not have faith in him the Gospel's message of life-saving grace will be preached to others, even to the Gentiles. The crowd's hostile reaction shows how little faith they did have in Jesus.

There is no record in the Gospels that Jesus ever set foot in Nazareth again.

Nazareth and its Principal Sanctuaries in History

From obscurity and disparagement to today's status as one of the Christian world's most venerated pilgrimage sites, Nazareth has endured a tumultuous history in the centuries since Jesus walked its streets and preached to the people. The archaeological artifacts and ruins help us understand some of what has happened here over more than three millennia.

Artifacts found on site indicate the presence of inhabitants in the area of what would one day become Nazareth dating back to the Middle Bronze Age (2100-1550 BC). However, archaeological evidence suggests that Nazareth did not come into existence as a village until the third or second century BC. This may explain why Nazareth is not mentioned in the Hebrew Scriptures as most of the Old Testament canon was already established by that time.

Scholars estimate that the village's population in Jesus' time was a few hundred families. Its economy was primarily based on agriculture and the raising of livestock which is evident from the many silos, cisterns and stone feeding troughs uncovered in excavations by the Franciscan archaeologist Bellarmino Bagatti. A professor of biblical archaeology at the Studium Biblicum Franciscanum in Jerusalem, Bagatti conducted his excavations around the area of the Grotto of the Annunciation in the late 1950s prior to the construction of the modern basilica. Some of what he uncovered of the primitive village can be seen on the north side of the modern church from the stairwell leading to the upper terrace. It is also possible to visit the museum adjacent to the antiquities site which houses some of the artifacts uncovered by Bagatti and others from earlier excavation periods. See the curator for access to the museum.

The Grotto of the Annunciation is the central point of interest for pilgrims coming to Nazareth and today it rests in the very heart of the modern basilica. Tradition holds that Mary was in this grotto when the angel Gabriel appeared to her to announce that she had been chosen to be the Mother of our Savior.

Fortunately, much of the original grotto still remains today for pilgrims to view and before which they may pray, recalling what many spiritual writers have described as being one of the greatest mysteries of our faith: the Incarnation. One of the more popular prayers offered at this site is the Angelus prayer which begins with the words "The angel of the Lord declared to Mary, and she conceived by the Holy Spirit." In this Grotto *"the Word became flesh"* (Jn 1:14).

It's one of those moments of grace for which so many pilgrims make the journey here from all corners of the world: the mystery of God's love, which is so great that he would send his Son into the world to suffer and die for us, is revealed right here in this humble cave. This is where heaven meets earth. This is where Mary's "Yes" allowed God to enter the world as a man to bring to completion his plan for our redemption.

Based on his excavations of the site, Bagatti suggests that a synagogue/church used by Jewish Christians had been built over the grotto in the second to third century time frame. With the establishment of Christian rule in the Holy Land in the Byzantine period (fourth to seventh centuries) Christians were free to build houses of worship. A pilgrim woman known as Egeria visited Nazareth in the late fourth century, and in her diary she writes that there was no church there but that she did see the grotto. At the end of the fourth century St. Jerome, a resident of the Holy Land, indicated in a letter written to the Roman matron Marcella that her pilgrimage itinerary would include Nazareth, but there is no mention of a church. By the sixth century, however, an anonymous pilgrim from Piacenza (c. 570) writes that he saw a church on the site of Mary's house.

Archaeological evidence supports these observations. Today in front of the grotto to the southeast you can see remnants of the fifth-century basilica and a remnant of a mosaic floor to the southwest of the grotto, dating also to the fifth century, which contains Christian symbols of various kinds, including a crude form of the cross known today as the Jerusalem Cross. The Jerusalem Cross depicts one large cross with each of the four arms of equal length, and four smaller crosses of the same design placed in the four corners of the large cross.

After the conquest of the Holy Land by the Islamic armies in 638, Christian rule of the land came to an end after nearly three centuries, and Nazareth gradually became an Arab town with Christians and Muslims

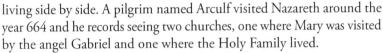

living side by side. A pilgrim named Arculf visited Nazareth around the year 664 and he records seeing two churches, one where Mary was visited by the angel Gabriel and one where the Holy Family lived.

The Crusaders arrived in 1099 and established Nazareth as an archbishopric. They began the work of building a large basilica over the Grotto of the Annunciation. Nearly as long as a modern football field and incorporating the ruined Byzantine church, this cathedral was mostly finished by 1106. Crowned by three apses at the east end, it became a major pilgrimage site and helped transform Nazareth into a flourishing Christian city.

Nazareth was probably abandoned by Christians in 1187 after the defeat of the main Crusader army by Saladin's Islamic forces. Later, the town and its cathedral church were destroyed by the Mamluke Sultan Baybars in 1263. Some of the remains of the Crusader basilica can be seen near the grotto. On either side near the entrance of the grotto the bases of two large pillars from the Crusader church can be seen. Behind the grotto, incorporated in the north wall of the modern basilica, are several courses of stone that once formed part of the north wall of the Crusader church.

In 1620, the Franciscans succeeded in acquiring the grotto through negotiations with the Druze Emir Fakr ed-Din, prince of Sidon. The Franciscans built a small chapel over the grotto in 1730. Over the next two centuries there were some modifications made to the chapel. This chapel was demolished in 1954 to make way for the modern basilica. Before work began on the modern basilica, excavations were conducted in order to better understand the historical developments of this sacred site.

Basilica of the Annunciation

With its massive, imposing concrete dome, the modern Roman Catholic basilica dominates the skyline of Nazareth, now one of the largest Arab cities in Israel. It is a symbol of the Church as a living, universal faith that unites people from all over the world. The basilica was commissioned by the Franciscans who asked the architect Giovanni Muzio for a design that would be "modern, multinational and mysterious." As the largest Christian house of worship in the Holy Land, it is one of Christianity's holiest shrines, commemorating that great mystery

of our faith, the Incarnation of the Word.

Many of the elements of previous structures on this site from the Judeo – Christian era, the Byzantine and Crusader churches, and from the Franciscan churches' religious art work from the eighteenth and nineteenth century churches were masterfully incorporated into the modern basilica. It is meant to give the pilgrim a sense of being part of a long and glorious history of fellow Christians who have come to see with their eyes of faith the great things God has done for us in sending his Son into our world at this sacred site.

When Pope Paul VI visited Nazareth in 1964, the basilica was only a shell. The modern basilica was consecrated on March 23, 1969 by Cardinal Gabriel Garrone. It was constructed on roughly the same foundations of the twelfth-century Crusader church. The unique shape and design of the dome, towering 180 feet above the town, is based on the Madonna lily, symbolizing the purity of the Virgin Mary, which appears as a visual motif in so many priceless paintings of the Annunciation.

Entering the enclosure of the basilica compound through the main gate from the street brings the pilgrim face to face with the massive west façade, which is crowned with a bronze statue of Jesus overlooking and blessing his home town of Nazareth. Below his statue, in stone relief, is an image of the angel Gabriel greeting Mary to announce her destiny and below, the words "The Angel of the Lord declared to Mary" (from the Angelus prayer) in Latin.

Further down the façade is a depiction of the four evangelists with the symbols associated with their respective Gospels (left to right): Matthew with the angel; Mark with the lion; Luke with the ox; and, finally, John with the eagle. To the left and the right of the evangelists are two Scripture passages related to prophesies about the role of Mary and Jesus in salvation history. To the left a passage in Latin from the Book of Genesis which reads in English: *"The Lord God said to the serpent … he shall bruise your head and you shall bruise his heel"* (Gen 3:15). Earlier in this passage God told the serpent that he would put *"enmity between you and the woman and between your seed and her seed"* (Gen 3:15). The woman mentioned in this passage is seen to be a prefiguring in Eve of Mary, and *"her seed"* is seen to be an allusion to Jesus' role in bringing about the redemption of humanity. To the right a passage in Latin from the

Book of the Prophet Isaiah which reads in English translation: *"Behold, a young woman shall conceive and bear a son, and shall call him Immanuel"* (Is 7:14). Beneath the evangelists are the Latin words, translated into English: *The Word became flesh and dwelt among us* (Jn 1:14).

On the portico walls on the south and west sides of the enclosure can be seen numerous portraits of Mary given by people from all over the world. There are more portraits of Mary in the upper church. Many of them present an image of Mary as she is venerated within their own respective nations or regions. For example, the people of Mexico donated a mosaic panel depicting Our Lady of Guadalupe which can be seen in the upper church. Of all places in the world, it is entirely appropriate that Christians should want to honor this simple maiden woman here in the town of Nazareth where she became the Mother of God.

Entrance to the basilica is through the right door directly ahead which leads to the lower level. One of the unique features of this basilica is its two levels; most basilicas have an open nave reaching from the floor to the ceiling. The lower level invites the pilgrim to approach the sacred grotto where Mary encountered the angel Gabriel and which is the principal point of interest for pilgrims visiting Nazareth. This area is mostly unadorned and dimly lit to help create an atmosphere of awe and reverence for the mystery being recalled at the site. The oculus above the grotto allows some natural light from the upper basilica to fall on this sacred site. Looking up through the oculus, pilgrims can see the magnificent interior of the Madonna-lily dome which features the letter "M", for Mary, repeated many times in rows which climb to the top of the dome. Pilgrims are permitted to walk by the Grotto stopping for a brief prayer, but access to the interior is blocked by an iron gate.

Inside the Grotto under the altar is an inscription with the words in Latin, "Verbum Caro Hic

The Grotto of the Annunciation

29

Factum Est," translated into English: "Here the Word became flesh."

A spiral staircase in the northwest corner of the basilica leads to the upper church. More Marian portraits can be seen on both the north and south walls. One of the more striking portraits of Mary is the mosaic panel given by the people of Japan which features hundreds of pearls used to form her mantle.

A large mosaic above the high altar depicts the Holy Trinity in the center and Mary seated on a throne. Members of the Church look toward the center. The theme of the mosaic as proclaimed by the Latin words at the top is "One, Holy, Catholic, Apostolic Church," from the Nicene Creed. The upper level is used by both pilgrim groups and the local parish for the celebration of the Eucharist. There are about 4000 members of this parish, mostly Arabs. The Franciscans in the community attached to the basilica look after the pilgrims and staff the parish, celebrating Mass, hearing confessions, and performing other ministries.

Take the exit through the door on the north side of the upper church to an elevated terrace. A museum that displays some of the antiquities of the ancient village of Nazareth discovered here is located under the terrace at the northern end. It is well worth a visit to better understand the ways of the people in the olden time when Jesus lived here.

Among its artifacts are several beautifully carved capitals found in 1908 in a nearby cave. These exquisite capitals were covered with debris and were likely being prepared for installation in the Crusader church, but were never put in place. There is also a base of a column on which was inscribed the words "Hail Mary" in Greek, the first words of the Ave Maria, the most popular of all Marian prayers. Scholars believe this inscription was made well before Marian devotion became popular after the Council of Ephesus in 431, at which the Council Fathers declared Mary to be the Mother of God.

St. Joseph Church

After the magnificent, overwhelming grandeur of the basilica, St. Joseph's Church offers an intimate, peaceful sanctuary away from the hustle and bustle of the crowds. A visit here is like going back in time centuries ago, epitomized by the medieval Romanesque exterior, with rough unadorned stone walls, and inside, an airy vaulted interior.

To get there, walk north about 100 yards across the terrace and up some steps to reach the rustic-looking church. As mentioned earlier, the pilgrim Arculf (c. 664) wrote that he saw the place where the Savior grew up and that there was a church on the site, known by the locals as the Church of the Nutrition of Jesus. It is thought that the site he refers to is the location of the present-day church.

The Crusaders built a church on the site in the twelfth century. After their expulsion from Nazareth it was destroyed, most likely at the same time as the Crusader cathedral church in 1263. In 1734 the Franciscans bought the site and in 1914 finished the work of building the modern Church of St. Joseph, honoring the site as being, according to tradition, the home of the Holy Family.

The present-day church was built on the ruins of the Crusader church and has two levels. In the crypt, there is a mosaic-covered basin which is thought to have been a pre-Constantinian baptismal font or pool. A cave system can be seen which also includes remains of cisterns and silos, apparently used for storage of grain and water in pre-Byzantine times.

Ornate stained glass windows decorate the upper part of the church, depicting in symbols, the Litany of St. Joseph; and near the altar frescoes depicting scenes from the life of Jesus and the death of St. Joseph. This upper part of the church is used by pilgrim groups as well as by the local parish community for the celebration of the Eucharist.

Synagogue Church

Exit the main gate of the basilica's enclosure then turn right (north) and walk through the souk (market place) a distance of about 100 yards to reach the Synagogue Church. Tradition holds that the Crusader structure on site today marks the location of the synagogue of Jesus' time. The Greek Catholic Church cares for this shrine. Here we recall Jesus reading from the scroll of the prophet Isaiah followed by his commentary, where he proclaimed their fulfillment as himself as the anointed one, which prompted the locals to want to throw him off the brow of the hill on the edge of town (Lk 4:16-30). The synagogue of Jesus' time is where he would have studied the Scriptures and learned to read Hebrew.

Church of St. Gabriel – Church of Mary's Well

About a mile northeast of the basilica is the Church of St. Gabriel, which is under the care of the Greek Orthodox Church. It was finished in 1750 and recalls, according to tradition, an encounter between Mary and the angel Gabriel at the spring of Nazareth. According to the apocryphal gospel of St. James, Mary was drawing water from the spring when the angel Gabriel first appeared to her. Since this is the site of the only fresh water spring in Nazareth, Mary would have come here often to draw water for the needs of the Holy Family. Upon entering the church, walk straight ahead until you see steps descending beneath a vaulted ceiling, likely dating to the Crusader period, to the source of the spring. On the left is a small recess with a shaft into which a cup can be lowered to draw water from the spring.

Fellow Pilgrims: Nazareth

Few places in the Holy Land have inspired more devotion and love from pilgrims than Nazareth. Among prominent early pilgrims was **St. Jerome**, accompanied by the Roman noblewoman **Paula** and her daughter **Eustochium,** who stopped here on pilgrimage in the late fourth century.

By the time that **Arculf,** a Bishop from Gaul, made his visit in the seventh century, Christians from far and near were flocking to shrines in the sleepy town, now a popular destination point. Arculf gives a description of what these early pilgrims would have seen on their visit:

"We remained two days and two nights at Nazareth, which is on a hill, and is also without walls, but it has large houses of stone, and two very large churches. One of these is raised upon mounds and arches connecting them, and under it, between the mounds, is a clear fountain, from which all the citizens draw water in vessels, which they raise up into the church by means of pulleys.

St. Jerome, painting by El Greco

On this site stood formerly the houses in which our Lord was nursed when an infant. The other church was built on the site of the house in which the archangel Gabriel came to the blessed Mary."

For a sense of reverence and piety, modern-day pilgrims can learn from the example of **St. Louis of France**, who visited in 1254. He gives us the scene of a medieval king humbling himself before his royal retinue, as he dismounts from his horse to pay his respects to the place that gave the world its Savior. "As soon as he came in sight of the holy town, he left the saddle and threw himself on both knees in prayer. Then proceeding on foot in all humility, he came to the holy town and entered the holy place of the Incarnation. That day he fasted on bread and water, in spite of his fatigue. With what devotion he behaved, with what solemnity and splendor."

More than four centuries later, Protestants had joined the throngs of travelers who continued to make the arduous journey to Palestine, even with some of the landmarks and shrines reduced to rubble. **Henry Maundrell**, a clergyman with the Church of England, shows how much had been lost since the days of the Crusaders:

"We went to see the house of Joseph, being the same, as they tell you, in which the Son of God lived for near thirty years, in subjection to man. Not far distant from hence they show you the synagogue where our blessed Lord preached that sermon by which he so exasperated his countrymen. Both these places lie north-west from

St. Louis of France

the convent, and were anciently dignified each with a handsome church, but these monuments of Queen Helena's piety are now in ruins."

Despite the ravages of time and wars that can make church buildings as ephemeral as man, the dusty little town of Nazareth itself remained as a witness to the past and, most importantly, to the life of Jesus.

Even a famous skeptic such as **Mark Twain** was touched by what he saw there in 1869, as part of a pilgrimage group from the United States. What struck the great author and satirist most about Nazareth was the same thing that has drawn so many here through the ages: the palpable sense that here one can truly walk in the footsteps of Jesus. As the creator of those timeless heroes of boyhood, Tom Sawyer and Huck Finn, Twain was charmed and disarmed by the small-town ambience of Nazareth, where he could easily picture to himself the carpenter's son growing up here and having the same sort of adventures as Tom and Huck did in the hamlet of Hannibal, Missouri. It was almost as if Twain could see traces of Jesus as a boy around every corner, as real as the place where he was raised.

"Nazareth is wonderfully interesting because the town has an air about it of being precisely as Jesus left it, and one finds himself saying, all the time, 'The boy Jesus has stood in this doorway – has played in that street – has touched these stones with his hands – has rambled over these chalky hills.'"

It was the site of the tiny Grotto of the Annunciation that humbled Twain the most, as he writes with a tone of awe and wonder not usually associated with one of the greatest-and

Mark Twain

most merciless-satirist of the modern era:

"We entered the great Latin Convent which is built over the traditional dwelling place of the Holy Family. We went down a flight of fifteen steps below the ground level and stood in a small chapel tricked out with tapestry hangings, silver lamps and oil paintings. A spot marked by a cross in the marble floor, under the altar, was exhibited as the place forever made holy by the feet of the Virgin when she stood up to receive the message of the angel. So simple, so unpretending a locality to be the scene of so mighty an event!"

Chapter Two

Ein Kerem

Ein Kerem in the Gospels

The title of this section is a bit misleading, as the episodes in Luke's Gospel associated with the village of Ein Kerem – Mary's visitation to her pregnant cousin, Elizabeth, and the subsequent birth of St. John the Baptist – do not mention a specific site by name. Luke simply informs us that, *In those days Mary arose and went with haste into the hill country, to a city of Judah* (Lk 1:39). We are left to rely on tradition to locate the places linked with these joyful events, which inspired Mary and Zechariah, priest and the husband of Elizabeth, to give us two of the most beautiful canticles in all the Scriptures: the Magnificat and the Benedictus.

When the angel Gabriel greets Mary in Nazareth to announce that God had chosen her to be the Mother of *"the Son of God"* (Lk 1:35) he also tells her: *"behold, your kinswoman Elizabeth in her old age has also conceived a son; and this is the sixth month with her who was called barren. For with God nothing will be impossible"* (Lk 1:36-37). With her cousin in the advanced stages of her pregnancy, Mary did what was natural; she went to assist Elizabeth in her time of need.

Mary entered the house of Zechariah and greeted Elizabeth. And when Elizabeth heard the greeting of Mary, the babe leaped in her womb; and Elizabeth was filled with the Holy Spirit and she exclaimed with a loud cry, "Blessed are you among women, and blessed is the fruit of your womb! And why is this granted to me, that the mother of my Lord should come to me? For behold, when the voice of your greeting came to my ears, the babe in my womb leaped for joy. And blessed is she who believed that there would be a fulfillment of what was spoken to her from the Lord." And Mary said,

"My soul magnifies the Lord,
and my spirit rejoices in God my Savior,
for he has regarded the low estate of his handmaiden.
For behold, henceforth all generations will call me blessed;
for he who is mighty has done great things for me,
and holy is his name.
And his mercy is on those who fear him
from generation to generation.
He has shown strength with his arm,
he has scattered the proud in the
imagination of their hearts,
he has put down the mighty from their thrones,
and exalted those of low degree;
he has filled the hungry with good things,
and the rich he has sent empty away.
He has helped his servant Israel,
in remembrance of his mercy,
as he spoke to our fathers,
to Abraham and to his posterity for ever."

And Mary remained with her about three months, and returned home (Lk 1:39-56).

Mary's journey from her hometown of Nazareth to the village of Judah, Ein Kerem, would have been an arduous one. It was 100 miles across a remote and lawless region with bandits and other dangers. And this risky excursion was undertaken by a teenage maiden who was pregnant as well. Such was Mary's concern for Elizabeth that she accepted the hardships so that she might give comfort and aid to her beloved cousin.

Luke does not tell us whether Mary had any companions or how she managed to complete the trek through the mountains of Judea. This has led to speculation by artists through the ages who have offered their own interpretations. A lovely example of this tradition is what we see in the large mosaic built into the façade of the present-day Church of the Visitation. The artist depicts Mary on a donkey leaving Nazareth as she rides toward Ein Kerem where Elizabeth awaits. Who accompanies the Mother of God on this perilous journey? Angels, of course!

When Mary greets her elderly kinswoman, Elizabeth is filled with the Holy Spirit and exclaims *"Blessed are you among women, and blessed is the fruit of your womb!"* (Lk 1:42). Elizabeth knew that Mary carried the Savior in her womb because the Holy Spirit had enlightened her to perceive what the eye could not see. And she is humbled that the Mother of the Lord would grace her with such a visit. While deeply grateful for Mary's presence, Elizabeth is also overwhelmed by the mystery of God's singular gift to Mary, of choosing her to be the Mother of his Son.

Elizabeth tells Mary that, upon hearing her cousin's voice, the babe in her womb leaped for joy. John, the unborn child of Zechariah and Elizabeth, rejoiced when his mother heard the voice of Mary because John, whose role will be to prepare the way of the Lord, has a premonition of the glory to come. He knows that God's plan for salvation is now upon them.

In a wonderful parallel from the Book of Samuel in the Old Testament, this Visitation event is foreshadowed

The Visitation, Miguel Cabrera (18th century)

in the story of David dancing before the Ark of the Covenant as it is being brought to Jerusalem, its new home (see 2 Sam 6:14-15). Just as David danced for joy before the symbol of the old covenant – the Ark containing the Law of God – John now leaps for joy before Mary, the Ark of the new and eternal covenant carried within her womb.

Mary's response to Elizabeth, a canticle of praise and gratitude to God, the Magnificat, recalls words that, throughout the centuries since, have resounded around the world. Its verses reveal Mary's profound humility in recognizing herself as the one chosen by God. She attributes to God all that has been bestowed upon her; she recognizes his works of justice and mercy through the ages, and his faithfulness to his people Israel.

Mary stayed with Elizabeth at her home for three months. Since the angel Gabriel had told Mary in Nazareth that her kinswoman was six months pregnant, this indicates Mary was likely present for the birth of John.

Earlier in this narrative from Luke's Gospel, we learn about the visit of the angel Gabriel to Zechariah while he was performing his priestly duties in the Temple in Jerusalem. The angel tells him that his wife, Elizabeth, will conceive and bear a son, and that his name is to be John. He asks how this can be, since he was an old man and his wife was barren and advanced in years. Because he does not trust in God's power to achieve his purposes, he is struck dumb until the moment his son John is named on the day of his circumcision.

Luke tells us that Elizabeth, upon becoming aware of her pregnancy, goes into seclusion for five months. This suggests Elizabeth went to live at another, perhaps a second home, such as a summer home, when Mary arrived to greet her. This traditional version of the account has been passed down through the ages, and locates the Visitation event at the present site of the Church of the Visitation on a hillside above Ein Kerem.

On the eighth day after the child was born to Elizabeth, the circumcision rite took place with friends and neighbors, as ordained by Jewish law. Those present asked Zechariah what the boy's name was to be. He motioned for a writing tablet and wrote: *"His name is John."And they all marveled. And immediately his mouth was opened and his tongue loosed, and he spoke, blessing God… And his father Zechariah was filled with the Holy Spirit, and prophesied, saying,*

> *"Blessed be the Lord God of Israel,*
> *for he has visited and redeemed his people,*
> *and has raised up a horn of salvation for us*
> *in the house of his servant David,*
> *as he spoke by the mouth of his holy prophets from of old,*
> *that we should be saved from our enemies,*
> *and from the hand of all who hate us;*
> *to perform the mercy promised to our fathers,*
> *and to remember his holy covenant,*

the oath which he swore to our father Abraham, to grant us
that we, being delivered from the hand of our enemies,
might serve him without fear,
in holiness and righteousness before him all the days of our life.
And you, child, will be called the prophet of the Most High;
for you will go before the Lord to prepare his ways,
to give knowledge of salvation to his people
in the forgiveness of their sins,
through the tender mercy of our God,
when the day shall dawn upon us from on high
to give light to those who sit in darkness
and in the shadow of death,
to guide our feet into the way of peace."

And the child grew and became strong in spirit, and was in the wilderness till the day of his manifestation to Israel (Lk 1:63-80).

Zechariah's words of thanksgiving and praise of God have become popularly known as the Benedictus, Latin for "Blessed," the first word in his canticle. The verses of this canticle speak about the fulfillment of God's promises and about John's role in preparing the way for the Savior.

Luke's mention of John being in the wilderness is the biblical basis for the local tradition identifying a cave about two miles from Ein Kerem as the place where John lived until he began his work of preparing the way of the Lord. Today, a Franciscan sanctuary with a chapel and monastery, known as St. John in the Wilderness, welcomes pilgrims to commemorate this tradition.

Birth of St. John the Baptist, Luca Giordano (between 1670 and 1679)

An apocryphal source called the *Proto-Gospel of James* contains a passage relevant to a tradition set in Ein Kerem. It relates a story connected with

Herod's slaughter of the innocents. Soldiers had raided Elizabeth's village on orders to kill all male infants according to the decree of Herod: "And Elizabeth, having heard that they were searching for John, took him and went up into the hill-country, and kept looking where to conceal him. And there was no place of concealment. And Elizabeth, groaning with a loud voice, says: O mountain of God, receive mother and child. And immediately the mountain was cleft, and received her. And a light shone about them, for an angel of the Lord was with them, watching over them."

The place in the mountain which opened to receive Elizabeth and John is associated with the grotto enclosed by the lower chapel in the present-day Church of the Visitation.

Ein Kerem and its Sanctuaries in History

As mentioned earlier, Ein Kerem is not identified in Luke's account by name as the site where Mary visited her cousin Elizabeth and where John the Baptist was born. We owe the association of those events with Ein Kerem to local tradition. It should be noted that the term *hill country of Judah* aptly describes the location of Ein Kerem, as it rests in a mountainous region of the biblical territory of Judah.

There is archaeological evidence demonstrating that Ein Kerem has been inhabited from the Middle Bronze Age (2100-1550 B.C.) through to the modern era. In particular, artifacts show that the village flourished during the Roman and Byzantine periods and later in the Crusader period. Among the ancient relics found were coins, the torso of a marble statue of Venus, oil lamps, shards of pottery, and remnants of Byzantine and Crusader churches.

The earliest account supporting the claim that Ein Kerem was Elizabeth's home is from the Archdeacon Theodosius, a pilgrim and chronicler, who wrote in his travel guide to the Holy Land (530 AD): "From Jerusalem to where St. Elizabeth lived, mother to St. John the Baptist, five miles." As it turns out, Ein Kerem is precisely five miles from the center of Jerusalem. In the late Byzantine period, early Arab period (seventh to eight centuries), a liturgical text called the *Jerusalem Lectionary* records these words celebrating a feast day: "28 August. In the village of Encharim [Encharim referring to Ein Kerem], in the church of the just Elizabeth, her commemoration."

The oldest textual eyewitness to the existence of two separate sanctuaries, one commemorating the visit of Mary and the other John's birth, dates from the fourteenth century: "Zechariah's house is in the mountains of Judea," wrote Brother Giovanni di Fedanzola of Perugia in 1330 after a pilgrimage to the Holy Land. "In this place there are two churches…and between these churches flows a spring that is quite full of water. At the site of the first church, it is said, Elizabeth was greeted by the Blessed Virgin Mary. It is also said that the blessed John the Baptist was hidden there during the Slaughter of the Innocents. At the site of the second church, the blessed John the Baptist was born."

There is little evidence to show the presence of a church in the Byzantine era on the site where the Visitation and the Rock of Hiding traditions are commemorated today. Remains of a cistern, the remnants of a foundation wall in the grotto and a portion of the tunnel above the well from this period suggest a structure that could have been a sanctuary.

At the site of John's nativity, though, there are considerable archaeological remains dating to the Byzantine period which indicate the presence of a church or churches. Excavations revealed a Byzantine era chapel (fifth century) on the west side of the present church under the porch. It is called the Chapel of the Martyrs due to a mosaic found in the ruins with the inscription: "Hail, martyrs of God." The identities of the martyrs remain unknown. This mosaic also displays figures of peacocks, doves, flowers and fruit. Perhaps the artist meant these symbols to represent Paradise, the eternal home of the martyrs commemorated in the chapel that once stood on this site.

The archaeological remains show that after the arrival of the Crusades in 1099, churches once stood at both the site of the Visitation and the site of John's birth. The Church of St. John, built by the Crusaders on the northern hill of the village, incorporated the grotto which local tradition held to be the birthplace of St. John. The Crusaders also accepted the local tradition that on the southern hill of the village, the Virgin Mary visited her cousin Elizabeth where she was staying when she went into seclusion upon learning of her pregnancy. Here, they built a church on two levels. The lower crypt chapel, containing the grotto of the spring, is also the site associated with the Rock of the Hiding.

After the departure of the Crusaders in 1187, the churches fell into ruin due to neglect and adaptation of the buildings by the locals. When the Franciscans arrived in the seventeenth century to take possession of the two sites, they found the churches in poor condition, both in need of major repair and restoration.

The Church of the Visitation

In a small verdant valley between Mount Herzl and the Hadassah Hospital, about five miles southwest of Jerusalem, sits the picturesque village of Ein Kerem, which means in Hebrew "the spring of the vineyard." Even today, one can see vineyards and terraced gardens on green slopes crowned with Italian cypress and Lebanese cedar and native pine trees. Here on the edge of town is an ancient spring, which gives Ein Kerem its name. The spring, located below an abandoned mosque, reminds visitors that this was once an Arab village.

This pastoral landscape was the setting for two of the most joy-filled stories recorded for us in the Gospels: the Visitation of Mary with Elizabeth and the birth of John the Baptist, now commemorated by beautiful Franciscan churches on sites that have beckoned pilgrims since early in the Christian era.

On the hillside a steep hike above Ein Kerem, tradition marks the mystical meeting of Mary and Elizabeth, known as the Visitation. For Christians, this encounter is an event shrouded in mystery as we learn how the Holy Spirit enlightened Elizabeth to understand that Mary carried in her womb the Divine Savior.

Today, a majestic church on the site commemorates this sublime mystery. Franciscans, the caretakers of the shrine on the hillside overlooking Ein Kerem, built the church, having purchased the property in 1679. Due to difficulties securing permission from the local authorities, they did not begin construction on the crypt chapel until 1862. In 1938, the Italian architect Antonio Barluzzi [see Sidebar on Antonio Barluzzi] began the design of the upper church. The church was consecrated on May 31, 1939. Further work on the church, including the creation of the frescoes, was interrupted by World War II. The frescoes were completed in 1953-4.

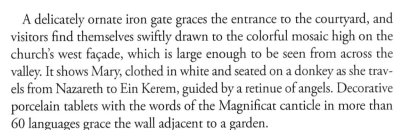
A delicately ornate iron gate graces the entrance to the courtyard, and visitors find themselves swiftly drawn to the colorful mosaic high on the church's west façade, which is large enough to be seen from across the valley. It shows Mary, clothed in white and seated on a donkey as she travels from Nazareth to Ein Kerem, guided by a retinue of angels. Decorative porcelain tablets with the words of the Magnificat canticle in more than 60 languages grace the wall adjacent to a garden.

Recalling the sacred encounter, in the presence of the Holy Spirit, between these two expectant women at this site, visitors often find themselves deeply moved. Here, God's mysterious plan for our salvation takes on a maternal dimension as we recall the two principal persons in this story, kinswomen upon whom God bestowed his special favor. Each will give birth to a son whose name was given by an angel sent by God. John, born of Elizabeth, will be the Precursor of the Lord, and Jesus, born of Mary, will be the Lord and Savior of the world.

From the courtyard, the entrance to the crypt chapel is on the left at ground level. This modern sanctuary, a masterpiece of design and devoutness, provides a loving tribute to Mary to remind us that all generations call her blessed. Barluzzi was careful to incorporate ruins from the existing Byzantine structure and Crusader church. Like the Crusader church, the modern church has two levels.

The lower-crypt chapel was built against the hillside at the spot where tradition says the mountain opened to protect the infant John and Elizabeth from Herod's soldiers. Today, a remnant of the rock which hid John can be seen on the right in a niche in the wall. The Latin inscription in the niche reads, "According to tradition Elizabeth hid John [behind] this rock." A small barrel-vaulted passageway in the east wall leads to an ancient well.

In the crypt chapel, three frescoes by the Italian artist Angelo della Torre adorn the walls. On the left, the priest Zechariah in his vestments offers incense in the Temple in Jerusalem. Above the well, a lovely pastoral scene shows Mary and Elizabeth together – the Visitation. On the right, the artist depicts the massacre of the Holy Innocents and the legend of the Hiding of John. In this scene, Elizabeth flees while carrying the baby John to a place where the angel directs them. Nearby, Herod's soldiers slaughter the innocent babes while their horrified mothers look on helplessly.

After exiting the crypt chapel, turn right and climb the steps through a garden to the upper church. Inside the Italianate bronze doors, the floor is covered with mosaics depicting plant and animal life. The imagery invites the visitor to join with Mary and Elizabeth in singing the praises of God for all of creation. The twelfth-century Crusader apse has been incorporated into the modern church. Part of the altar also derives from the Crusader period.

In the apse above the altar are five fresco panels by the Italian artist Fernando Manetti. In the central panel, Mary stands gracefully in the hill country of Judea flanked by her devotees, including the Franciscan Custos, Fr. Faccio, who presents her with a model of the church dedicated to her honor. Nearby is the Latin Patriarch of Jerusalem, Alberto Gori, in a gray robe, along with St. Francis, crowned by a halo. In the panel on the top left, Christians present Our Lady with models of important Marian churches from around the world. In the bottom left panel, Elizabeth receives Mary at her home. The top right panel features members of the many and diverse religious communities whose spirituality is centered on Marian devotion. On the bottom right, an unnamed woman in the Gospels calls out to Jesus after he had just expelled a demon from a man: *"Blessed is the womb that bore you, and the breasts that you sucked!"* (Lk 11:27).

High on the wall opposite the entrance are another series of fresco panels; these by the Italian artist Cesare Vagarini in the style of the late Renaissance Tuscan masters, celebrating Mary's titles and her intercession in salvation history. The Latin titles given by the Church for Mary have been placed under each panel. Nearest to the altar, one finds a scene of the Council of Ephesus (431), which decreed Mary to be the "Mother of God." In the next panel, Mary is depicted as "Refuge of those who hope in you" in her flowing robe, enveloping sinners from every race and nation who find refuge in her mantle, as she stands ready to intercede on their behalf before her Son's Throne of Mercy. Barluzzi, the church's architect, had himself painted into this panel, perhaps to show that he considers himself a sinner in need of Mary's maternal care. Look for the bearded gentleman in a suit and bowtie.

The middle panel shows the wedding feast at Cana, the place of Jesus' first miracle, which was prompted by a request from his Mother. It is the biblical basis for Mary's title "Mediator Most Powerful," and the root of our faith in her intercession. The next fresco depicts Don Juan of Austria receiving a blessing from the papal legate at the Battle of Lepanto (1571) when the Holy League armada led by Don Juan defeated the Turkish Ottoman fleet and saved Europe from Muslim invasion; this despite the fact that the Christian alliance was vastly outnumbered. The miraculous victory was attributed to Mary's intervention, and hence her title "Help of all Christians." Finally, in the last panel, the medieval Franciscan theologian, Blessed John Duns Scotus, defends the Immaculate Conception at the University of Paris (1307), representing yet one more title of Mary as the "Immaculate Conception."

The Church of St. John the Baptist

The forerunner of the Messiah, the one who was to *"prepare the way of the Lord"* was born on the site where today stands an imposing limestone sanctuary bearing his name, the Church of St. John the Baptist. Its spire rises above the town of Ein Kerem, where it has

Marble floor beneath the altar marking the birth place of St. John the Baptist

been a familiar landmark for over a century. From a cave within this church came forth the Precursor who would bear witness that Jesus is the Son of God. He would one day point out Jesus to the crowds gathered at the Jordan River and say: *"Behold, the Lamb of God, who takes away the sins of the world"* (Jn 1:29).

Inside the church to the left of the main altar are steps which lead down to a grotto, the traditional birthplace of John. The Franciscans found mostly ruins from the Crusader church and made minor repairs after purchasing the site in 1621. Later, with funding from the Spanish monarchy, they undertook extensive restorations during the next 200 years, taking care to retain as much of the Crusader-era church as possible. By the late nineteenth century, the renovated church, featuring a Spanish design with decorative glazed tiles and finely detailed iron work, was completed.

In the front courtyard, a wall bears tiled panels with the Benedictus canticle inscribed in more than three dozen languages. Climb the steps to the porch at the front entrance. Here a circular wrought-iron fence encloses an opening in the floor, allowing the visitor to see a mosaic remnant of the Byzantine chapel. Written in Greek, it reads "Hail Martyrs of God." Above the main entrance to the church, a plaque with a Latin inscription, roughly translated, reads: "This church, dedicated to the birthplace of the Holy Precursor, was restored by the Custody of the Holy Land through the generosity of the Catholic Kingdom of Spain. A. D. 1895"

Six massive pillars divide the dimly lit interior into three aisles. The walls and pillars are covered with marvelous blue and white tiles in the Majolica style, a gift from the Spanish royal family that sponsored the renovation. Sculptures, oil paintings and other works of sacred art, mostly by Spanish artists of the seventeenth and eighteenth centuries, adorn the church. To the right of the altar, above the sacristy door, the words, "The Beheading of St. John the Baptist," powerfully attest to this holy man's martyrdom.

Two paintings in the nativity grotto also deserve mention. The first, located above the steps leading down to the marble-encased grotto, "The Baptism of Jesus," offers an exquisite portrayal of the Gospel episode the moment when the Spirit of God in the form of a dove descends and rests upon Jesus. Above the white marble altar at the base of the grotto, a painting depicting the birth of John can be seen. And on the floor beneath the altar, a marble medallion with the Latin inscription, "Here the Precursor of the Lord was born," marks the site where the joyful words of the Benedictus were heard for the first time.

St. John in the Desert

About two miles from Ein Kerem sits a site on a wooded slope of the Judean hills which local tradition records as having been the place where John lived in seclusion before starting his public ministry. Apparently, the area had been deserted and isolated during John's lifetime; it served him well as a hermitage, where he could prepare for his work by dedi-

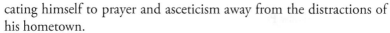
cating himself to prayer and asceticism away from the distractions of his hometown.

Some remains of a twelfth-century Crusader monastery and church still exists here, giving witness to the fact that the Crusaders accepted the local tradition that identifies the site as John's place in the wilderness. In 1586, Belgian pilgrim Jean Zuallart visited the ruins, and made drawings of what he saw, which made a deep impression:

"Leaving the Visitation, we decide to continue for another two or three miles, to visit the Desert where St. John the Baptist, guided and comforted by the Holy Spirit, spent his childhood until the day of his manifestation to Israel, preaching the Baptism of Repentance," he wrote. "When we reached this Desert, following a very difficult and dangerous path, we were filled with joy at seeing a place that was both so austere and beautiful, although now there are not as many trees as apparently there were in the past and it is very rough and harsh and far from any settlement."

The community of local Arabs, well known for maintaining traditional names of places for centuries, called the site Ain el-Habis, which translates as "Spring of the Hermit," due to the existence of a spring in the cave where John lived.

In 1922, the Franciscans built a chapel and monastery above the remains of the Crusader church. Today, the friars welcome pilgrims and curious locals who are drawn here both for the biblical significance of the site as well as its natural beauty. Orthodox Christians, as a manner of custom, immerse themselves in a pool which collects fresh water from the spring.

Follow a path that leads up the hill about one hundred yards to the chapel which encloses the place where John's mother, Elizabeth, was once entombed.

With its canopy of trees and lush vegetation, the site today looks more like an oasis than an arid desert as its name implies. Nonetheless, the site offers refuge from the bustle of the world, a place of reprieve for reflection and meditation. It is a fitting memorial to John the Baptist, who calls us to be attentive to the quiet voice and presence of Jesus.

Fellow Pilgrims: Antonio Barluzzi (1884-1960)

The Church of the Visitation was designed by the Italian architect and secular Franciscan Antonio Barluzzi, who devoted his life to the building of shrines in the Holy Land. His other masterpieces, two dozen in all, include the Church of the Beatitudes, the Basilica of the Transfiguration, Dominus Flevit, and the Basilica of the Agony.

When Barluzzi received his first commission in 1919 for the churches of Gethsemane and Mount Tabor, he wrote in his diary words of joy that echoed those of Mary and Elizabeth: "My heart leaps for joy, and I say, 'It is God's will.'" While embarking on his projects, Barluzzi lived and prayed and attended Mass with the Franciscans as a brother. He said the purpose of his work was to "translate by architecture the majesty and simplicity of the Bible" and he designed his churches to express as eloquently he could the sacred events they commemorate.

In 1958, Barluzzi's design for the rebuilding of the Basilica of the Annunciation in Nazareth

Portrait of Antonio Barluzzi

was rejected, a hard blow for him to endure. He had a heart attack and never regained his health. A visitor who saw him convalescing in his bare room at the Franciscan Terra Sancta Delegation in Rome said that the gaunt, dying 76-year-old "resembled nothing so much as a saint by El Greco." His churches endure as monuments to the mystery of faith, and they continue to inspire pilgrims from around the world. As the saying goes, "There are three types of architecture in the Holy Land: Greco-Roman, Byzantine, and Barluzzi.

Chapter Three

Bethlehem

Bethlehem in the Old Testament

Bethlehem is first mentioned in the Scriptures as a place of reference connected to the tragic loss of Jacob's wife, Rachel. Rachel died giving birth to her son, Benjamin, *on the way to Ephrath, that is, Bethlehem.* Jacob buried her at the place where she died and placed a pillar upon her grave (see Gen 35:16-20). In another Old Testament reference to Bethlehem, an unnamed Levite was asked by Micah of Ephraim to serve as his priest in a shrine he had constructed. The Levite identified himself as *"a Levite of Bethlehem in Judah"* (see Judg 17:7-13).

Bethlehem also provides the setting for the touching story of a Moabite woman named Ruth. Ruth's mother-in-law, Naomi, was an Israelite who had gone to live among the Moabites with her husband and two sons following a famine in Bethlehem, their home village. Naomi's two sons married Moabite women, one of whom was Ruth. Ruth had such a deep devotion to her mother-in-law that she insists on following Naomi back to her home town of Bethlehem after the death of their husbands: *"for where you go I will go, and where you lodge I will lodge; your people will be my people, and your God my God"* (Ruth 1:16). After settling in Bethlehem Ruth meets and marries *a man of wealth* named Boaz. From their progeny came one of the greatest figures of the Old Testament; they became the great-grandparents of King David (see Ruth 4:1-22). David's birth in Bethlehem secures its place in history since it is from his line that the Messiah (Christ) would descend (see Is 9:7); and it was in his home village that the *one who is to be ruler in Israel* would be born (Micah 5:2).

After the Lord had rejected Saul as king of Israel, he sends Samuel to

Bethlehem to anoint one of Jesse's sons to be Saul's successor. David, Jesse's youngest son, is called from tending the sheep, and when he comes into the presence of Samuel, the Lord says to Samuel *"Arise, anoint him; for this is he"* (1 Sam 16:12). The anointing of David with the horn of oil by Samuel foreshadows the coming of the Christ (from the Greek word "Christos," which means "anointed one") who will be anointed not with oil but with the Holy Spirit.

When David became king, it would have been natural for him to make Bethlehem his capital. But for reasons of political expediency, he chose Jerusalem to be his capital city. He needed to convince the tribal leaders that he was king of all the tribes and so he chose the neutral, centrally-located city of Jerusalem.

Once, while with some of his soldiers, David expressed a desire for some water from the well of Bethlehem, which, at that time, was occupied by the Philistines. Three of his men went to the well, and after returning safely with the water, David refused to drink it because of the great risk they'd taken (see 2 Sam 23:13-17). Rehoboam, king of Israel, fortified the city of Bethlehem, among other cities, *for defense in Judah* (2 Chron 11:5-6).

As mentioned above, the prophet Micah gives us the name of the humble village from which the future ruler of Israel would come: *But you, O Bethlehem Ephrathah, who are little to be among the clans of Judah, from you shall come forth for me one who is to be ruler in Israel* (Micah 5:1). After King Herod learned of the birth of a new king of Israel from the wise men who came from the East, he asked the chief priests and scribes where the Christ was to be born. Citing Micah's prophecy they told him *"in Bethlehem of Judea"* (Mt 2:5).

Bethlehem in the Gospels

Of the four Gospels only two evangelists, Matthew and Luke, give us an account of Jesus' birth. Fortunately, both narratives give different details related to Jesus' birth, enriching our encounter with this great mystery. Matthew begins his Gospel with the genealogy of Jesus, whom he describes as being *the son of David, the son of Abraham* (Mt 1:1). This genealogy was intended to establish Jesus' "Jewish credentials" – *the son of Abraham* – and to show that he was a descendent of David, which prophecy required of the Messiah. Scholars suggest Matthew's audience to be a Jewish Christian community, and his mission, to strengthen their faith in Jesus as being the long-awaited Messiah.

After giving Jesus' genealogy Matthew gets right to the point: *Now the birth of Jesus Christ took place this way* (Mt 1:18). Mary is found to be with child, and while after her betrothal to Joseph, the news comes before they came together. Joseph planned to divorce her quietly, but an angel of the Lord, in a dream, told him that he should not fear to take Mary as his wife; that she has conceived of the Holy Spirit. The angel also tells him to give the child the name Jesus, which means, "God is salvation," because he will save his people from their sins. Joseph did as the angel commanded him and took Mary as his wife (see Mt 1:18-25).

When wise men from the East arrive in Jerusalem and inform King Herod that they have come to worship the newborn king of the Jews, Herod became troubled. Extra-biblical historical sources describe Herod as a brutal ruler and capable of great cruelty toward anyone who threatened his rule (see Josephus' *Antiquities of the Jews*). He saw Jesus as just such a threat (see Mt 2:1-4).

Herod consulted with his chief priests and scribes regarding where the Christ was to be born, and they cite for him the prophecy of Micah, pointing to Bethlehem of Judea. The wise men are then told that they will find the child in Bethlehem but that they should return to Herod to give him word of their encounter, so that he could also worship the newborn king. Herod had no such intention of worshipping the child; rather, he planned to kill him. There could be only one king of the Jews (see Mt 2:5-8).

The star which the wise men saw in the East now led them to Bethlehem, to the house where the infant Jesus was with his Mother, Mary. They presented gifts of gold, frankincense and myrrh to the newborn Jesus, giving rise to the tradition that there were three wise men, since three gifts had been offered. In fact, Matthew does not mention the number of wise men. The wise men were told in a dream not to return to Herod, so they departed to their own country by a different route (see Mt 2:9-12).

Herod was furious when he discovered the wise men had tricked him. In his earlier conversation with them, he had asked them when the star

The Adoration of the Magi, Giuseppe Bartolomeo Chiari (1654-1727)

which they followed first appeared. Basing his calculations from the information they gave him, Herod ordered the killing of all male infants two years of age and younger in Bethlehem and its environs. The Holy Family escaped Herod's plans, since Joseph had been told in a dream to take the child and Mary and flee to Egypt. They stayed in Egypt until the death of Herod (see Mt 2:13, 16).

In those days a decree went out from Caesar Augustus that all the world should be enrolled. This was the first enrollment, when Quirinius was governor of Syria. And all went out to be enrolled, each to his own city. And Joseph also went up from Galilee, from the city of Nazareth, to Judea, the city of David, which is called Bethlehem, because he was of the house and lineage of David, to be enrolled with Mary, his betrothed, who was with child. And while they were there, the time came for her to be delivered. And she gave birth to her firstborn son and wrapped him in swaddling cloths, and laid him in a manger, because there was no place for them in the inn (Lk 2:1-7).

Luke makes no mention of the wise men; instead, he writes about the visit of some shepherds to the Christ child. It was night and shepherds were in the region of Bethlehem tending their flocks. Suddenly an angel appeared and they were filled with fear. The angel assures them that they need not fear; he had come to bring good news of great joy: *"for to you is born this day in the city of David a Savior, who is Christ the Lord."* Then a host of angels appear praising God: *"Glory to God in the highest, and on earth peace among men with whom he is pleased!"* The shepherds make their way to Bethlehem, where they found Mary and Joseph and the babe lying in a manger. The shepherds told Mary and Joseph what the angel had told them about the child. How mysterious these words must have sounded to the ears of Mary and Joseph. Who was this child destined to be (see Lk 2:8-20)?

Bethlehem and its Sanctuaries in History

The first mention of Bethlehem in history comes from a pre-biblical account in the *Amarna Letters* (fourteenth century BC) in which the king of Jerusalem asks the king of Egypt to send archers to help him in his efforts to recover Bit-Lahmi (Bethlehem), which had broken away from his jurisdiction. The *Amarna Letters*, found in Upper Egypt at Amarna, refers to correspondence on clay tablets between the Egyptian administration and its representatives in Canaan and Amurru during the New Kingdom.

Bethlehem's place in biblical history has been described above so we will now move to the post-biblical period.

Neither Matthew's nor Luke's account of Jesus' birth make mention of a cave. But Justin Martyr, a native of Palestine (born in Neapolis, present day Nablus) and a Christian apologist, writing in about the year 153, mentions that Jesus was born in a cave. The *Protoevangelium of James*, written about 150, also speaks of the cave in which Jesus was born. Origen, a prominent and sometimes controversial theologian from Alexandria, came to reside in Palestine in 216. He likely took advantage of time there to visit some of the holy sites and would have seen the Nativity cave with his own eyes. He, too, describes Jesus' birth as having taken place in a cave: "In Bethlehem you are shown the cave where he was born, and, within the cave, the manger where he was wrapped in swaddling clothes."

In order to dissuade Christians from visiting and venerating the site of Jesus' birth, the Roman emperor Hadrian had a grove of trees dedicated to the pagan god Adonis on the site of Jesus' birth. St. Jerome, writing in 395, gives this testimony: "From Hadrian's time (c. 135) until the reign of Constantine, for about 180 years, the Gentiles used to worship an image of Jupiter set up in the place of the Resurrection and on the rock of the Cross a marble statue of Venus... Bethlehem, now ours, and the earth's most sacred spot... was overshadowed by a grove of Thammuz, which is Adonis, and in the cave where the infant Messiah once cried, the paramour of Venus was bewailed." In attempting to desecrate the site, Hadrian reinforced efforts of local Christians entrusted with keeping in living memory the site's location. St. Cyril of Jerusalem supports Jerome's testimony by writing in 348 that the site was "wooded." The sacred grove was gone by the time St. Cyril wrote his comment about this site; a large basilica had been constructed over the cave in which Jesus was born.

Bishop Eusebius Pamphili of Caesarea, sometimes referred to as the first church historian, offers the most concrete information regarding construction of the first sanctuary on the site of Jesus' birth. In his *Life of Constantine*, we learn that he, Bishop Eusebius, and the Bishop of Jerusalem, Makarios, met Emperor Constantine at the Council of Nicaea (325). They may have been responsible for Constantine's decision to construct three churches on the sites commemorating the principal mysteries in Jesus' life: the birth of Jesus, his Death and Resurrection, and his Ascension into heaven. St. Helen, the mother of the emperor and a devout Christian, was present at the beginning of the construction of the basilica (a Greco-Roman model adopted by Christian architects) which began in 326. The Basilica of the Nativity was dedicated on May 31, 339.

The Constantinian basilica had an octagonal-shaped sanctuary situated directly over the Nativity Grotto with stairs nearby giving access to the cave. At the center of the sanctuary sat an altar directly above the Grotto. To the west of the sanctuary was a central nave and four side aisles created by four rows of ten columns each. The floor of the basilica was covered with mosaics, portions of which were uncovered during excavations carried out by the British Mandatory Department of Antiquities in the 1930s. These excavations, together with Eusebius' comments on the basilica, provide our principal sources of information regarding the Constantinian basilica. In the floor of the present basilica, trap doors in the floor, when open, reveal the mosaics of the Constantinian basilica.

In 382, at Pope Damasus I's commission, St. Jerome provided a revision of the old Latin translations of the four Gospels. Later, on his own accord, he decided to translate more books of the Bible, including a translation of the Hebrew Bible (Old Testament) into Latin. Moving to Palestine would have put him in close contact with learned rabbis and Hebrew scholars who could provide the manuscripts of the Hebrew Bible he needed for his translation work. In 384, he arrived in Bethlehem and began his work of translating the Hebrew Bible into Latin. The Bible he gave the Latin Church, the Vulgate, from the Latin word *vulgata (editio)*, means "(edition) prepared for the public."

About two years after his arrival in Bethlehem, St. Paula and her daughter, St. Eustochium, joined him. He had met these women of nobility in Rome and eventually became their spiritual director. St. Paula used her resources to construct two monasteries in Bethlehem; one for herself and her nuns, and another for St. Jerome and his monks.

Beneath the Basilica of the Nativity exists a series of caves said to have been used by Jerome for his translation work, and as a burial site for St. Paula (404), followed by her daughter St. Eustochium (c. 417), St. Jerome (420) and finally for the successor to St. Jerome as monastery abbot, St. Eusebius of Cremona. The Church today recognizes all four of these Bethlehem figures as saints; their images can be seen in bronze relief on the main doors of the modern Franciscan parish church of St. Catherine of Alexandria, on the north side of the Nativity basilica.

In 527 Justinian became the emperor of the Byzantine Empire. Christians living in the Holy Land during his reign experienced prosperity and growth. The non-Christians, however, did not always receive such favorable treatment, leading to the Samaritan revolt in 529 against Christian rule in the Holy Land, and resulting in serious damage to the Constantinian church in Bethlehem. After the defeat of the uprising, the Patriarch of Jerusalem decided to send a delegation, headed by St. Sabas, to Justinian to petition for help in restoring the church in Bethlehem. Justinian responded by sending an architect with instructions to restore the Constantinian church to its former glory.

Justinian's basilica retained the basic form of the previous church, but the octagonal sanctuary was replaced with a triple-apse structure. The nave was slightly extended to the west and a narthex was added. The Justinian church has been in continual use ever since.

But in 614, the arrival of a Persian army began a period of great suffering for the Christians in the Holy Land; countless thousands were massacred, including many monks, nuns and members of the clergy. The Persians' fourteen-year occupation of the land resulted in the destruction of nearly all the churches and monasteries across the land of the Bible built over the previous 300 years. It was a crushing defeat for the Byzantine Empire and traumatized Christians everywhere. The Persians did not, however, destroy the Nativity basilica. According to a letter written in 836 during the Synod of Jerusalem, the discovery of a mosaic on the façade of the church prevented its destruction;

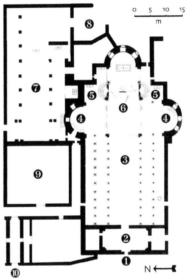

BASILICA OF THE NATIVITY: 1. Entrance. 2. Narthex. 3. Nave. 4. Transept. 5. Entrance to the Grotto. 6. Grotto of the Nativity and the Manger. 7. Parochial Church of St. Catherine. 8. Sacristy. 9. Medieval Cloister. 10. Entrance to the Franciscan Convent.

it depicted the Magi (from the East) presenting their gifts to the Christ Child wearing Persian garments. The letter from the Synod states that the Persian soldiers were amazed at the image of the Magi dressed like their fellow countrymen and that, "In respect and affection for their ancestors, whom they venerated as if they were alive, they spared the church."

In 628, the Byzantine emperor Heraclius successfully expelled the Persians from the land, but only ten years later, the Arab armies arrived from the Arabian Peninsula with their new religion – Islam - and overwhelmed the Byzantine defenses of the land. The Holy Land would be under Islamic rule for most of the next five centuries. In 638, Caliph Omar visited Bethlehem and prayed in the southern apse of the church. The Caliph gave the Patriarch of Jerusalem, Sophronius, a written guarantee that Moslems would only pray in the church singly and without chanting the Call to Prayer. This practice likely contributed to the church being spared, since, in 1009, the fanatical Fatimid caliph of Cairo, al-Hakim, ordered the destruction of all Christian monuments across the land.

When the first Crusader army arrived in the Holy Land in 1099, Bethlehem was secured before Jerusalem, since many feared the Nativity church would be destroyed by the Muslims. A force of about a hundred knights was dispatched by Godfrey de Bouillon, leader of the first Crusade, who, led by their captain, Tancred, claimed the Nativity basilica and placed it under Christian protection for the first time in nearly 500 years.

The Crusader period (1099-1187) was a time of rebirth for the town of Bethlehem and its holy sanctuary. The Nativity basilica became the setting for the coronation of the first king (Godfrey de Bouillon, the first ruler of the kingdom, refused to accept the title of king) of the Latin Kingdom of Jerusalem, established after the capture of Jerusalem on July 15, 1099. King Baldwin I was crowned king by the Patriarch of Jerusalem on Christmas day in the year 1100.

During the Crusader era, clergy for the Greek and Armenian churches continued to celebrate their rites in the Church of the Nativity along with Latin-rite Canons of St. Augustine, who took up residence next to the church. The Augustinian Canons built a monastery on the north side of the basilica, which is mostly intact today and currently occupied by the Franciscans. A general restoration of the church included the installation of mosaics on the interior walls and the painting of the images of saints from both the western and eastern traditions on the columns of the Justinian basilica. The Crusaders also installed a new cedar roof covered with lead. Pilgrims came in ever-increasing numbers, bringing prosperity and renewed hope for the few Christian inhabitants of the city of David.

But the Crusaders were obliged to relinquish control of the city to the newly victorious Saladin, the Islamic warrior who succeeded in defeating the main Crusader army at the Horns of Hittin in 1187. The Crusaders withdrew to the coastal areas of the land following their defeat by Saladin, and in 1291, were expelled from their last stronghold in the Holy Land at Acre.

In the post-Crusader period, different Islamic regimes gained control of the Holy Land, including the Ayyubids, followed by the Mamelukes and finally the Ottomans. It was a Mameluke sultan who allowed the Franciscans to take up residence in Bethlehem in 1347. In the subsequent centuries, the Franciscans and the Greeks both struggled to gain possession of the Nativity basilica. The two church communities sought support for their claims to the church from their respective governing authorities. In 1757, a decree by the Ottoman Turkish Sultan gave possession of the basilica to the Greeks, with some concessions to the Franciscans and the Armenian Apostolic Church. This arrangement, known as the *Status Quo*, is still in force today.

The Basilica of the Nativity of Our Lord Jesus Christ

Standing in the plaza in front of the church, one can gain some insight into how the history of this sacred site has developed over the centuries. Three church communities have acquired the right to officiate in the Church of the Nativity: the Greek Orthodox Church; the Armenian Apostolic Church; and the Roman Catholic Church, which is represented by the Franciscans. Each community has built a monastery adjacent to the basilica. While facing the western façade of the church, the Armenian monastery is on the right. Farther back to the southeast of the basilica is the Greek monastery. The Franciscan monastery is to the left on the north side of the church. The Franciscans also have a parish church, St. Catherine's, situated against the north wall of the Nativity church.

Notice in the masonry of the façade how the door has been lowered twice since the original door of Justinian's time, located just below the projecting lintel. The Crusaders lowered the door in the twelfth century, as indicated by the pointed arch in the masonry, then sometime after the departure of the Crusaders, it was lowered again, likely to prevent looting from the basilica. A small door called the Gate of Humility marks the main entrance to the Church of the Nativity today. To enter, all but small children must bow. For Christians, we symbolically recall our need to humble ourselves before our Divine Savior, who was born in such poor circumstances so that our lives might be enriched by his poverty.

Passing through the narthex and standing in the nave, the forty-four red limestone columns lining the north and south sides of the basilica come into view. The upper parts of the columns contain images of saints painted during the Crusader period. The saints depicted come from both the eastern (like St. Onuphrius and St. Macarios) and western traditions (such as St. Olaf, king of Norway; and St. Leo the Great) and include some biblical figures (Elijah, and St. John the Baptist among them) as well. In the southern aisle, sits an octagonal font, likely was constructed for the Justinian church. In the upper part of the nave, remnants of mosaics installed during the Crusader period can be seen. They depict ecumenical and regional councils in which various doctrines of the church were codified. At the top of the walls above the columns, one can see the mosaics depicting angels facing the Nativity grotto. Directly ahead is a raised platform and at its eastern end, the iconostasis (icon wall), constructed in 1764, which conceals the Greek altar behind it. The main body of the Nativity basilica is used by the Greek Orthodox Church as their parish church for the local Orthodox Christians.

On either side of the raised platform, steps lead down into the Nativity grotto. It is an accepted arrangement that large groups enter the grotto on the right, or south, side of the raised platform and individuals or small groups can enter from the north side. The entrance to the grotto is framed by a marble structure built by the Crusaders. After descending the steps from the south side and reaching the grotto, look to the right for a small altar. The Greek Orthodox and the Armenian Church share this altar for their liturgies. Under the altar, a fourteen-point star has been embedded in the floor with the Latin phrase, "HIC DE VIRGINE

MARIA JESUS CHRISTUS NATUS EST – 1717" (Here of the Virgin Mary Jesus Christ was born – 1717). The "HIC (Here)" in the inscription identifies this place as being where Jesus Our Savior was born into this world. The year 1717 apparently refers to the date of the placement of the star. Streams of pilgrims down through the centuries have wept tears of joy at this site, recalling the unfathomable love God has for us in sending his Son into our world to bring about our redemption. Many,

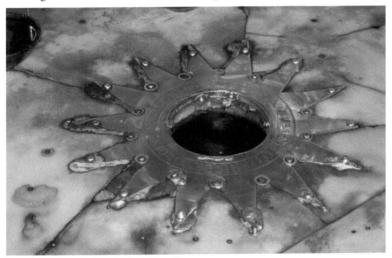

Star of Bethlehem marking the birthplace of Jesus

in a spontaneous show of affection, kiss the star and gently touch it with their fingers in recalling this joyous mystery of our Christian faith.

To the left at a lower level, the Chapel of the Manger comes into view. Its altar houses a painting above it showing the Magi presenting their gifts to the Christ child. The Franciscans and other Catholic groups alike share this altar for the celebration of Mass. Opposite the Altar of the Magi, one sees a marble-covered manger. From Christmas until the Feast of Epiphany, the manger includes a life-size statue of the infant Jesus lying on a bed of straw.

The grotto has a vaulted roof and an irregular, oblong shape. Asbestos tapestries line the walls. They were installed in 1873 after a fire in 1869 destroyed the furnishings and mosaics of the grotto. Oil lamps belonging to the three communities hang from the ceiling. Exiting the

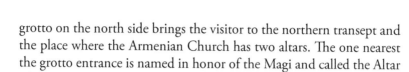

grotto on the north side brings the visitor to the northern transept and the place where the Armenian Church has two altars. The one nearest the grotto entrance is named in honor of the Magi and called the Altar of the Kings. The other altar is named for the Virgin.

Exit the Nativity basilica through the door in the north transept, which leads to the Church of St. Catherine (1881), the parish church for the roughly 4000 Arab Roman Catholics living in Bethlehem and neighboring villages. Turn right upon entering the Church of St. Catherine and descend a flight of stairs to reach a cluster of caves, which now serve as chapels for the celebration of Mass for visiting pilgrim groups. The first chapel encountered upon reaching the foot of the steps was named in honor of St. Joseph, who was given charge to serve as guardian of the Holy Family. Look left and you will find a small chapel with an altar honoring the Holy Innocents, the male infants put to death on Herod's orders. Notice the burial niches in the recesses of the cave. Turning west, a passageway leads first to St. Eusebius's tomb on the right, then farther along on the west wall of this chamber, to St. Jerome's burial site, and finally on the east wall, the burial site of the two Roman noblewomen St. Paula and her daughter St. Eustochium. A door on the north of this chamber leads to the Chapel of St. Jerome. St. Jerome is said to have used this space as his study while producing for the Roman Catholic Church a translation of the Bible into Latin known as the Vulgate. Above the altar, a mosaic panel shows the four saints whose bodies were once buried in these caves.

Exiting the cave structure, go directly ahead and look to the right for a side chapel with an image of Mary, and above her head, the Latin inscription "Tota Pulchra Es Maria" (You are all fair Mary). Beneath the altar, a statue of the Christ Child resting on a bed of straw. This statue is placed under the main altar of the Church of St. Catherine during the midnight Mass on Christmas. At the end of Mass, the Latin Patriarch blesses the people with the statue in his hands and then carries the "Bambino" (baby Jesus) to the Nativity grotto, where it is placed in the manger. The Church of St. Catherine, named in honor of St. Catherine of Alexandria, is the parish church for the local Catholics, and the site of the Christmas midnight Mass celebrated by the Latin Patriarch, usually attended by the political leaders of the Palestinian Authority. In

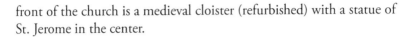

front of the church is a medieval cloister (refurbished) with a statue of St. Jerome in the center.

Milk Grotto

A short distance southeast of the Nativity Church, a shrine honors Mary as the mother who nourishes her divine child. The shrine is called the Milk Grotto, as local tradition holds that Mary, Joseph and the Christ child lived in this cave for some time after the birth of Jesus, and at one point while Mary was nursing the child some milk fell from her breast, turning the color of the stone in the cave milky-white. Local women from both the Christian and Moslem communities sometimes come here to pray that they will have a sufficient milk supply to nurse their child.

Few historical witnesses to the Milk Grotto exist prior to the arrival of the Franciscans to Bethlehem in 1347. We know the friars once planned to build a friary and chapel over the Milk Grotto in the late fourteenth century, but these plans never materialized. After many difficulties, the friars managed to build, in 1871, an oratory in the grotto with a friary and bell tower above the grotto.

As a sign of their devotion to the Milk Grotto, the locals donated the façade of the grotto. It displays some of the local talent featuring biblical scenes carved in stone relief. Among the imagery to be found on the façade is a depiction of the dream of Joseph being told by the angel to flee Bethlehem; and another relief of the Holy Family's Flight to Egypt. The oratory is decorated with mother-of-pearl carvings (a local craft) made by Bethlehem artisans. Even the steps leading down to the grotto are inlaid with mother-of-pearl.

Shepherds' Field

Just about a mile, but a world away from the crowds that throng the Church of the Nativity, sits a quiet hillside retreat where often the only sound is the breeze rustling through the tall, swaying cypress and long-needled pine trees. This is Shepherds' Field, where tradition says an angel told the shepherds of the birth of the Savior.

Today it is commemorated with a chapel and garden grounds that provides pilgrims with a peaceful setting to pause for reflection on the meaning of the Incarnation.

And an angel of the Lord appeared to them, and the glory of the Lord shone around them, and they were filled with fear. And the angel said to them, "Be not afraid; for behold, I bring you good news of a great joy which will come to all the people; for to you is born this day in the city of David a Savior, who is Christ the Lord.

And this will be a sign for you: you will find a babe wrapped in swaddling cloths and lying in a manger." And suddenly there was with the angel a multitude of the heavenly host praising God and saying, "Glory to God in the highest, and on earth peace among men with whom he is pleased!" (Lk 2:9-14).

While it cannot be known with certainty the location of this glorious event, the Shepherds' Field shrine provides an ideal place for recalling the moment when the news of our Savior's birth was first revealed to the world, beginning with the humble shepherds. The Franciscan caretakers of the shrine today welcome pilgrims to take a moment to give thanks for the gift of our Savior in a setting which evokes the kind of pastoral setting which the Gospel story relates. A cave east of the modern Shepherds Chapel likely has been used by shepherds down through the ages as a place in which to seek refuge from the elements and safeguard their flocks. Today, pilgrim groups celebrate the Mass in that cave.

Nearby are ruins of a Byzantine monastery, active from the fourth to the seventh centuries. Today outdoor altars have been set up among the ruins to provide prayer areas for the many groups who come to this site.

The Shepherds Chapel sits atop a small hill overlooking the site. Designed by the Roman architect Antonio Barluzzi, it was meant to resemble a shepherd's tent. Consecrated on Christmas day in 1954, the chapel was built with donations given by the people of Canada. An acknowledgement of their generosity can be seen in the image of a maple leaf inscribed on the front of the altar. The Latin inscription on the face of the altar translates: "Built with the help [of the people] of Canada, 1954." In the dome of the chapel, glass discs have been inserted to allow the sun to shine through, giving the effect of stars shining in the heavens, a scene common in the life of shepherds who often slept under the stars when the weather conditions allowed it. The beautiful frescoes by Italian artist Umberto Noni depict Luke's account of the appearance of the angel to the shepherds.

Chapter Four

Jordan River
and Jericho

The Jordan River in the Scriptures

Celebrated in countless hymns and spirituals, the Jordan River has watered the countryside of the Holy Land since time immemorial, and most importantly, it has fed the devotion of the faithful as a wellspring of spiritual renewal.

Formed by the union of three streams – the Senir, Hermon and Dan – which rise in southern Lebanon, northern Israel and the Golan Heights, the Jordan follows a meandering path for nearly 250 miles as it winds its way south to empty into the Dead Sea. The source of water for these streams is the winter rain and the melting snow from Mount Lebanon and Mount Hermon.

It is believed that the name for the river originates in a Hebrew root word meaning "to go down" or "to descend." Dropping in elevation more than 2,000 feet from its source streams to the Dead Sea, the lowest point on earth, the Jordan earns its title as "the descender." The river lies in a geographic trench known as the Great Rift Valley, which stretches across a vast distance of countries and climate from northern Syria to east Africa.

The portion of the Great Rift Valley between Mt. Hermon and the Dead Sea was known in the Scriptures – and even today – as the Jordan Valley.

The river, and the valley through which it flows, course their way throughout the entire span of the Scriptures. As one of the most familiar place names in the Bible, the Jordan appears nearly 200 times in the Old and New Testaments.

It is first mentioned in the story of the separation of Abraham and Lot, in the Book of Genesis. Abraham and his nephew Lot had possessions of flocks and herds and tents too great in number for them to dwell together peaceably. Abraham decided they needed to separate to avoid strife. Lot chose first: *And Lot lifted up his eyes, and saw that the Jordan valley was well watered everywhere like the garden of the Lord... So Lot chose for himself all the Jordan valley* (Gen 13:10-11). Abraham went west and settled in the land of Canaan.

In the Books of Deuteronomy and Joshua, the Jordan plays a major role in the destiny of the Chosen People. At the end of their 40-year journey in the desert following the exodus from Egypt, Moses and the children of Israel reached Mount Nebo, which overlooks the Jordan Valley and the Canaanite city of Jericho. Moses died on Mount Nebo, leaving Joshua to lead the Israelites across the valley into the Promised Land, which the Lord had pledged to Abraham and his descendants. The Lord instructed Joshua to have his priests carry the ark of the covenant of the Lord into the Jordan and have them stand on the river's bed. When they did so the current miraculously stopped, allowing the Israelites to cross over on dry ground to begin their settlement of the land of Canaan (see Deut 34:5; Josh 1-4).

In the Book of Joshua, the Jordan River provides an important bound-

Joshua Passing the River Jordan with the Ark of the Covenant, Benjamin West (1800)

ary marker to help divvy up the territories given as an inheritance to the tribes of Israel. The section of the river north of the Sea of Galilee served as an eastern boundary for the territory of the tribe of Naphtali (see Josh 19:33-34); the river south of the Sea served as an eastern boundary for the tribal territories of Judah (see Josh 15:5), Ephraim (see Josh 16:7), Benjamin (see Josh 18:12) and Issachar (see Josh 19:22).

The signs and wonders continued, as the waters of the Jordan were divided yet again, this time for Elisha, as the Lord had done for Elijah and for Joshua before him.

In the Second Book of Kings, the Lord instructed Elijah to anoint Elisha as his successor as the prophet of Israel. When he found Elisha in Abel-meholah, he placed his mantle on Elisha's shoulders, and by this action Elisha understood that he was being called into service of the Lord. Together they traveled to Jericho.

Later, Elijah informed his successor that they must part because the Lord had instructed him to go to the Jordan. Elisha insisted on accompanying him. When they arrived at the Jordan, Elijah rolled up his mantle and struck the water, which divided, allowing them to cross over on dry land. After reaching the east side of the Jordan, a flaming chariot and horses of fire appeared and separated them. Riding in the chariot of fire, Elijah was taken up in triumph to heaven in a whirlwind. As Elijah went away to heaven, his mantle fell to the ground. Elisha took up the mantle and went to the bank of the Jordan and struck the water, which divided, allowing him to cross on dry land (see 1 Kgs 19:16; 2 Kgs 2:4-14).

The healing power of the Jordan is highlighted in the story of Naaman. As the commander of the Syrian army, Naaman was held in high favor by his king *because by him the Lord had given victory to Syria. He was a mighty man of valor, but he was a leper.* Naaman's wife had an Israelite servant girl captured in a raid and she advised her mistress to have her husband go to see a prophet among her people *"who is in Samaria! He would cure him of his leprosy."* Armed with a letter from his master, Naaman went to the king of Israel, along with gifts of gold, silver and festal garments. The letter asked the king of Israel to heal his stricken commander. When the king of Israel read the letter from his arch enemy, he rent his garment *and said, "Am I God, to kill and make alive, that this man sends word to me to cure a man of leprosy? Only consider, and see how*

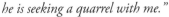

he is seeking a quarrel with me."

Elisha learned that Naaman had met with his king, hoping for a cure. He sent word to Naaman to come see him *"that he may know there is a prophet in Israel."* When the Syrian commander arrived at Elisha's house, a messenger was sent out to tell Naaman to wash in the Jordan seven times. Naaman became angry, convinced that the mighty rivers of Syria were far superior to the waters of the humble Jordan. But his servants persuaded him to do as the prophet had said. After he dipped himself in the water seven times, he was made clean, and his flesh was like that of a little child (2 Kgs 5:1-14).

Jesus made reference to this story in his sermon while visiting a synagogue in Nazareth. He took Elisha's healing of the foreigner Naaman as predictive that his Gospel message would be carried to all the nations (see Lk 4:27).

"Behold, the Lamb of God!"

Clothed in a garment of camel's hair homespun with a leather belt and living alone in the Judean wilderness on a diet of locusts and wild honey, John the Baptist recalled the hermetic and ascetic tradition of prophets like Elijah. He warned the crowds gathered around him at the Jordan River that it was time to *"Repent, for the kingdom of heaven is at hand."* He preached his fiery sermons at a place the evangelist John called *Bethany beyond the Jordan* near a busy crossroads and principal gateway to Jerusalem. The multitudes who were ready to accept John's words were baptized by him in the Jordan River, confessing their sins.

John's baptism was a baptism with water, a purification ritual meant to prepare the people for the arrival of the one called *"the Lamb of God, who takes away the sins of the world."* John knew his role was as a herald to rouse the people and proclaim the coming of the Messiah. He explained to his followers that there is one who would come after him *"whose sandals I am not worthy to carry; he will baptize you with the Holy Spirit and fire."* John was the Precursor, the voice of one called by God to prepare the way of the Lord. The time had come for Jesus to reveal himself as the long-awaited Messiah (Jn 1:19-36; Mt 3:1-11).

Then Jesus came from Galilee to the Jordan to John, to be baptized by him. John would have prevented him, saying "I need to be baptized by you, and do you come to me?" But Jesus answered him, "Let it be so now; for thus it is fitting for us to fulfill all righteousness." Then he consented. And when Jesus was baptized, he went up immediately from the water, and behold, the heavens were opened and he saw the Spirit of God descending like a dove, and alighting on him; and lo, a voice from heaven, saying, "This is my beloved Son, with whom I am well pleased" (Mt 3:13-17).

The Baptism of Christ in the Jordan River, Karoly Marko (1840-1841)

Why would Jesus come to the Jordan to be baptized by John? Was he not free from all sin? It is a reasonable question. The answer is not immediately clear until one begins to understand that Jesus journeyed to the Jordan not for himself, but for us. He came not to be made holy by the water, but to make the water holy by allowing his sacred body to purify and consecrate the water. By consecrating the water of the Jordan, Jesus consecrates the water used for all who come to the baptismal font to receive the grace of baptism. As the first baptized with water and the Spirit, Jesus prepares the way for all who pledge themselves to him, and are reborn through water and the Spirit.

When Jesus came up from the water, John the Baptist testified that: *"I saw the Spirit descend as a dove from heaven, and it remained on him"* (Jn 1:32). Jesus took on flesh so that he could receive the Spirit as one who shares our human condition; in doing so he fulfills God's plan for

restoring humanity to its original condition before the Fall of Adam.

Jesus received the Spirit so that we may receive the Spirit in him. It is this Spirit of adoption which makes us sons and daughters of God by our adoption in Christ Jesus. Once again, we see that Jesus came to be baptized in the Jordan not for himself, but for us:

"If we reason correctly, and use also the testimony of Scripture, we can see that Christ did not receive the Spirit for himself, but rather for us in him; for it is also through Christ that all gifts come down to us" (St. Cyril of Alexandria).

The Jordan River Today

Today there are no ancient ruins in the immediate area where pilgrims gather on the banks of the Jordan to commemorate our Lord's baptism. Instead, wooden platforms with access steps and handrails lead down to the river's edge, making it possible to safely enter the water. Some pilgrims, mostly Orthodox Christians, fully immerse themselves in the water three times to recall the moment they were born into the family of God. [See sidebar on Theodoric] Others take handfuls of water and bless themselves, or are blessed by a priest sprinkling them with the sacred water. Here at the Jordan, they recall their own baptism, the moment when they were *born, not of blood nor of the will of the flesh, nor of the will of man, but of God* (Jn 1:13). Christians come to this peaceful site from all over the world to recall the moment they became adoptive sons and daughters of the Father, a member of Christ's body and a temple of the Holy Spirit.

Some pilgrims are initially disappointed at the humble dimensions of the Jordan. Most of the year, the river is only 30 or 40 feet wide, and in most spots it is as shallow as a creek or a backyard swimming pool. It is possible to cross the Jordan, but not advisable! The river forms an international border between the West Bank and The Kingdom of Jordan. Israeli soldiers stationed on the west side and Jordanian soldiers on the opposite side keep a sharp eye on the pilgrims and other visitors to make sure the border remains secure.

About a hundred yards from the water's edge on the Jordanian side, ruins of ancient Byzantine churches still stand next to a dry river bed where the Jordan once flowed. Over the centuries, the river has changed

Traditional site of the baptism of Jesus with ruins from Byzantine-era churches

course due to earthquakes and other natural forces. These ruins mark the place venerated in the Byzantine period as the baptismal site of the Lord. A remnant also exists of a chapel built to honor St. Mary of Egypt, a former prostitute who converted to Christianity and came to live near the Jordan as a hermitess until her death in the mid-fifth century. [See sidebar on St. Mary of Egypt]

Less than a mile east of the Byzantine ruins is a small mound locals have for centuries called Tel Mar Elias, Arabic for the Hill of St. Elijah, said to be the place from which Elijah was taken up into heaven in a fiery chariot (see Kgs 2:2).

Today there are a number of churches under construction on the Jordanian side on land that the king of Jordan has given to Christian communities of various denominations. Nearest the river looms the gold dome of the Greek Orthodox Church. The other churches under construction – a total of about 12 planned – are being built by the Russians, Roman Catholics, Copts, and others.

About a mile from the Baptismal Site on the West Bank side of the

Jordan lies a sprawling, forlorn building on a hill to the left. This abandoned medieval monastery is named in honor of St. John the Baptist; a tablet above the entrance is inscribed with the Greek initials ICXC NIKA, which stands for "Jesus Christ Conquers," befitting its Crusader-era architecture. With its thick stone parapet walls, above which fly the national flag of Greece and the flag of the Greek Orthodox Patriarchate, it has the appearance of a fortress. For this reason, locals call it Qasr al Yahud, or Castle of the Jews in Arabic, in tribute to the crossing of the Jordan by Joshua and the Israelites, which tradition says happened in this vicinity.

Farther down the road are ruins of a Franciscan chapel and guest house (1935), and ruins of several other Orthodox churches. The churches and monasteries on the west side of the Jordan had to be abandoned after the war of 1967. During this conflict, known as the Six Day War, the West Bank fell into Israeli hands. Because this area was so close to a hostile border, the decision was made to plant land mines along the border to deter terrorist infiltrations and to slow the advance of any invading army.

Today the site, enclosed by a fence to prevent visitors from wandering into areas where land mines are still present, is under the supervision of the Israel Nature and Parks Authority. Modern structures have been built nearby to provide for both the material and spiritual needs of the visitors. White robes can be rented from the gift shop for those who wish to immerse themselves in the Jordan, with changing rooms and showers for the convenience of the pilgrims who take the opportunity to perform this ritual.

Jericho in the Scriptures

After a forty-year sojourn following their exodus from Egypt, Moses brought the children of Israel to the frontier of the Promised Land. The Lord then instructed Moses to *"Ascend this mountain of the Abarim, Mount Nebo, which is in the land of Moab, opposite Jericho; and view the land of Canaan, which I will give to the people of Israel for a possession; and die on the mountain which you ascend, and be gathered to your people"* (Dt 32:48-49). After blessing the people of Israel, Moses climbed to the summit of Mt. Nebo and saw below *the valley of Jericho the city of palm trees* (Dt 34:3). In addition to seeing the valley of Jericho, Moses was given a miraculous view of the Promised Land in its entirety, and then he died. The Lord told him that he would not enter the land because he *"broke faith with me in the midst of the people of Israel at the waters of Meribath-kadesh, in the wilderness of Zin"* (Dt 32:51).

After Joshua and the Israelites crossed the Jordan, they encamped at a place called Gilgal and made preparations for the siege of Jericho. Earlier, before the Israelites crossed the Jordan, Joshua had sent two spies to reconnoiter the land, especially Jericho. After the spies entered Jericho, the king of Jericho learned of their presence and sent soldiers to find them. A harlot, named Rehab, offered to hide the spies if they agreed to spare her life, and the lives of her family, after the city was taken. The spies agreed. The spies returned to Joshua, saying *"Truly the Lord has given all the land into our hands"* (Josh 2).

While encamped at Gilgal the Israelites kept Passover on the fourteenth day of the month in the evening, their first Passover in the Promised Land. The next day they ate the fruit of Canaan for the first time and the manna ceased. They had arrived in the Promised Land, the land flowing with milk and honey (see Josh 5).

In a story which has vexed readers of the Bible for ages, the Lord assumes the role of commander of the army of Israel when the time came for the conquest of Jericho. The Lord gave instructions to Joshua on how he was to take Jericho. He was told to have his men of war march around the city once every day for six days, accompanied by seven priests blowing their trumpets of rams' horns (shofars). The priests were to march in front of the ark of the covenant of the Lord. On the seventh day they were to march around the city seven times *"in the same manner."* The seventh time around, with the priests blowing their trumpets, Joshua said to the people *"Shout; for the Lord has given you the city."* The walls of the city fell flat and the Israelite men of war entered the city, putting all to the edge of the sword, including *men and women, young and old, oxen, sheep, and asses* sparing only Rahab and her family (Josh 6).

The territory allotted to the tribe of Benjamin included the city of Jericho (see Josh 18:21). In the period of the Judges the city was ruled by Eglon, the king of Moab, and *the people of Israel served Eglon the king of Moab for eighteen years.* When the people of Israel cried out to the Lord, *the Lord raised up for them a deliverer, Ehud.* Ehud led the Israelites in a successful battle against the Moabites, *And the land had rest for eighty years* (Judg 3:12-23).

After Elisha saw his master taken up into heaven, he returned to Jericho as the newly appointed prophet of Israel. Among their other duties, prophets in the biblical period oftentimes found themselves handling the complaints of the people. Elisha soon learned this lesson. Upon arriving in the city, the residents complained about the water from the spring saying it *"was bad, and the land was unfruitful."* Elisha took some salt from a new bowl and threw it into the water, and said, *"Thus says the Lord, I have made this water wholesome; henceforth neither death nor miscarriage shall come from it."* So the water has been wholesome to this day (2 Kgs 2:19-22).

During the period of the Maccabees, Ptolemy, the governor of the plain of Jericho, lured Simon the high priest and his two sons to the stronghold of Dok (known today as Jebel Quruntul, the Mt. of Temptation) for a great banquet. After his guests were drunk, in an *act of great treachery,* Ptolemy had them killed (1 Macc 16:11-17).

Then Jesus was led up by the Spirit into the wilderness to be tempted by the devil.

Immediately after Jesus was anointed by the Spirit and confirmed by the Father for his mission as Messiah and Savior, he is led by the Spirit into the wilderness to be tempted by the devil:

And he fasted forty days and forty nights, and afterward he was hungry. And the tempter came and said to him, "If you are the son of God, command these stones to become loaves of bread." But he answered, "It is written, 'Man shall not live by bread alone, but by every word that proceeds from the mouth of God.'"

Then the devil took him to the holy city, and set him on the pinnacle of the temple, and said to him, "If you are the Son of God, throw yourself down; for it is written, 'He will give his angels charge of you,' and 'On their hands they will bear you up, lest you strike your foot against a stone.'" Jesus said to him, "Again it is written, 'you shall not tempt the lord your God.'"

Again, the devil took him to a very high mountain, and showed him all the kingdoms of the world and the glory of them; and he said to him, "All these I will give you, if you will fall down and worship me." Then Jesus said to him, "Begone Satan! For it is written, 'You shall worship the Lord your

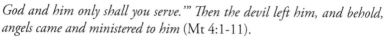

God and him only shall you serve.'" Then the devil left him, and behold, angels came and ministered to him (Mt 4:1-11).

Spiritual writers have often noted that when we successfully resist temptation to sin we demonstrate our love for God: *For this is the love of God, that we keep his commandments* (1 Jn 5:3). We demonstrate that love by choosing what God wants for us and not what we want for ourselves. When Jesus allowed himself to be tempted by the devil he did so not that he might demonstrate his love for his Father – the Father, Son and Holy Spirit are eternally joined in a perfect union of love – but rather, that he might give us, by his example, courage in resisting the temptations of the evil one. Jesus became like us in all things, except sin, and that includes being tempted to do that which is contrary to the will of his Father.

"If in Christ we have been tempted, in him we overcome the devil. Do you think only of Christ's temptation and fail to think of his victory? See yourself as tempted in him, and see yourself as victorious in him. He could have kept the devil from himself; but if he were not tempted he could not teach you how to triumph over temptation" (St. Augustine).

According to local tradition, the place of Jesus' first and third temptations was a mountain located less than a mile west of Jericho, called by the locals Jebel Quruntul, the Arabic form of Mount Quarantana (its name in the medieval period, which means Mount of Forty, referring to the forty days of Jesus' fast). Today it is more commonly known as The Mount of Temptation by Christian pilgrims who come to this site to remember how our Lord rebuked the evil one: *"Begone Satan!"*

As Jesus, accompanied by a large crowd, was leaving Jericho on his way to Jerusalem, he passed by a blind beggar named Bartimaeus. When the beggar learned that among the great multitude passing him by was Jesus of Nazareth, he cried out *"Jesus, Son of David, have mercy on me!"* The crowd tried to silence him, but he called out all the more *"Son of David have mercy on me!"* Jesus called for him and asked what he wanted. *"Master, let me receive my sight." And Jesus said to him, "Go your way; your faith has made you well." And immediately he received his sight and followed him on the way* (Mk 10:46-52).

Luke records that as Jesus was passing through Jericho, he saw a tax collector named Zachaeus in a sycamore tree. Zachaeus was a man of small stature and because the crowds made it difficult to get close to Jesus, he needed to gain some elevation if he was to see him. So he climbed a sycamore tree. When Jesus saw him he called him to come down and told him *"I must stay at your house today."* The people murmured *"He has gone in to be the guest of a man who is a sinner."* Zachaeus then declared to the Lord that he repented of his past evil deeds and that he would make restitution to those he defrauded. *And Jesus said to him, "Today salvation has come to this house, since he also is a son of Abraham. For the Son of man came to seek and to save the lost"* (Lk 19:1-10).

Pilgrims today stop at a large sycamore tree about a hundred yards from the modern city center to recall this story. It's situated on property which belongs to the Russian Orthodox Church. Near the tree the Russians built a museum which presents a history of Russian pilgrimages to the Holy Land.

Jericho in History

In the prehistoric period, a semi-sedentary people known as the Natufians settled next to a powerful perennial spring at a site known as Tel es Sultan. ("Tel" is an Arabic word which refers to a mound which has the remains of multiple layers of human-occupation debris.) They built a small brush-hut village, hunted the local wildlife, gathered wild barley, and buried their dead in nearby cemeteries.

Tel es Sultan is identified as the site of Jericho of the Old Testament. It was occupied then either destroyed or abandoned many times since people first settled on the site. In the 1950s, a British archaeologist named Kathleen Kenyon dug a trench on the west side of the Tel to investigate the different levels of occupation debris to learn more about the people who inhabited the site. Above the level of the occupation debris of the Natufians, she uncovered a 25-foot-high stone tower with internal steps which has been dated to around 8,000 BC, a period of history archaeologist call the Neolithic Age (New Stone Age). Evidence of a massive defensive wall from this period was also uncovered. These discoveries have led locals to boast that their city is the oldest city (10,000 years old) in the world. At an elevation of about 850 feet below sea level, Jericho can also make the boast of being the lowest city in the world.

Kenyon's interpretation of the archaeological finds uncovered at Tel es Sultan led to the controversial claim that there was no evidence of a walled city on the site during the period when it is thought Joshua destroyed the city, around 1200 BC. This is a claim which even today stirs debate.

On the east side of Tel es Sultan, across the modern road, is the spring which has made it possible for people to occupy the site for millennia. Known locally as Ain es Sultan (Arabic for Spring of the Sultan), but pilgrims call it the Spring of Elisha in honor of the prophet who healed its waters with salt. A modern red-roofed building covers the ground from which the spring rises. Today, the spring helps to sustain the modern city of Jericho, with a population of about 20,000 inhabitants.

The Mount of Temptation lies less than a mile to the west of the Tel. The summit has been identified as the place of the third temptation of Christ. A wall surrounding the summit gives it a fortress-like appearance. In 340, St. Chariton built the Laura of Douka on the site. The monastery was later destroyed, either by the Persians or the Arabs. The Crusaders built a church and fortress on the summit. They also built a church above the sacred grotto which marks the site of the first temptation. The churches and fortress were destroyed after their departure in 1187.

In 1874 the Greek Orthodox Patriarchate took possession of the summit and the site of the first temptation – a small cave in the side of the mount facing east about a third of the way down from the summit. The Greeks built the wall which surrounds the summit and made plans to build a church there, but it has not yet been realized. Ruins from the previous churches and monasteries of the Byzantine and Crusader periods can be seen within the enclosure of the wall. In 1895, the Greeks completed the construction of the monastery and the chapel in front of the sacred grotto. The chapel of the temptation, the southernmost chapel in the monastery, has a small white dome which can be seen from the plain of Jericho below. In this chapel, pilgrims can see the rock on which our Lord sat during his period of fasting and where he endured the first temptation.

During the Hasmonean (164-63 BC) and Herodian (37-4 BC) periods, the settlement of Jericho moved to the southwest of the Tel by about a mile, along the banks of Wadi Qelt. A hippodrome and theatre were constructed at this time to provide entertainment for the residents. Numerous palaces built by Jewish aristocrats also existed. Inhabitants of that period enjoyed spending time in Jericho during the winter months because of its mild weather conditions.

Herod the Great built an aqueduct system, which brought water from springs located farther west in Wadi Qelt. He also built a fabulous winter palace here, which included a swimming pool. The Jewish historian, Flavius Josephus, described in some detail Herod's death (4 BC) in Jericho and the elaborate royal funeral procession which brought his body to the Herodium Fortress for burial, a distance of about 25 miles (*Antiquities of the Jews*).

FELLOW PILGRIMS: JORDAN RIVER
St. Mary of Egypt (Fifth Century)

A pilgrimage to the Holy Land can be a life-changing experience. The legend of Mary of Egypt, the hermitess of the Jordan, reminds us that it is never too late to live the words of John the Baptist, to repent and be saved. Mary was a prostitute who accompanied pilgrims from Alexandria to Jerusalem, not to pay homage to the Lord but to continue her lustful ways. Out of curiosity, she joined the celebrants for the Feast of the Exaltation of the Holy Cross, hoping to gain new customers.

St. Mary of Egypt, Jusepe de Ribera (1651)

But when Mary tried to enter the Church of the Holy Sepulcher for the celebration, she was repelled by an unknown force. Realizing this was due to her wicked life, she prayed for forgiveness before an icon of the Blessed Virgin in the courtyard. Then she went into the church and venerated a relic of the true cross, when a voice told her to go live in the desert beyond the Jordan River where she would find peace for her soul and be saved.

Mary spent nearly 50 years as a solitary ascetic in the wilderness east of the Jordan, where she did penance for her sins, and was delivered of her temptations "by the spiritual meat of the word of our Lord." This is what she told a monk named Zosimus, who discovered an aged Mary with her clothes rotted away, her body wasted and sunburnt from years of exposure in the harsh desert climate. She asked him to meet her at the Jordan on Holy Thursday evening with the Holy Eucharist. Tradition says that Mary walked on the water to where Zosimus waited across the Jordan. Then she received Communion, asking him to come the following year to the spot where he had first met her.

There at the appointed hour, he found her corpse and next to it, scrawled in the sand, was her final request: "Zosimus, bury Mary's little body, return her dust to the earth, and pray for me to the Lord, at whose command I left this world."

Theodoric (Twelfth Century)

The custom of the faithful

Battle of Cresson, Sebastian Mamerot 1474 Knights of Templar

bathing in the Jordan River, as eastern Orthodox pilgrims still do today, is a tradition of great antiquity. Those pilgrims of olden times, however, often faced dangers that their modern counterparts could hardly imagine.

In the mid-twelfth century, the German monk Theodoric journeyed to the Holy Land and he described how pilgrims encamped on the banks of the Jordan under a military escort from the Knights Templars and Hospitallers, as protection against Muslim warriors. Here he tells of the beautiful, haunting spectacle of the candle-bearing throngs of pilgrims under the watchful eyes of the enemy along the Jordan one night long ago:

"When our humble selves had also visited this place in order to pray there, desiring to wash in the waters of the Jordan with the rest, we descended the mountain after sunset, just as darkness was coming on: and looking out from its heights over the flat plain below us, we saw, according to our reckoning, more than sixty thousand men standing thereon, almost all of them carrying candles in their hands-all of whom could be seen by the infidels from the mountains of Arabia beyond Jordan."

Chapter Five

Galilee

GALILEE

The dream of every pilgrim is to walk where Jesus walked, and the Galilee has the most places in the Holy Land where pilgrims can do just that. Along the peaceful shores of the Sea of Galilee are the sites where Christ worked his earthly ministry. Here is the hallowed ground where God, clothed in human form, lived and breathed and broke bread among his followers and performed miracles to help them believe.

From the scenic ruins of Capernaum to the Mount of Beatitudes, the region has a power to inspire and to renew one's faith in the unspoiled countryside, little changed from the Days of the Apostles. Let us begin with the place where Jesus came to live when he began his public life – Capernaum.

CAPERNAUM

Capernaum in the Gospels

There is no mention of Capernaum in the Old Testament, nor do we have any archaeological evidence of any settlement here during the Israelite period (1200-587 BC) when most of the Hebrew Scriptures were compiled.

However, by the time of the Roman rule of Palestine, Capernaum had become a prosperous, bustling Jewish town on the northwest shore of the Sea of Galilee. In the Gospels, Capernaum takes center stage as the adopted home of Jesus and the scene for many of Jesus' teachings and miracles. With Jerusalem as sole exception, Capernaum is the privileged setting of more Gospel stories than any other place in the Holy Land.

Matthew tells us that Jesus chose to live for a time here in this fishing village during his public ministry: *Now when he heard that John had been arrested, he withdrew into Galilee; and leaving Nazareth he went and dwelt in Capernaum by the sea.* Later in his Gospel, Matthew calls Capernaum Jesus' *own city* (Mt 4:12-13; 9:1).

After settling in Capernaum, Jesus called two local

Jesus walking on the Sea of Galilee, Paul Brill (1590s)

fishermen to be his disciples as they were casting their net into the water, Simon (*who is called Peter*), and his brother Andrew: *Follow me and I will make you fishers of men.* Farther along the shore line, he summoned another pair of brothers and fishermen, James and John, as his followers (Mt 4:18-22). In Luke's Gospel the call of these first disciples is preceded by the Miraculous Catch of Fish (see Lk 5:1-11).

Unlike Mark and Luke, Matthew does not explicitly say that Jesus' healing ministry began in Capernaum; instead he simply notes that Jesus *went about all Galilee, teaching in their synagogues and preaching the gospel of the kingdom and healing every disease and every infirmity among the people.* The people marveled at Jesus' miraculous healing powers and his authoritative teaching. His fame soon spread *throughout all Syria…and great crowds followed him from Galilee and the Decapolis and Jerusalem and Judea and from beyond the Jordan* (Mt 4:18-25).

In Mark's Gospel, Jesus came to Galilee after his baptism at the Jordan River. While walking along the Sea of Galilee, he calls four fishermen – Simon (Peter), Andrew, James and John – to be his disciples, to *become fishers of men.* Jesus would later nickname James and John "Sons of Thunder," apparently for their stormy temperament, always quick to rebuke the enemies of Jesus. Together they walk to nearby Capernaum and go to the synagogue because it is the Sabbath day. Jesus began to teach the people in the synagogue, and *they were astonished at his teaching, for he taught them as one who had authority, and not as the scribes.* Like Matthew, Mark also makes it clear that Capernaum became Jesus' home: *And when he returned to Capernaum after some days, it was reported that he was at home* (Mk 1:16-22; 2:1; 3:17).

Capernaum, in Mark's Gospel, has the honor and distinction of being the place where Jesus began his teaching and healing ministries, starting with an exorcism. As Jesus taught in the synagogue, a man possessed by an unclean spirit cried out: *"What have you to do with us, Jesus of*

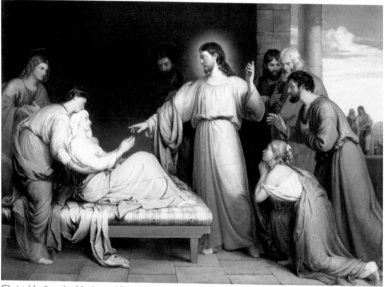

Christ Healing the Mother of Simon Peter's Wife, John Bridges (1839)

Nazareth? Have you come to destroy us? I know who you are, the Holy One of God." Jesus rebuked the unclean spirit, which shook the man with convulsions as it left his body with a shriek. Witnesses spread the news of the teachings and miracles of the Nazarene, and his fame spread like wildfire throughout Galilee (Mk 1:24).

After the synagogue service, Jesus visits the house of Simon (Peter) and Andrew and they tell him that Simon's mother-in-law has fallen ill with a fever. Jesus takes her by the hand and the fever leaves her immediately. That evening, Jesus heals many townspeople who had gathered outside Simon's (Peter's) house after hearing about the miracles Jesus had wrought. He also expels demons from others who are brought to him (see Mk 1:29-32).

Luke tells us that in the days after Jesus was rejected by his townspeople in Nazareth, he *went down to Capernaum, a city of Galilee*. Luke's account of Jesus' teaching in the synagogue of Capernaum, the expulsion of the demon, and the cure of Simon Peter's mother-in-law echoes closely that of Mark's (Lk 4:31-41).

John describes Jesus' first miracle as taking place at a wedding in Cana; it was the miracle of Jesus turning the water into wine. After the wedding feast, Jesus *went down to Capernaum, with his mother and his brethren and his disciples; and there they stayed for a few days.* It's interesting to note that John does not give his readers the impression that Capernaum became Jesus' permanent home; rather, it seemed to be more of a temporary base to minister to the growing crowds that came to hear his preaching and see his healing miracles (Jn 2:1-12).

Later, while visiting Cana once again, Jesus is approached by an official whose son is gravely ill at his home in Capernaum, about 15 miles away, a day's walking journey from Cana. He begs Jesus to heal his son. *Jesus said to him, "Go; your son will live."* When the official returns to Capernaum, he discovers that his son had been cured at the same hour Jesus had told him that he would live (Jn 4:46-54).

Now that it has been established that Capernaum became Jesus' *own city,* let us turn to some other healing miracles; to the momentous calling of the disciple Matthew; and to some shocking revelations Jesus publicly declares about himself and his true mission, all of which all took place in this Gospel city.

In Matthew's Gospel, Jesus stays engaged in his ministry all throughout Galilee for some time before he makes another visit to Capernaum. Just before his return, he delivers the Sermon on the Mount, one of his lengthiest and most luminous Gospel teachings. On his way down the mountainside, Jesus attracts a large crowd while heading to Capernaum, about a half-hour's walking distance. In the throng following him, a leper appears, kneeling before him saying, *"Lord, if you will, you can make me clean." And he stretched out his hand and touched him saying, "I will; be clean." And immediately his leprosy was cleansed.* Though a mere look or a word from Jesus could have accomplished the healing, he wants to make physical contact with the leper, considered an "untouchable," which shows us that Jesus excludes no one from the circle of his restorative love (Mt 8:1-4).

Unlike the other two Synoptic Gospels (Mark and Luke), Matthew does not mention Jesus teaching in the synagogue before visiting the house of Simon Peter. In Matthew's account, a Roman centurion approaches Jesus just as he arriving in Capernaum. One of the town's leading citizens, the centurion beseeches Jesus, saying, *"Lord, my servant is lying paralyzed at home, in terrible distress." And he said to him, "I will come and heal him." But the centurion answered him, "Lord, I am not worthy to have you come under my roof; but only say the word, and my servant will be healed."* Jesus is moved by the staunch faith of this Gentile, stronger than any he's seen thus far in his ministry, and tells him, *"Truly, I say to you, not even in Israel have I found such faith."* At this very moment, the centurion's servant is healed. Astute Catholics will recognize the words of the centurion declaring his unworthiness to have Jesus enter his house as being the words – with slight alteration – which communicants say before receiving Holy Communion at Mass (Mt 8:5-13).

Up to this point in Matthew's Gospel, Jesus' miracles and his authoritative teaching convinced many witnesses that Jesus is much more than any ordinary man. But who is he, really? In the story of the cure of the paralytic, Jesus reveals his divine nature with just one statement: *"Take heart, my son; your sins are forgiven."* The reaction is one of shock and fear. The bold claim that Jesus makes about himself here for the first time - authority to forgive sins, implying divine authority - will ultimately lead to his Passion in Jerusalem (Mt 9:2).

After returning by boat from *the other side* (the region of the Gadarenes on the northeast shore of the Sea of Galilee), Matthew tells us that Jesus *came to his own city.* Some locals brought a paralytic on his mat and set him before Jesus. Jesus simply tells the man his sins are forgiven. Some of the scribes there understand what Jesus claims about himself - that he has the power to forgive sin; a power reserved to God himself. Their hostile reactions are predictable: *"This man is blaspheming."* Jesus can read their thoughts and proceeds to demonstrate his authority to forgive sins by healing the paralytic. Upon witnessing this, the crowds become afraid *and they glorified God who had given such authority to men* (Mt 8:28; 9:1-8).

A remarkable call to discipleship follows this controversial healing. Matthew was a collector of taxes for the Roman government. It was considered a disreputable profession whose practitioners were often reviled as social outcasts. *As Jesus passed on from there, he saw a man called Matthew sitting at the tax office; and he called him, "Follow me." And he rose and followed him.* Matthew records no conversation between him

The Calling of Saint Matthew, Caravaggio (1599-1600)

and Jesus. He simply gets up from his desk and follows Jesus, leaving behind what was a lucrative (even if it was despised) profession to follow a vocation filled with physical want and hardship. Perhaps Matthew was well aware of Jesus' reputation and felt privileged to be called to be his disciple; hence the lack of any hesitation to follow him (Mt 9:9).

Matthew then records Jesus' teaching on the need for mercy in our relations with one another. This occurs as Jesus dines with guests whom the Pharisees considered sinners. The disciples of John the Baptist ask Jesus why his disciples do not fast, and he explains by drawing a parallel to the joy and celebration of a wedding feast, with Jesus as the bridegroom. He says that now is not the time for them to fast since the bridegroom is present; later when the bridegroom is taken away from them, then it will be the time to fast (see Mt 9:10-17).

While Jesus dines, an unnamed ruler (identified as a synagogue ruler named Jairus in Mark's Gospel, 5:22 and in Luke's Gospel, 8:41) comes and kneels before Jesus saying *"My daughter has just died; but come and lay your hand on her, and she will live."* Jesus rises and while on his way to Jairus' house, a woman suffering from a hemorrhage for twelve years approaches and touches the fringe of Jesus' garment, saying to herself, *"If*

I only touch his garment, I shall be made well." She was immediately cured. Jesus then goes into the house of Jairus, takes his daughter's hand and brings her back to life. Moving on from the house, two blind men approach Jesus, asking to be healed. They are healed after having professed to Jesus they believe he had the power to do so (Mt 9:18-31).

In chapter ten of Matthew's Gospel, Jesus described to his twelve disciples, in words with an

The Raising of Jairus' Daughter, Paolo Veronese, (1540s)

ominous tone, what discipleship required: *"Beware of men; for they will deliver you up to councils, and flog you in their synagogues, and you will be dragged before governors and kings for my sake, to bear testimony before them and the Gentiles."* This crucial part of Jesus' mission will prepare the twelve for the hardships ahead; for the rejection they will meet for preaching the name of Jesus, and the persecution they will experience, with most ultimately giving witness to their faith in martyrdom (Mt 10:5-42).

In the next chapter, Matthew tells us that Jesus has denounced Capernaum along with Chorazin and Bethsaida, nearby places that were part of his ministry, as cities which failed to repent after having witnessed so many of Jesus' mighty works. Like the rejection he receives in Capernaum, his disciples can expect the same while bringing the Gospel to all the nations. For its failure to repent, Jesus condemns Capernaum: *"And you, Capernaum, will you be exalted to heaven? You shall be brought down to Hades. For if the mighty works done in you had been done in Sodom, it would have remained until this day"* (Mt 11:20-24).

Matthew dedicates almost the entire chapter thirteen to examples of

Jesus teaching the crowds about the *kingdom of heaven* by way of parables, his signature teaching technique throughout the Gospels. *That day Jesus went out of the house and sat beside the sea. And great crowds gathered about him, so that he got into a boat and sat there; and the whole crowd stood on the beach.* A small bay located just south of Capernaum, known as the "Bay of Parables," is traditionally associated with this Gospel episode. After teaching the parables, Jesus *left the crowds and went into the house* where the disciples asked Jesus to *"Explain to us the parable of the weeds of the field."* Jesus does, and goes on to further describe in parables what the kingdom of heaven is like (Mt 13:1-52).

Capernaum's final appearance in Matthew's Gospel comes in the story of the payment of the temple tax. *When they came to Capernaum, the collectors of the half-shekel tax went up to Peter and said, "Does not your teacher pay the tax?"* Peter rushed to where Jesus is staying, and before he can speak, Jesus told him to cast a hook into the sea, and he will catch a fish with a shekel coin in its mouth, worth enough to pay the half-shekel tax for both of them. This story provides the basis for the popular name of the local tilapia fish, known as "St. Peter's Fish," so often served to pilgrims visiting the Sea of Galilee region (Mt 17:24-27).

The other two Synoptic Gospels, Mark and Luke, also record some of the stories that are, for the most part, quite similar to those found in Matthew's Gospel. It is worth noting that Luke gives an important detail related to the synagogue. He records the intervention of the Jewish elders to Jesus on behalf of the centurion: *"He is worthy to have you do this* [heal the centurion's servant] *for him, for he loves our nation, and he built us our synagogue"* (see Mk 2:1-12; 13-14; 15-17; 5:21-24; 25-34; 35-43; Lk 5:27-28; 29-39; 7:1-10; 8:40-42; 43-48; 49-56; 10:15).

Next, we turn our attention to Jesus' discourse on the "Bread of Life," set in the synagogue of Capernaum and recorded only in the Gospel of John. This teaching, one of Jesus' more perplexing ones, will stir great controversy among his enemies and followers alike. Many will find it too difficult, and abandon him as their spiritual leader.

Chapter six of John's Gospel begins with Jesus travelling to another place along the Sea of Galilee, opposite Capernaum on the northeastern shore. After he performs the Miracle of the Multiplication of Loaves and Fishes, Jesus withdrew to a mountain to pray alone. That evening, the disciples *went down to the sea, got into a boat, and started across the sea to Capernaum.* After they had rowed for some time Jesus appeared to them, walking on the water. The disciples gladly took Jesus into the boat and *immediately the boat was at the land to which they were going* (Jn 6:1-21).

The people who had witnessed the mighty Miracle of the Loaves and Fishes made their way to Capernaum seeking the wonder-worker from Nazareth. But Jesus admonished them saying, *"Truly, truly, I say to you, you seek me, not because you saw signs, but because you ate your fill of loaves. Do not labor for the food which perishes, but for the food which endures to eternal life, which the Son of man will give to you."* With these words Jesus has laid the groundwork for his "Bread of Life" discourse (Jn 6:22-27).

What does this labor *"for the food which endures to eternal life"* require? *"What must we do, to be doing the works of God?"* Jesus answered them, *"This is the work of God, that you believe in him whom he has sent."* Before they were willing to place their faith in Jesus, they wanted some sign from him, some work such as the miracle of the *"manna in the wilderness"* which sustained their Hebrew ancestors in their sojourn to the Promised Land. Jesus explains to them that it is *"my Father [who] gives you the true bread from heaven. For the bread of God is that which comes down from heaven, and gives life to the world."* They said to him, *"Lord, give us this bread always"* (Jn 6:27-34).

When the crowd asks Jesus for a sign such as *"the manna in the wilderness,"* Jesus seizes the opportunity to begin to open their minds and hearts to the mystery of the Eucharist. *"Jesus said to them, "I am the bread of life."* He explains that he came *"down from heaven."* It is now clear to the crowd that Jesus is claiming to be the *bread of God* which came down from heaven, and they began to murmur among themselves: *"Is this not this Jesus, the son of Joseph, whose father and mother we know?"* Jesus then invites them to place their faith in him: *"For this is the will of my Father, that every one who sees the Son and believes in him should have eternal life."* Earlier, they had asked Jesus to *"give us this bread always,"* but when they hear Jesus explain that he is this *bread of God* who has come down from heaven, their reaction is one of disbelief (Jn 6:31; 34-35; 38; 41-42).

In the synagogue at Capernaum, Jesus elaborates about the *bread of life* by saying *"I am the living bread which came down from heaven; if anyone eats of this bread, he will live forever; and the bread which I shall give for the life of the world is my flesh.* "Not surprisingly these words spark a dispute among the Jews: *"How can this man give us his flesh to eat?"* The Jews gathered in the synagogue may have thought that Jesus was teaching cannibalism, a practice abhorrent to them. But Jesus does not soften his words; he continues to insist emphatically: *"Truly, truly, I say to you, unless you eat the flesh of the Son of Man and drink his blood, you have no life in you; he who eats my flesh and drinks my blood has eternal life, and I will raise him up at the last day."* This he said in the synagogue, as he taught at Capernaum (Jn 6:51-59).

His discourse, in which he is trying to give plain talk on his true mission in the world, is not well received, even by those closest to him. *Many of his disciples, when they heard it, said, "This is a hard saying; who can listen to it?"* Finding the teaching too hard, many of Jesus' disciples *no longer went about with him.* Jesus then turned to the twelve to ask them if they were ready to leave him as well. *Simon Peter answered him, "Lord, to whom shall we go? You have the words of eternal life; and we have believed, and have come to know, that you are the Holy One of God."* Even though his mind may not understand the mysteries revealed in this discourse, Peter believes in his heart every word Jesus taught that day in the synagogue at Capernaum, providing an inspiring example for everyone who wrestles with this challenging teaching (Jn 6:60-69).

Jesus often met resistance to his teachings in the course of his public life. But in this discourse on the *bread of life,* he encounters not only murmuring but abandonment by *many of his disciples [who] drew back and no longer went about with him.* Jesus turns to the twelve and asks them if they were ready to leave him as well. Such was the scandalous nature of this teaching.

For the Jews, it was an abomination and a violation of the Law of Moses to eat flesh with its blood. And yet Jesus insisted that they eat his flesh and drink his blood, which, to the crowd, likely sounded like cannibalism. It is not surprising that they murmured among themselves, and considered this teaching blasphemous.

But Jesus does not back down. He even speaks more forcefully: *Truly, truly, I say to you, unless you eat the flesh of the Son of man and drink his blood you have no life within you.* Jesus will not allow for a symbolic or metaphorical interpretation of his words (Jn 6:53).

In the latter half of this discourse the word used for "eat" changes from the common verb form used to describe how a person eats to the verb form used to describe how animals eat, something like "gnaw" or "munch." By repeating his demand that his flesh be eaten several times and by using a rather crude and animalistic verb form of the word "eat," Jesus insists that we express our faith in him by consuming his flesh and drinking his blood in a real and physical way - in the sacrament of the Eucharist. Jesus' disciples will learn later at the Last Supper that in the mystery of the Eucharist his flesh and blood are hidden under the appearance of bread and wine.

Capernaum in History

Franciscan archaeologists Virgilio Corbo and Stanislao Loffreda conducted excavations of this site almost without interruption from 1968-1991. The results of their research have been recorded in an archaeological guide titled *Recovering Capharnaum* by Stanislao Loffreda. Much of this history section relies upon this report.

The earliest archaeological evidence of permanent settlement of Capernaum dates back to the second millennium B.C. But excavations have not yielded any archeological evidence of occupation of the site during the Israelite period (1200-587 BC). Excavations show that the construction of permanent dwellings resumes in the fifth century BC and marks the beginning of a long period of occupation which will end later in the thirteenth century A.D. After the thirteenth century the site is abandoned and falls into ruins. Travelers to the site in the nineteenth century report seeing a few Arabs occupying the site living among the ruins.

In 1894, the Franciscan Custody of the Holy Land purchased about two thirds of the ancient site from Bedouins. The purchase included the ruins of the synagogue which had been identified by the American explorer Edward Robinson earlier in the same century. It also included the yet-to-be uncovered "House of St. Peter." The Greek Orthodox Patriarchate came into possession of the remaining third of the site, located to the east of the Franciscan property.

There were a number of archaeologists involved in uncovering the ruins of Capernaum in the years following the acquisition of the property, beginning with Kohl and Watzinger of the Deutsch Orient-Gesellschaft in 1905. Franciscans Wendelin von Menden (1906-1915) and Gaudentius Orfali (1921-1925) also contributed to the excavations of the site. Wendelin von Menden's work partially uncovered the fifth-century octagonal-shaped church, which later excavations revealed was situated above the ruins of the house of St. Peter. Fr. Orfali is credited with the initial restoration of the synagogue. An inscription in Latin on one column in the north section of the synagogue recognizes this achievement. Over 40 years passed before excavation work resumed under Corbo and Loffreda (1968-1991).

The artifacts uncovered in Capernaum indicate the village economy depended largely on agriculture and on the manufacturing of glass vessels. Numerous olive presses and grinding stones for wheat and other cereals, made of the local basalt stone, were uncovered in the course of the excavations. The village's close proximity to the sea made fishing part of its economy as well.

The Via Maris (Latin for the "Way of the Sea"), an ancient trading route connecting Egypt in the south with empires to the north, passed near Capernaum making it possible for the locals to sell their olive oil, flour, fish, etc. to traders passing through the region. Matthew's presence as a tax collector here in Capernaum can be explained by the practice of taxing goods passing through the region.

Many small, private dwellings dating to the first centuries of the Christian era have been uncovered, giving the visitor some idea of what housing conditions were like at the time Jesus lived here. The floors and walls of the dwellings were made of the local basalt field stones, wood branches were laid across the tops of the walls with the spaces between the branches filled with beaten earth mixed with straw. The rooms of the houses centered around an open courtyard and many of the houses had steps in the courtyard leading to the roof. Windows in the walls faced not outward but inward toward the courtyard.

The Synagogues in Capernaum

Upon entering the ancient site, the visitor is greeted by two monumental structures; one a partially reconstructed synagogue, and the other, a modern octagonal-shaped memorial church. The synagogue is of special

interest to pilgrims as there are several stories in the Gospels which
make reference to the synagogue at Capernaum. Could this partially
reconstructed synagogue be the synagogue of the Gospels?

One of the first things visitors notice about the synagogue is that,
unlike all the other structures on site, it was construction consists not
of basalt stone but of beautiful white limestone. The high quality of the
stone-carving evident in the synagogue's artifacts scattered throughout
the site is impressive. One particularly interesting artifact is a Corinthian
capital on display near the synagogue, which depicts a menorah (cande-
labrum), an incense shovel and a shofar (ram's horn), all ritual objects
associated with Jewish worship services. Near the capital is another
architectural object from the synagogue, which depicts what appears
to be (still debated by scholars today) the Ark of the Law (a cabinet for

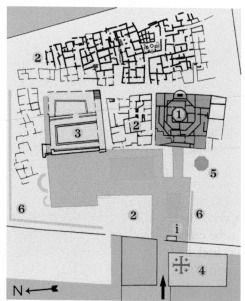

GROUND PLAN OF CAPERNAUM'S ARCHAEOLOGICAL SITE

1. Remains of the House of St. Peter and the Byzantine Church.
2. Dwellings of the ancient Capernaum.
3. Synagogue (4th-5th century BC).
4. Franciscan Convent of the Eucharistic Promise.
5. Mosaic of the octagonal church.
6. Architectural remains, mainly belonging to the synagogue.

the storage of the Torah scrolls) on wheels.

The synagogue complex consists of four sections; namely, the prayer hall, the eastern courtyard, the southern porch and a side room on the northwest corner of the prayer hall. Two rows of columns running north and south and one row of columns running east and west divide the prayer hall into a central nave, along with three aisles on the north, east and west sides. Stone benches line the east and west walls. The façade of the synagogue faces south toward Jerusalem. Jewish worshipers typically would enter through one of the three doors on the south side of the synagogue turn around and then take a seat facing south toward Jerusalem for the prayer service. Fr. Loffreda is of the opinion that the scrolls of the Law were kept permanently against the south wall of the central nave, where traces of two "bemas" (raised platforms) on either side of the central door have been discovered.

A single door on the east wall of the synagogue leads to the trapezoidal-shaped eastern courtyard. Three sides of the courtyard (the north, east and south sides) were covered with a roofed portico. Though its purpose unclear, the courtyard, we can speculate, may have been used for a number of activities, such as a place to accommodate travelers, for studies, and for social events.

Fr. Corbo and Fr. Loffreda dug trenches in and around the perimeter of the prayer hall, uncovering thousands of Late Roman coins and pottery. Based on an analysis of these artifacts, they concluded that the so-called "white synagogue" (the one made of white limestone) dates to the late fourth century AD. Trenches dug inside the prayer hall exposed remains dating prior to the construction of the white synagogue. The trenches cut in the central nave revealed a basalt (black stone) stone pavement dating back to the first century AD: *"Both Fr. Corbo and the writer [Fr. Loffreda] agree that the very large stone pavement of the first century A.D. uncovered beneath the central nave of the white synagogue does belong to the long-looked-for synagogue built by the Roman centurion and visited by Jesus"* (*Recovering Capharnaum*, Stanislao Loffreda).

The archaeologists explain the identification thus: the sheer size of the first-century pavement was too large to be considered part of a private dwelling. Also, in antiquity it was common to build religious structures on the same site when one structure needed to be replaced by another.

Finally, pilgrims (such as Egeria) seem to locate the first-century synagogue in the area of the white synagogue.

From outside the white synagogue on the west side, visitors can see beneath the white limestone foundation a basalt stone foundation which may be (according to Fr. Corbo) part the foundation of the first-century synagogue. Fr. Loffreda posits that this basalt stone foundation may be from an intermediate stage between the first-century synagogue and the white synagogue.

The House of St. Peter

It was known from historical sources that the house of St. Peter had been converted into a domus ecclesia (house church), a place of worship by the early Christians living in that village. For example, we have this testimony of Egeria who visited Capernaum in the late fourth century: "The house of the prince of the Apostles [St. Peter] in Capernaum was changed into a church; the walls, however, [of that house] are still standing as they were [in the past]." A later witness, an anonymous pilgrim from Piacenza who visited Capernaum around 570, mentions seeing St. Peter's house as being a basilica: "We came to Capernaum in St. Peter's house, which at present is a basilica." Where was this house church, later a basilica, of St. Peter's to be found? The Franciscan caretakers of the site set about to find an answer to that question.

In the early part of the twentieth century (1906-1915) Franciscan architect Brother Wendelin von Menden began excavations of the ruins of an octagonal-shaped church (the name of this Byzantine period church has not been discovered) located about 100 feet south of the white synagogue. When excavations of the site resumed in 1968, Frs. Corbo and Loffreda made a remarkable discovery under the octagonal church. They found the remains of what they concluded to be the house of St. Peter. Let us look at the evidence they present to support this claim.

The uncovered remains revealed evidence indicating that the house was built in the Late Hellenistic period (third-second century BC). In the late first century AD the house was converted into a house church, a place of Christian worship. This conclusion was based on several discoveries at the site. The floor and walls of this house had been plastered as many as six times. No other house that has been to date excavated at

Capernaum had plastered floors or walls. Tiny pieces of Herodian era lamps were discovered embedded in the plaster, dating to as early as the late first century AD, and certainly not later than the beginning of the second century.

Other artifacts discovered in this house dating to a later period reinforces the claim that this house had been converted into a house church in the first century AD. Plaster fragments with Christian graffiti, monograms and symbols were found embedded in some of the layers of plaster. The languages of the graffiti found inscribed on the plaster fragments were Greek, Paleo-Estrangelo, Aramaic and Latin. The diversity of languages found in the graffiti suggests that this house was both a place of worship for the local Christian community and a place of pilgrimage.

Jesus' name appears several times among the graffiti. He is called "Lord," "Christ," the "Most High", and "God." Some graffiti even bears the name "Peter." Liturgical expressions were also found in the graffiti including "Amen" and "Kyrie eleison." Based on paleographic analysis of the graffiti the archaeologists concluded that they date from the beginning of the third century to the early fifth century AD.

In the late fourth century AD, the house underwent some significant changes, having been set apart from the rest of the village by an enclosure wall some 350 feet in perimeter. Notably, the house, with its plaster floor and walls, was the focal point of the enclosure wall. The north wall of the house was rebuilt and a central arch was added to the interior of the house, perhaps to support a stronger, heavier roof. The arch showed evidence of having been plastered twice.

Based on all this evidence, the two Franciscan archaeologists concluded that the house was none other than that of the prince of the apostles, Simon Peter. This may explain why in the later part of the fifth century AD (Byzantine period), Christians built a basilica directly over the remains of Peter's house. The earlier house had been partially deconstructed, then filled with earth to provide a foundation for the new church. The octagonal-shaped fifth-century church comprised a small central octagonal-shaped wall, a larger octagonal-shaped wall enclosing the smaller one, and a half-octagonal-shaped wall partially enclosing the other two walls. Archaeologists also discovered, on the east side of the half-octagonal-shaped wall, remains of an apse and a baptistery. The

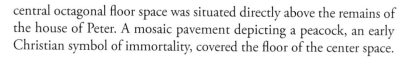
central octagonal floor space was situated directly above the remains of the house of Peter. A mosaic pavement depicting a peacock, an early Christian symbol of immortality, covered the floor of the center space.

The Memorial Church of St. Peter

Above the remains of the house of Peter and the Byzantine church, resting on eight pillars made of reinforced concrete clad in the local basalt stone, one finds the modern Memorial Church of St. Peter. This unique, hovering design feature provided shelter for the precious artifacts below, and served to give visitors an opportunity to view the remains of Peter's house, and offer a place of worship. A glass panel at floor level in the center of the church allows visitors to view the remains from above. Should the church be closed to visitors, they can view the ruins from the ground level as well.

On the feast of St. Peter and St. Paul, June 29, 1990, Cardinal Lourdusami, Prefect of the Congregation for the Oriental Churches, dedicated the Memorial Church of St. Peter. Designed by the Italian architect Ildo Avetta, the general shape of the church recalls that of the previous Byzantine octagonal-shaped church. Much of its exterior was covered in basalt slabs of stone to help make the church blend with the ancient site.

Several wood panels carved in relief, some of which depict Gospel scenes related to Capernaum, line the interior space. A bronze fence containing various Christian symbols follows the perimeter of the oculus. On the face of the altar a mosaic combines the two biblical accounts of the manna in the desert and the multiplication of the loaves and fishes. In the sanctuary near the altar, some excerpts of Jesus' "Bread of Life" discourse have been inscribed on the walls.

The question that begs to be asked by visitors is: "Where did Jesus live in Capernaum?" It would be reasonable to assume Jesus lived with Peter. This might explain the special care the Christians gave to Peter's house beginning in the late first century AD, making it first a house church and then later building a basilica over the site. The archaeological record cannot prove this assumption, but it certainly does not disprove it.

CANA
Cana in the Gospel of John

The name Cana appears four times in the Gospel of John; twice in the story of the first miracle of the wedding wine, once in the story of the cure of the official's son (already discussed in the Capernaum section), and once as being the home town of the disciple Nathaniel. Only John's Gospel includes these two miracles and the reference to Nathaniel's home town. The Synoptic Gospels do not name Nathaniel as being one of the twelve, but instead mention a disciple named Bartholomew (who is not mentioned in John's Gospel). It is generally understood that the Bartholomew of the Synoptic Gospels is the Nathaniel of John's (see Jn 2:1-11; 4:46-54; 21:2).

On the third day there was a marriage at Cana in Galilee, and the mother of Jesus was there; Jesus also was invited to the marriage, with his disciples. In this well-known Gospel story, we learn that the wedding couple's wine eventually gave out, prompting the mother of Jesus to intervene on behalf of the couple by telling her Son, *"They have no wine."* The mother of Jesus (Mary's personal name is not mentioned in John's Gospel) wants the couple to avoid the embarrassment of running out of wine, suggesting she may be a relative of the wedding couple. Jesus seems to object, telling his mother, *"My hour has not yet come."* Turning to the servants, the mother of Jesus utters her last recorded words in the Gospels: *"Do whatever he tells you,"* leaving powerful spiritual advice for all of Jesus' future followers (Jn 2:1-5).

Jesus instructs the servants to fill six stone jars with water, each with a capacity of twenty or thirty gallons, which were on hand for the purpose of fulfilling Jewish rites of purification. The servants were then told to draw out a sample and give it to the steward of the feast. The steward tasted *the water now become wine* and was astonished at the high quality of the wine. The steward called the bridegroom over and said to him, *"Every man serves the good wine first; and when men have drunk freely, then the poor wine; but you have kept the good wine until now."* John describes this as being the first of Jesus' signs (miracles), *and his disciples believed in him* (Jn 2:6-11).

John's Gospel is rich in symbols meant to draw the reader deeper into the mystery of Jesus' ministry. The story of the wedding feast provides the reader with just such an experience. In the evangelist's chronology of the beginning of Jesus' ministry, seven days have passed when Jesus appears at the wedding feast (see Jn 1:19-51; 2:1). It was on this seventh day of his ministry that he first reveals his glory in the miracle of the wedding wine; and it happened on the third day after his encounter with Nathaniel (see Jn 1:43-51). John wants the reader to recall the seven days in which God created the world (see Gen 1:1-2:3) and to understand that this same creation is now being transformed and renewed by Jesus. Furthermore, Jesus revealed his glory on the third day (after meeting Nathaniel) in Cana just as he revealed his glory on the third day after his death - by his Resurrection. In the person of Jesus, all of creation is being created anew.

John continues with this theme of a "new creation" by drawing parallels between the Genesis creation account and the wedding feast. After Mary points out to her son that the wine has given out, Jesus addresses his mother as *"woman"*: *"O woman, what have you to do with me? My hour has not yet come."* This is an allusion to chapters two and three of Genesis in which Eve is called woman. This woman (Eve) was deceived by the serpent and ate the forbidden fruit. Then she gave the fruit of the tree to Adam and he ate it, resulting in their expulsion from the Garden of Eden. Mary, the new Eve, reverses Eve's action by prompting (*"Do whatever he tells you."*) her Son, the new Adam, to begin his mission of salvation (Jn 2:4).

In yet another example of symbolic language, we learn that the six stone jars, which together held more than 120 gallons of water, were turned into good wine by Jesus. An abundance of good wine is a biblical symbol which could have numerous meanings. One interpretation holds that an abundance of wine is a sign of the messianic age (see Is 25:6; Joel 3:18; Amos 9:13). Another way to understand this miracle is to see that it anticipates the transubstantiation of wine into the blood of Jesus in the Eucharistic celebration.

The Church of the First Miracle

The village most pilgrims visit today to recall the wedding miracle is known as Kafr Kanna. Since the nineteenth century this village has been the one most visited by pilgrims who desired to see the place where Jesus turned the water into wine.

In 1879, Franciscan Father Egidio Geissler, pastor of the Church of the Annunciation in Nazareth, purchased the property which local tradition held to be the site of the first miracle. A new church was built on the site, consecrated in 1881, named, appropriately, the Church of the First Miracle of Our Savior Jesus Christ; it was later enlarged between 1897 and 1905. Ancient columns and capitals from a Jewish synagogue dating from the Roman-Byzantine period (fourth-fifth century AD) were uncovered at the site in the course of the excavations for the new church. These ancient artifacts were incorporated into the porch of the present church.

One artifact worth noting in the present church is the Aramaic inscription in a mosaic floor piece located about two feet below floor level on the right side of the nave about half way to the altar from the front entrance. The inscription reads (in translation): "Blessed be the memory of Joseph, son of Talhum, son of Butah and his sons who made this picture [mosaic]. Blessings be upon them." It is thought that this artifact was part of the Jewish synagogue previously mentioned.

In 1969 Franciscan Father Loffreda conducted excavations in the courtyard north of the present-day church. He discovered remains of a synagogue (forth-fifth century AD) which extended beyond the property of the Franciscans. During a recent restoration of the church, further excavations were conducted underneath the church, bringing about the conclusion that the Aramaic inscription mentioned above had been placed in the porch of the synagogue. Part of the synagogue's ruins can be seen under the present church, which can be accessed by doors on both the right and left side of the middle of the nave. Pilgrims may also view remains from private dwellings (first-fourth century AD), a building from the Middle Ages (fourteenth century) and from the first Franciscan church (1881).

The Church of the First Miracle comprises local white limestone, its most prominent features being its two bell towers and a red dome. Above the altar, an oil painting depicts Jesus attending the wedding festival. The church today serves both as a shrine for pilgrims and the parish church for a few hundred local Latin-rite Arab Christians. Married

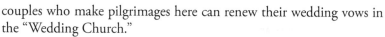
couples who make pilgrimages here can renew their wedding vows in the "Wedding Church."

About 100 yards north of the First Miracle Church is a small Franciscan chapel, built in 1885 to honor the disciple who called this village his home: Nathaniel (or Bartholomew).

Khirbet Cana

Early Christian pilgrims' testimonies concerning Cana are not detailed enough to give us an undisputed location of the site where Jesus' first sign was performed. Today, many scholars point to a different site about five miles north of Kafr Kanna (site of the Franciscan Church of the First Miracle) in the Bet Netofa Valley, known as Khirbet Cana (Arabic for "ruin of Cana"), as being the more likely location of the Cana of John's Gospel. A considerable amount of evidence supports this claim. For example, a cave complex discovered at the site reveals the presence of Christian worship within the complex. Parts of the cave had been covered with several layers of plaster. Greek graffiti found inscribed on some of the plaster mentions the name, "Lord Jesus." The lime plaster covering the floor included three layers, indicating use of the cave dating from the Byzantine period through the Crusader period.

A sarcophagus lid, with three Maltese-style crosses inscribed on its side, was found in the cave. Turned on its side, it may have been used as an altar. Examination of the plaster used to cover the lid revealed that it dated to the fifth to sixth centuries. Above the lid was a shelf in which two stone vessels were found *in situ* (Latin for "in position"). There was space for four more vessels, bringing the total to six; the number of jars Jesus instructed the waiters to fill (see Jn 2:6)!

Pilgrim diaries, guide books and maps from the Byzantine Period through the Late Middle Ages give additional support to the claim that Khirbet Cana was the site venerated by pilgrims as the place of the wedding feast mentioned in John's Gospel.

Those who argue against the Franciscan Wedding Church (Kafr Kanna) as being the place of the first miracle, point out that no archaeological evidence exists showing that the site was venerated by Christian pilgrims prior to the nineteenth century when the present church was built.

JACOB'S WELL
Jesus and the Samaritan Woman

The setting for this Gospel story is in the region of Samaria, a territory devout Jews typically avoided due to the unorthodox beliefs of the Samaritan people: *For Jews have no dealings with Samaritans* (Jn 4:9). It is included in this chapter on Galilee since it will be one of only two Gospel stories (the site of the healing of the ten lepers is the other) covered in this book with a setting in Samaria.

The story of Jesus' encounter with the Samaritan woman is only recorded in John's Gospel. In chapter four of John's Gospel, Jesus is returning to Galilee from Judea after having celebrated the feast of Passover in Jerusalem. The most direct route for Jesus and his disciples would be through Samaria, but they always risked being unwelcome. In Luke's Gospel, Jesus was journeying to Jerusalem through Samaria when he learned that, *the people would not receive him, because his face was set toward Jerusalem* (Lk 9:53).

Christ with the Samaritan Woman at the Well, Angelica Kauffman (1796)

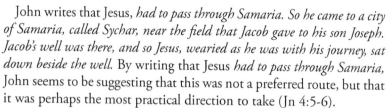

John writes that Jesus, *had to pass through Samaria. So he came to a city of Samaria, called Sychar, near the field that Jacob gave to his son Joseph. Jacob's well was there, and so Jesus, wearied as he was with his journey, sat down beside the well.* By writing that Jesus *had to pass through Samaria,* John seems to be suggesting that this was not a preferred route, but that it was perhaps the most practical direction to take (Jn 4:5-6).

There came a woman of Samaria to draw water. Jesus said to her, "Give me a drink." For his disciples had gone away into the city to buy food. The Samaritan woman said to him, "How is it that you, a Jew, ask a drink of me, a woman of Samaria?" For Jews have no dealings with Samaritans. Jesus answered her, "If you knew the gift of God, and who it is that is saying to you, 'Give me a drink,' you would have asked him, and he would have given you living water." The woman said to him, "Sir, you have nothing to draw with, and the well is deep; where do you get that living water? Are you greater than our father Jacob, who gave us the well, and drank from it himself, and his sons, and his cattle?" Jesus said to her, "Every one who drinks of this water will thirst again, but whoever drinks of the water that I shall give him will never thirst; the water that I shall give him will become in him a spring of water welling up to eternal life." The woman said to him, "Sir, give me this water, that I may not thirst, nor come here to draw."

The story continues with Jesus revealing knowledge about certain aspects of her personal life that convinced her that he was a prophet. The dialogue then turns to the subject of worship, with the Samaritan woman pointing out that they worship on a nearby mountain while the Jews worship in Jerusalem. At this point, Jesus shifts the conversation from a discussion about where people worship to how the Father wants to be worshiped. Jesus reveals to her that the time has come for true worshipers to worship *"the Father in spirit and truth, for such the Father seeks to worship him. God is spirit, and those who worship him must worship in spirit and truth."* Jesus then goes on to reveal to the woman that he is the Messiah (Jn 4:16-26).

History

The first mention of Jacob's well in the post-biblical historical record comes from the anonymous pilgrim of Bordeaux, who wrote in 333 about the presence of a baptistery on the site which used water drawn from Jacob's well for the Rite of Baptism.

A church built in the form of a Latin cross, erected on the site around 380, likely was destroyed during a Samaritan uprising in 484 or 529. The Emperor Justinian rebuilt the church in the early sixth century and may have stood as late as the ninth century.

The Crusaders arrived in 1099 and later built a church, placing the altar near the well which was located in a crypt below. The church may have been constructed with the support of Queen Melisande, who, in 1152, had been exiled to the nearby city of Nablus, where she died in 1161. Theodoric (who wrote a guide to the Holy Land in 1172) mentions the presence of nuns in service at the site. The church was dependent on the Benedictine Abbey of Bethany. Following the collapse of the Crusader kingdom in 1187, the site fell into ruins.

In 1860 the Greek Orthodox Patriarchate purchased the site, and in 1893, the well was restored for Christian worship. In 1914, construction of a new church on the site began with funds provided by the church of Czarist Russia. The revolution of 1917 ended the work on the church, leaving unfinished walls in place until work recommenced in the modern era, bringing it to completion in 2007. At the time of this writing, the current caretaker of the shrine for over 35 years, Fr. Justinos, welcomes pilgrims graciously. He is the artist responsible for the stunning paintings which can be seen filling the interior of the church with icons of Christ and other images depicting stories found in the Gospels.

The Sermon on the Mount, Carl Bloch (1877)

Pilgrims have access to the well by descending 19 steps to the crypt filled with icons and lamps. A winch above the well head allows the visitor to lower a bucket about 114 feet to the fresh water below. Tradition holds that this is the place Jesus revealed himself as the

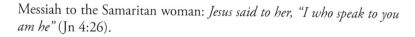

Messiah to the Samaritan woman: *Jesus said to her, "I who speak to you am he"* (Jn 4:26).

MT. OF BEATITUDES
The Mt. of Beatitudes in the Gospel of Matthew

Seeing the crowds, he went up on the mountain, and when he sat down his disciples came to him. And he opened his mouth and taught them, saying: "Blessed are the poor in spirit, for theirs is the kingdom of heaven. Blessed are those who mourn, for they shall be comforted. Blessed are the meek, for they shall inherit the earth. Blessed are those who hunger and thirst for righteousness, for they shall be satisfied. Blessed are the merciful, for they shall obtain mercy. Blessed are the pure in heart, for they shall see God. Blessed are the peacemakers, for they shall be called sons of God. Blessed are those who are persecuted for righteousness' sake, for theirs is the kingdom of heaven. Blessed are you when men revile you and persecute you and utter all kinds of evil against you falsely on my account. Rejoice and be glad, for your reward is great in heaven, for so men persecuted the prophets who were before you" (Mt 5:1-12).

Jesus *went up on the mountain,* an allusion to Moses going up Mt. Sinai to receive the Law (see Ex 19-24). After Moses received the Law he brought it down to the people. In contrast, Jesus invites the crowds to follow him up the mountain where he will give them the new Law of the Covenant. Matthew wants the reader to understand that the giving of these new precepts *on the mountain* shows the new Law of Jesus will be higher than the Law given by Moses.

He *sat down,* the posture a rabbi takes when teaching with authority, and began to teach. In one of Jesus' most luminous teachings, he describes for the crowds what it means to be blessed. By observance of the eight Beatitudes (derived from the Latin word for "blessed") Jesus assures his followers that they will find happiness (blessedness), in as much as possible, in this world, and perfect happiness when the fullness of the Kingdom arrives.

The Church of the Beatitudes

About one mile south of Capernaum in a region today called Tabgha (the Arabic name, derived from the Greek word "Heptapegon," meaning seven springs) is the site where three Gospel stories are set: the place of the multiplication miracle, the setting for the post-Resurrection appearance of Jesus to Peter and the disciples, and the site of the Sermon on the Mount.

After describing the site of the multiplication story, Egeria (383) wrote: "Past the walls of this church [Church of the Multiplication] goes the public highway on which the Apostle Matthew had his place of custom. Near there on a mountain is the cave to which the Savior climbed and spoke the Beatitudes." The cave she mentions is likely the cave which can be seen today about two hundred yards east of the modern entrance to the Church of the Multiplication. It's called the Hermit's Cave, due to the belief by some that it was used by hermits in the Byzantine era. The small plain above the Hermit's Cave may be the site Egeria identifies as the place where Jesus delivered his Sermon on the Mount (see Mt 5-7).

The modern Basilica of the Beatitudes is situated up the hill from the Hermit's Cave. Normally, the modern shrines commemorating the Gospel stories are built on the site of the traditional site of the story. But in this case the decision was made to locate the modern shrine in a place where the topography was more amenable for the construction, first of a guest house for pilgrims, then later the church and a convent for the sisters. It was a wise decision, as the modern shrine's higher elevation offers the visitors a magnificent panoramic view of the Sea of Galilee and the rising Golan Heights on the opposite shore of the sea. Looking out from the porch of the church pilgrims are able to see many of the sites connected with Jesus' Galilean ministry.

The land on which the guest house and church were constructed was ceded by the Franciscan Custody of the Holy Land to the National Association for Aid to Italian Missionaries in 1905. Guest house accommodations for pilgrims were scarce in the early part of the twentieth century, and the number of pilgrims visiting the region was increasing with the passing of time, making the need for lodging more pressing. The Association decided to first construct a guest house, completed in 1912, and in more recent years, recognizing the need to accommodate a growing number of pilgrims, built a newer facility, inaugurated on Oct. 30, 2009.

An octagonal-shaped church, designed by Antonio Barluzzi to commemorate the eight Beatitudes, dominates the mountain top. Barluzzi, the designer of many modern shrines in the Holy Land, often incorporated a special design feature in the architecture to assist the pilgrims in reflecting upon the mystery being commemorated; hence the octagonal (eight-sided) shape for the church, symbolizing the eight Beatitudes. Built with black basalt stone and white limestone, the basilica stands as an elegant witness to Jesus' Sermon on the Mount.

Consecrated in 1937, the Basilica of the Beatitudes and the surrounding landscaped gardens provide an ideal setting for meditating on Jesus' teachings on Christian living. Religious sisters on site, members of a community called the Franciscan Missionary Sisters of the Immaculate Heart of Mary, welcome pilgrims and assist with Masses, and also serve as custodians of the shrine.

Inside the church, just below the dome, eight windows inscribed with the Beatitudes in Latin become visible. A mosaic pavement surrounding the altar contains the names of the three theological virtues (faith, hope and love) and four cardinal virtues (justice, prudence, temperance and fortitude), which all symbolically flow (indicated by wavy lines in the pavement) from the altar, their source - Jesus, present in the tabernacle.

When Pope Paul VI visited the shrine on January 5, 1964, he left a gift of a priest's stole (liturgical garment), now kept in a display cabinet near the entrance. Pope John Paul II visited the shrine on March 24, 2000, and left, as a gift, a chasuble (a priest's outer garment worn at Mass) and stole for the shrine, which is also on display near the entrance.

SEA OF GALILEE
Sea of Galilee in the Scriptures

In the Old Testament period, the Sea of Galilee, a body of fresh water, was known as Yam Kinneret (Sea of Kinneret; alt. sp. Chinnereth, Chinneroth). All three times it is mentioned as being a boundary marker (see Num 34:11; Josh 12:3; 13:27). The name "Kinneret" is thought to be derived from the name of a village called Kinneret, dating to the Bronze and Iron Age, and located on a hill on the northwest side of the sea.

The minor role the sea plays in the Old Testament starkly contrasts its central role in the Gospels. A significant portion of the Synoptic Gospels' stories are set on and around the Sea of Galilee, also known as the Sea of Tiberias and the lake of Gennesaret in the Gospels.

The name, *Sea of Galilee,* is mentioned in the two Synoptic Gospels of Matthew and Mark, and in the Fourth Gospel (see Mt 4:18; 15:29; Mk 1:16; 7:31; Jn 6:1). In John's Gospel both names, the *Sea of Galilee* and the *Sea of Tiberias,* can be found (see Jn 6:1); and, toward the end of John's Gospel (see Jn 21:1), there is also another mention of the *Sea of Tiberias.* Only in Luke's Gospel do we find the name *lake of Gennesaret* (Lk 5:1).

In both the Greek (in which the Gospels were written) and English languages, the word sea denotes a body of salt water. In the first century AD, the locals called this body of fresh water a lake (see Lk 5:1; Josephus, *War of the Jews*). Why do Matthew, Mark and John refer to it as a sea?

Some scholars believe that the early Christian community gave the name "sea" to the Sea of Galilee, or Sea of Tiberias, because of their belief that Jesus is the fulfillment of the prophecy of Isaiah (9:1):

Now when he heard that John had been arrested, he withdrew into Galilee; and leaving Nazareth he went and dwelt in Capernaum by the sea, in the territory of Zebulun and Naphtali, that what was spoken by the prophet Isaiah might be fulfilled: "The land of Zebulun and the land of Naphtali , toward the sea, across the Jordan, Galilee of the Gentiles - the people who sat in darkness have seen a great light, and for those who

The Storm on the Sea of Galilee, Rembrandt van Rijn (1633)

sat in the region and shadow of death light has dawned" (Mt 4:12-16).

Isaiah's reference to *toward the sea, across the Jordan* and *Galilee of the Gentiles* inspired them to associate these descriptions with the region of Jesus' ministry. The sea mentioned in Isaiah's prophecy was, in the minds of the early Christian community, the fresh water lake in *Galilee of the Gentiles*. This is how a fresh water lake became a sea.

The Gospel stories of interest set on the sea include: the miraculous catch of fish, the calming of the sea, and Jesus walking on the sea. In chapter five of Luke's Gospel, Jesus was standing by the *lake of Gennesaret* near two empty boats. The fishermen were nearby washing their nets. Jesus stepped into Simon's boat and asked him to *"put out a little from the land." And he sat down* [the posture of a rabbi teaching] *and taught the people from the boat.* After speaking for a while, he told Simon (Peter), *"Put out into the deep and let down your nets for a catch."* Simon initially objected stating that they had fished all night and caught nothing, but then relented and did as Jesus had asked. They caught a large shoal of fish in the nets to the point where the nets were ready to break. Simon called for his partners, and when they hauled in the fish in both boats, they were close to sinking. *But when Simon Peter saw it, he fell down at Jesus' knees, saying, "Depart from me, for I am a sinful man, O Lord."* All those present who witnessed this miracle were *astonished,* including Simon's fishing partners, James and John. *And Jesus said to Simon, "Do not be afraid; henceforth you will be catching men." And when they had brought their boats to land, they left everything and followed him* (Lk 5:1-11).

After healing many who were sick in Capernaum, a large crowd gathered around Jesus. He gave instructions to the disciples to make preparations to go to the other side by boat. *And when he got into the boat, his disciples followed him. And behold, there arose a great storm on the sea, so that the boat was being swamped by the waves; but he was asleep. And they went and woke him saying, "Save, Lord; we are perishing." And he said to them, "Why are you afraid, O men of little faith?" Then he rose and rebuked the winds and the sea; and there was great calm. And the men marveled, saying, "What sort of man is this, that even winds and sea obey him"* (Mt 8:23-27)?

After performing the miracle of the loaves and fishes Jesus instructed his disciples to get into the boat and go over to the other side. Meanwhile Jesus dismissed the crowds and then went up the mountain by himself to pray. When the boat was *many furlongs distant from the land* Jesus appeared to the disciples walking on the sea. The disciples were terrified thinking Jesus to be a ghost, but Jesus reassured them, saying, *"Take heart. It is I; have no fear"* (Mt 14:22-27).

And Peter answered him, "Lord, if it is you, bid me come to you on the water." He said, "Come." So Peter got out of the boat and walked on the water and came to Jesus; but when he saw the wind, he was afraid, and beginning to sink he cried out, "Lord, save me." Jesus immediately reached out his hand and caught him, saying to him, "O man of little faith, why did you doubt?" And when they got into the boat, the wind ceased. And those in the boat worshiped him, saying, "Truly you are the Son of God" (Mt 14:28-33).

The disciples had earlier witnessed Jesus performing healing miracles, and demonstrating his power over evil spirits by expelling them from those who had become possessed. They had also seen Jesus bring Jairus' daughter back to life, showing his power over death. With these three miracles on the Sea of Galilee, they have witnessed Jesus manifest his power over the forces of nature. In all these miracles, Jesus has shown his authority over evil spirits, disease, the forces of nature, and even death. Is it no wonder that the disciples *marveled* at Jesus and *worshiped him, saying, "Truly you are the Son of God"*?

General Information

Lying in the Great Rift Valley at about 700 feet below sea level, the Sea of Galilee, the lowest freshwater lake in the world, stretches approximately thirteen miles long from north to south and about eight miles at its widest point east to west. Its depth of about 140 feet can vary according to weather conditions; its circumference spans thirty-three miles. The mountains and wadis (valleys) which surround the sea create the right conditions for winds (tunnel effect) to sometimes come rushing down forcefully through the valleys onto the surface of the sea, creating high waves which could make sailing very dangerous.

The sea supports a thriving fishing industry today as in ages past. According to Mendel Nun, a professional fisherman who lived for decades around the Sea of Galilee, "The indigenous population consists of 18 species, ten of which are commercially important and the majority is endemic to the lake or to Jordan's aquatic system." This is due to the sea's isolation for millions of years. Among the species of fish that can be found in the sea are: St. Peter's Fish (Latin name: tilapia galilea), Damascus Barbell, Longhead Barbell, Grey Mullet, Silver Carp, Kinneret Bleak, Catfish, and so on.

The Gospels make mention of two types of nets used by fisherman. In Matthew's Gospel we have the only mention of a dragnet. The term dragnet is not used but by its description it is obvious that it is a dragnet. In the thirteenth chapter of Matthew's Gospel Jesus teaches in several parables what the kingdom of heaven is like. In one of the parables he says: *"Again, the kingdom of heaven is like a net which was thrown into the sea and gathered fish of every kind; when it was full men drew it ashore and sat down and sorted the good into vessels but threw away the bad. So it will be at the close of the age"* (Mt 13:47-49). About a dozen fishermen would stand on shore, in two groups separated by a distance of about 50-100 yards, while a boat played out the net (as long as 600-1,000 feet) into the water. Once an area of water was surrounded by the net the fishermen on shore would drag the net ashore with ropes tied to both the top of the net and the bottom of the net. The top of the net floated thanks to corks attached to it, while the bottom of the net was weighted with rocks or heavy metal bringing it close to the bottom of the lake.

The casting net, also used by fishermen of Jesus' time, was circular and much smaller than the drag net, measuring about 16-26 feet in diameter. *And passing along by the Sea of Galilee, he saw Simon and Andrew the brother of Simon casting a net in the sea; for they were fishermen* (Mk 1:16). The perimeter of the net had weights attached so that when the net was cast, it would spread out like a parachute and then fall down over the fish below, trapping them until the net reached the bottom of the lake. Normally, fishermen used the casting net in shallow water.

KURSI: THE MIRACLE OF THE SWINE
The Story of the Expulsion of the Demon in the Gospels

All three Synoptic authors record the account of Jesus expelling a demon on the northeastern shore of the Sea of Galilee, but different names are given for the site of this miracle. Matthew calls it *the country of the Gadarenes* (Mt 8:28). Mark refers to it as *the country of the Gerasenes* [other ancient authorities read Gergesenes, some Gadarenes] (Mk 5:1). In Luke's Gospel, the site is named *the country of the Gerasenes* [some ancient authorities read Gadarenes, others Gergesenes] (Lk 8:26).

This confusion may be explained by the sacred authors' lack of knowledge of the topography of this region. Gerasenes, thought to be associated with the city of Jerash (located about thirty-three miles east of the Sea of Galilee in Transjordan), and Gadarenes, thought to be associated with the city of Gadara (located six miles southeast of the Sea of Galilee) do not fit the account of the expulsion story, as the Synoptic authors describe it as taking place upon disembarkation from the boat after sailing to *the other side of the sea.* Origen, an early Church Father who lived in the Holy Land in the late third century, makes reference to "an ancient city ... by the lake now called Tiberias, by which is a cliff overhanging the lake, from which they show that the swine were cast down by the devils." This "ancient city," called Gergesa, was located in the Nahal Samak delta, identified today as Kursi, the name of a fishing village mentioned in ancient Jewish texts, the Talmud and the Mishna. This village of Gergesa (Kursi)-*the country of the Gergesenes*-seems to be the best candidate for the site of the Miracle of the Swine.

They came to the other side of the sea, to the country of the Gerasenes. And when he had come out of the boat, there met him out of the tombs a man with an unclean spirit, who lived among the tombs; and no one could bind him any more, even with a chain; for he had often been bound with fetters and chains, but the chains he wrenched apart, and the fetters he broke in pieces...And then he saw Jesus from afar, he ran and worshiped him; and crying out with a loud voice, he said, "What have you to do with me, Jesus, Son of the Most High God? I adjure you by God, do not torment me." For he had said to him, "Come out of the man, you unclean spirit." And Jesus asked him, "What is your name?" He replied, "My name is Legion; for we are many." And he begged him eagerly not to send him out of the country. Now a great herd of swine was feeding there on the hillside; and they begged him, "Send us into the swine, let us enter them." So he gave them leave. And the unclean spirits came out and entered the swine; and the herd, numbering about two thousand, rushed down the steep bank into the sea, and were drowned in the sea (Mk 5:1-13).

History

In 1970, workers constructing a new road in this area discovered the ruins of a Byzantine monastery complex. Excavation of the site, carried out over a period of four years by Dan Urman and Vassilios Tzaferis of the Israeli Department of Antiquities and Museums, uncovered the largest known Byzantine monastery in the Holy Land. The rectangular enclosure wall of the fifth-century monastic complex measures 390 feet by 455 feet. The walls, made of dressed basalt stones, were covered in plaster.

The church, built in the basilica style with a central nave and two side aisles formed by two rows of white limestone columns, is located in the center of the complex. An apse located in the eastern part of the church marks the site where the altar once stood, and benches line the apse where the clergy would sit during the liturgies. The church had a large colonnaded atrium with two cisterns in front of its entrance. At one time, the nave was covered with mosaics, but today only damaged mosaics in the two aisles and in some of the rooms on the sides of the church remain. Many of the images in the mosaics were intentionally damaged, perhaps during the iconoclasts' crisis of the seventh century or by the Muslims who considered representations of humans and animals as idolatrous. On the right (south) side of the apse is a room covered in a mosaic with an inscription stating that the baptistery was constructed in 585 under the abbot Stephanos and Byzantine emperor Mauricius. On the south side of the church a crypt was found containing six sarcophagi and the skeletons of twenty-four men and one child. On the north side, a room harbors an ancient olive press.

A path on the south side of the church leads to ruins of a small chapel, also built in the Byzantine era, located at the entrance of a cave on the side of a hill. The chapel and cave have mostly disappeared due to earthquakes, the effects of weather and possibly by intentional destruction. The chapel has the remains of three separate layers of mosaic pavement. It's thought that this chapel marked the site where the demoniac resided, and where Jesus expelled the demon. The hill's steep slope leans toward the direction of the sea. Some have suggested that the swine ran into the sea at this place. Others have suggested a hill a few hundred yards to the south, which has a very steep slope leading down to the sea, was the more likely point from which the swine plunged to their death into the sea.

After the Persian invasion of the Holy Land in 614, the monasteries and dependent buildings were damaged. Christians later returned and rebuilt the church and occupied the site until the great earthquake of 749 destroyed most of the church and monastery, leading the local Christian community to abandon the site. Later, the, Arabs who made some alterations to the buildings, occupied it. From the ninth century until the present, the site ceased to serve as a place of pilgrimage for Christians.

Following the excavations of the site, parts of the church and monastery were reconstructed. The site was opened to the public in September, 1982 and is administered by the Israel National Parks Authority.

NAIN: THE RAISING OF THE WIDOW'S SON
The Gospel Account

The village of Nain ("Nein" in Hebrew) sits on the north slope of the Hill of Moreh in southern Galilee, a few miles southwest of Mt. Tabor. On the south side of the Hill of Moreh lies a modern Arab village called Sulam. Its name comes from an ancient biblical village (Shunem) mentioned in the Second Book of Kings, which served as the setting for the story of Elisha and the raising of the Shunammite couple's son. Elisha was a friend of the childless couple, whose names are not given. During one visit with the couple, Elisha blessed them, and later the woman gave birth to a son. Sometime later, the child died unexpectedly, and Elisha was summoned. After Elisha prayed over the body of the boy, *the child sneezed seven times, and the child opened his eyes* (2 Kgs 4:8-37).

Soon afterward he went to a city called Nain, and his disciples and a great crowd went with him. As he drew near to the gate of the city, behold, a man who had died was being carried out, the only son of his mother, and she was a widow; and a large crowd from the city was with her. And when the Lord saw her, he had compassion on her and said to her, "Do not weep. And he came and touched the bier, and the bearers stood still. And he said, "Young man, I say to you, arise." And the dead man sat up, and began to speak. And he gave him to his mother. Fear seized them all; and they glorified God, saying, "A great prophet has arisen among us!" and "God has visited his people!" And this report concerning him spread through the whole of Judea and all the surrounding country (Lk 7:11-17).

The people of the village of Nain would know the story of Elisha's

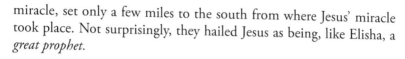

miracle, set only a few miles to the south from where Jesus' miracle took place. Not surprisingly, they hailed Jesus as being, like Elisha, a *great prophet.*

History

Bishop Eusebius of Caesarea (260/265-339/340) and Saint Jerome (347-420) both mention Nain in their writings, indicating that it was located near Ein Dor. During the Crusader period, a pilgrim named Peter the Deacon mentions seeing a church on the site in 1137: "In the village of Nain is the house of the widow whose son was brought back to life, which is now a church, and the burial place where they were going to lay him is still there to this day."

Following the expulsion of the Crusaders, the church was converted into a mosque, which later was abandoned. Another mosque was later built nearby. The Franciscan Custody of the Holy Land purchased the site of the Crusader church in 1878, after lengthy negotiations. The modern Church of the Miracle of the Raising of the Widow's Son, consecrated in 1880, has very simple lines forming the shape of a rectangle and is decorated inside with two oil paintings of the miracle.

At this writing, the church is not open to the public. But plans have been approved by the Franciscan authorities to build a convent next to the church and to invite a community of religious sisters to become the caretakers of the shrine.

THE MIRACLE OF THE LOAVES AND FISHES
The Gospel Accounts

Egeria (she was a pilgrim in the Holy Land 381-384) described in her diary a place "not far from there [Capernaum]" that has a "grassy field with plenty of hay and many palm trees. By them are seven springs, each flowing strongly." The presence of seven springs in this area gave rise to the name, "Heptapegon," which means "seven springs" in Greek. After the conquest of the land by the Arabs in 638 the name "Heptapegon" eventually became corrupted into the present Arab name, "Tabgha." In Tabgha today, visitors can see the sites associated with three Gospel stories: the site commemorating the Sermon on the Mount; the site of the multiplication of the loaves and fishes; and the place of Jesus'

Jesus Feeding a Crowd with Five Loaves and Two Fish, Bernardo Strozzi (early 1600s)

post-Resurrection appearance to the disciples.

For the first three centuries of the Christian era, local Christians would visit the site of the miracle of the loaves and fishes at Tabgha, recalling the only miracle recorded in all four Gospels (with the exception of the Resurrection). The Gospels of Matthew and Mark record two multiplication miracles; the first one set on the western shore at Tabgha and the second multiplication on the eastern shore at a place called Tel Hadar (see Mt 14:13-21; 15:32-39; Mk 6:30-46; 8:1-10). In both Gospel accounts there were twelve baskets of leftovers collected after the meal for the first account of the multiplication, and seven baskets of leftovers collected after the second multiplication story. Biblical commentators note that the twelve baskets, which were collected in territory inhabited predominantly by Jews, symbolize the Twelve Tribes of Israel. The seven baskets of the second story, collected in territory mostly inhabited by pagans, symbolize the seven nations conquered by the Israelites, that is, the Gentile world (see Dt 7:1; Acts 13:19).

Luke locates the multiplication story in the village of Bethsaida (see Lk 9:10-17). John describes the multiplication as taking place when the Jewish feast of Passover (Feast of Unleavened Bread) was at hand, and places the miracle on the northeastern shore of the sea, on *the other side of the Sea of Galilee* (Jn 6:1-13).

And when it grew late, his disciples came to him and said, "This is a lonely place, and the hour is now late; send them away, to go into the country and villages round about and buy themselves something to eat." But he answered them, "You give them something to eat." And they said to him, "Shall we go and buy two hundred denarii worth of bread, and give it to them to eat?" And he said to them, "How many loaves have you? Go and see." And when they found out they said, "Five, and two fish." Then he commanded them all to sit down by companies upon the green grass. So they sat down in groups, by hundreds and by fifties. And taking the five loaves and the two fish he looked up to heaven, and blessed, and broke the loaves, and gave them to the disciples to set before the people; and he divided the two fish among them all. And they all ate and were satisfied. And they took up twelve baskets full of broken pieces and of the fish. And those who ate the loaves were five thousand men (Mk 6:35-44).

History

Around 350, a small church was built around the rock marking the site of the miracle of the loaves and fishes with the side of the church running parallel to the Via Maris (ancient trade route linking Egypt in the south with the empires to the north) located a short distance to the north. Some scholars attribute the construction of the church to a Judeo-Christian nobleman from Tiberias named Josepos. In the modern church, remnants of that fourth-century church can be seen under a glass panels in the floor, one next to the altar, and the other in the northern transept.

A larger church replaced this primitive church around 450. The foundation lines of the fifth-century church shifted some twenty-eight degrees, so that the new church would be oriented directly to the east.

Over the next several decades, floor mosaics, many of which are still intact today, were installed, and are considered to be among the most beautiful in the Holy Land.

Colorful mosaic tiles depicting geometric patterns, floral and animal motifs, cover the north and south transepts and the area between the columns. Perhaps the most important Christian mosaic in all the Holy Land is the depiction of a basket of four loaves and two fish. The artist intentionally created an image of only four loaves (in the Gospel account there were five loaves) so as to help the pilgrim to understand that the fifth loaf is the Eucharist on the altar, located above the mosaic, with which Jesus continues to feed us today. The rock directly beneath the altar is said to mark the site where the miracle was performed. The rock's original location, a few feet to the west, had been moved when the fifth-century church was constructed.

In the southern transept, a depiction of a nilometer can be seen. Tax authorities used the nilometer to measure the depth of the Nile River, which helped the authorities to determine the amount of taxes they might expect from the farmers. The higher the Nile rose, the greater the yield from the fields, resulting in higher tax revenue. The Greek letters on the nilometer represent the numbers 6 to 10 cubits. The depiction of a Lotus flower, a flower not indigenous to the Galilee region but common in northern Egypt, and the image of a nilometer, suggests the artist's familiarity with the region of the Nile Delta.

The presence of Egyptian motifs in the floor mosaics might be explained by a Greek inscription located to the north of the altar which reads: "To the memory and the repose of the sponsor, the holy Patriarch Martyrios." He was the patriarch of Jerusalem from 478-486, and as a young man spent some time in Egypt. It's likely he brought one or more a mosaicists from Egypt to create these remarkable mosaics. Different artistic styles are noted in the mosaics indicating the work of at least two different artists. The memorial inscription indicates the mosaics were installed sometime after his death in 486. Another Greek inscription in the northern transept reads: "Lord, remember Saurus at this holy site," which suggests Saurus may have been one of the mosaic artists.

Some of the mosaic floor has been restored in recent years. The tiles which have a glossy sheen are original to the fifth century, while those tiles with a dull finish result from restoration work in the modern period. Placed among the flora and water vegetation are images of herons, cranes, cormorants, ducks, peacocks, a flamingo and a swan.

After the Persian invasion of 614, the church was destroyed. The Gallic bishop Arculf visited the site in 670 and reported seeing only columns lying among the springs of the area. The site of the church was forgotten until a survey by G. Schumacher in July 1889 indicated the remains of the mosaic floor and other ruins of the fifth-century church. The site had been purchased (1889) by the German Holy Land Association in order to build a German Catholic agricultural colony. In 1932, German archaeologists Father Andreas E. Mader and Father Alfons Maria Schneider excavated the site of the ruins of the church. During restoration work of the mosaics by Bernhard Gauer in 1936, the foundations of the fourth-century church were discovered.

The present Church of the Multiplication of the Loaves and Fishes, built on the foundation walls of the fifth century church, was consecrated by the archbishop of Cologne, Germany, Josef Cardinal Höffner on May 23, 1982. Two architects from Cologne, Germany, Anton Goergen and Fritz Baumann, designed the church so that its architectural style mimicked that of the fifth-century church. German Benedictine monks (since 1939) and Filipino Benedictine nuns are the caretakers of the shrine.

CHURCH OF THE TEN LEPERS
The Gospel Account

Luke is the only evangelist to record the miracle of the healing of the ten lepers. In his account, Jesus was making his way to Jerusalem with his disciples when he encountered ten lepers who kept their distance from him. They had no doubt heard about Jesus' powers over disease and sickness, so when they saw him coming their way they did not hesitate to beg for help from the Supreme Healer.

On the way to Jerusalem he was passing along between Samaria and Galilee. And as he entered a village, he was met by ten lepers, who stood at a distance and lifted up their voices and said, "Jesus, Master, have mercy on us." When he saw them he said to them, "Go and show yourselves to the priests." And as they went they were cleansed. Then one of them, when he saw that he was healed, turned back, praising God with a loud voice; and he fell on his face at Jesus' feet, giving him thanks. Now he was a Samaritan. Then said Jesus, "Were not ten cleansed? Where are the nine? Was no one found to return and give praise to God except this foreigner?" And he said to him, "Rise and go your way; your faith has made you well" (Lk 17:11-19).

History

The name of the village where Jesus encountered the ten lepers is not given in Luke's account. Christian tradition identifies the Arab village of Burqin as the site of the miracle. The village, located about two miles west of Jenin, has a population of 7,500, of which there are only about 60 Christians.

The present church, named in honor of St. George, rests on the site where one of the earliest churches in the Holy Land was built. According to local tradition, St. Helen, the mother of Emperor Constantine, passed this site on her journey through the Holy Land (326-328) and left instructions that a church should be built on the site of the cave where the ten lepers lived, the place where Jesus performed the miracle.

The fourth-century church was one of the earliest to be built in the Holy Land. This church was later expanded sometime between the sixth and ninth centuries. In the twelfth century the Crusaders built a church on the site with a stone wall around it. The Greek Orthodox Patriarchate built the present church in the eighteenth century, refurbishing it in 1997. The present church is built against the cave of the lepers. At some point in time, one side of the cave was removed to allow pilgrims to see where the lepers lived. The cave has a round opening at the top through which food and water would have been given to the lepers.

While its official name is the Church of St. George, its popular name is the Church of the Ten Lepers. Numerous icons adorn the walls of the church and the cave depicting Jesus and the ten lepers. In the nave of the church a bishop's chair made of limestone can be seen. The local caretaker claims the chair dates back to as early as the fifth century, and is quite possibly the oldest bishop's chair in the world.

Chapter Six

Passion,
Death
and
Resurrection

BETHANY
Bethany in the Gospels

On one occasion, Jesus entered a small village near Jerusalem, over the Mount of Olives and eastward on the Jericho side. Here he was received into the home of Martha. Luke does not give the name of the village, but we learn from the other evangelists that Martha and her sister, Mary, lived in Bethany with their brother Lazarus. At this house in Bethany, Jesus found rest on his journeys to the Holy City and enjoyed precious moments of warm friendship. After Jesus took his seat, Mary came and sat at his feet and listened to his teaching.

But Martha was distracted with much serving; and she went to him and said, "Lord, do you not care that my sister has left me to serve alone? Tell her then to help me." But the Lord answered her, "Martha, Martha, you are anxious and troubled about many things; one thing is needful. Mary has chosen the good portion, which shall not be taken away from her" (Lk 10:38-42).

It is a simple but profound story about two sisters and their different ways of showing reverence and love for their honored guest. The practical, hospitable Martha wants to insure that Jesus will find comfort and pleasure in the food she is preparing; while Mary, the mystic of the sisters, is keen to learn from the Master, so she sits at his feet clinging to his every divine word.

Spiritual writers have long discovered in these women the two dimensions of the spiritual life. Martha represents the active life as she devotes her time and energy to honoring the Lord through her attention to his material needs. Mary, on the other hand, represents the contemplative life as she devotes her attention to listening to Jesus and focusing on the

Word of God. Both dimensions are necessary for the life of a Christian. But the latter is essential for the nourishment of the soul and is a surer path to reaching the life of perfection to which Jesus calls us: *"You, therefore, must be perfect, as your heavenly Father is perfect"* (Mt 5:48). In heaven, there is no active life in the sense of our earthly existence, only contemplation of the infinite love of God.

As Jesus' earthly mission was drawing to a close, he made it known to the disciples that he was going to Jerusalem where, *"the Son of man will be delivered to the chief priests and scribes, and they will condemn him to death, and deliver him to the Gentiles to be mocked and scourged and crucified, and he will be raised on the third day"* (Mt 20:18-19). It was soon after Jesus' Transfiguration that he and his disciples began making their way to the Holy City. Their journey took them on a rugged hike through Jericho and then up into the Judean Mountains. They were making their way to Martha's house in Bethany when they received word from Lazarus' sisters:

"Lord, he whom you love is ill." But when Jesus heard it he said, "This illness is not unto death; it is for the glory of God, so that the Son of God may be glorified by means of it" (Jn 11:3-4).

After receiving word of Lazarus' illness, Jesus delayed his journey to Bethany by two days. He explained to his disciples that he was going to *"awake him [Lazarus] out of sleep."* When the disciples did not understand Jesus' use of this metaphor (sleep) for death, *Jesus told them plainly, "Lazarus is dead; and for your sake I am glad that I was not there, so that you may believe"* (Jn 11:5-15).

When Jesus arrived in Bethany he went to console the grieving sisters. He learned that Lazarus had been in the tomb four days. Martha came to Jesus while Mary remained in the house and Martha said,

"Lord, if you had been here, my brother would not have died. And even now I know that whatever you ask from God, God will give you." Jesus said to her, "Your brother will rise again." Martha said to him, "I know that he will rise again in the resurrection at the last day." Jesus said to her, "I am the resurrection and the life; he who believes in me, though he die, yet shall he live, and whoever lives and believes in me shall never die. Do you believe this?" She said to him, "Yes, Lord; I believe that you are the Christ, the Son of God, he who is coming into the world" (Jn 11:17-27).

Jesus came to the tomb and he was greatly moved, weeping tears of compassion for the bereaved. He gave instructions to remove the stone covering the entrance. Martha objected, claiming there would be an odor from a corpse that had been buried for four days. Jesus said to her, *"Did I not tell you that if you would believe you would see the glory of God?"* When the stone was removed, Jesus lifted his eyes and offered a prayer of thanksgiving to his Father: *"I know that thou hearest me always, but I have said this on account of the people standing by, that they may believe that thou didst send me."* When he had said this, he cried with a loud voice, *"Lazarus, come out."* The dead man came out of the tomb still bound with his burial cloths. *Jesus said to them, "Unbind him, and let him go"* (Jn 11:38-45).

It was Jesus' third raising of the dead, and this miracle crystalized the hatred of the Jewish authorities, who determined to have Jesus put to death. In order to take refuge out of the public eye, Jesus and his disciples retreated to the wilderness area in the nearby village of Ephraim.

With the feast of Passover, and the beginning of Jesus' Passion, only six days away Jesus returned to Bethany with his disciples. A meal was prepared for Jesus and his disciples.

The Raising of Lazarus, Rembrandt van Rijin (c. 1630-1632)

Martha served at the meal, and Lazarus also sat at the table where they were joyfully received. John does not record the name of the host of this supper; it is Mark who reveals his name as Simon the leper (see Mk 14:3). In the course of the meal, *Mary took a pound of costly ointment of pure nard and anointed the feet of Jesus and wiped his feet with her hair; and the whole house was filled with the fragrance of the ointment.* Judas

Iscariot objected to this extravagant use of such a costly ointment, saying it could have been sold and the money given to the poor. *Jesus said, "Let her alone, let her keep it for the day of my burial. The poor you always have with you, but you do not always have me"* (Jn 12:1-8).

Once again, we see Martha representing the active role in the spiritual life and Mary providing an example of the contemplative role. Martha is busy serving the guests at table. Mary is prostrate before her Lord as she wipes his feet with her hair. It is the posture of a person in prayer, recalling the penitent woman in the house of the Pharisee (see Lk 7:38).

History

Renowned archaeologist W.F. Albright identifies the region in which the village of Bethany is located with Ananiah, one of the areas settled by the tribe of Benjamin after their return from Babylonian Exile (see Neh 11:32) . This may explain the etymology of the name of Bethany: a village located in the region of Ananiah becomes Beth Ananiah (house of Ananiah in Hebrew) and then, in the Gospels, it is rendered Bethany.

In 1863, Marchioness Pauline de Nicolay purchased a tract of land about 30 yards to the east of Lazarus' tomb and then transferred the title to the Franciscan Custody of the Holy Land. This property contained important archaeological remains of churches that were built in both the Byzantine and Crusader eras. About a hundred yards to the west of Lazarus' tomb, a plot of land associated with the home of Simon the leper was purchased by the Franciscans in 1889.

From 1949 to 1953, Franciscan archaeologist Fr. Sylvester J. Saller supervised the excavations of the site near Lazarus' tomb where remains of previous churches lay buried. His excavations revealed the presence of churches in the fourth, fifth and twelfth centuries. Remains of a Crusader-era abbey for Benedictine nuns also were excavated.

In the historical record, one of the earliest witnesses we have of Lazarus' tomb is Bishop Eusebius of Caesarea, who wrote in 330 that it was in Bethany that "the place of Lazarus." was to be found. The anonymous pilgrim of Bordeaux, who stayed in Jerusalem in 333 for about two months, records this description: "A mile and a half eastwards from there [Mount of Olives] is the village called Bethany, and in it is the vault in which was laid Lazarus, whom the Lord raised."

The pilgrim Egeria records in her *Itinerary*, in about the year 384, that on the Saturday before Palm Sunday "as the seventh hour approaches, all go up to the Lazarium, that is Bethany, situated at about the second milestone from the city." Bishop Eusebius wrote in his *Onomasticon* from 330: "They still show you the place of Lazarus." In 390, St. Jerome, already a resident of Bethlehem for four years, translated Eusebius' *Onomasticon* and he substituted these words of Eusebius with his own update: "A new church, now built on this site, has his memorial," that is, the tomb of Lazarus.

In 570, Antoninus of Piacenza visited the shrine and writes that he found Lazarus' tomb in a church. A Frankish priest named Arculf lived in the Holy Land for about nine months in 670 and he notes that in Bethany there was a large monastery and basilica "built above the grotto where the Lord had recalled Lazarus to life after he had been dead four days."

The Anglo-Saxon pilgrim, Saewulf, visited the Holy Land in 1102-1103 and observed: "there is the church of Saint Lazarus where you can see his tomb and that of many bishops of Jerusalem." Also in the early twelfth century, 1106, we have this report from a Russian abbot named Daniel: "In the middle of the area, there is a great, high church, richly adorned with paintings. The distance from the church to the tomb [of Lazarus] is about 12 sagena [about 27 yards]."

The archaeological record supports the descriptions of these early pilgrims. The first church was built sometime between 333 and 390. Fr. Saller believes it was destroyed by an earthquake in the late fourth or the early fifth century. Another church was built on the same site sometime in the fifth century, and a third during the Crusader era in the twelfth century. A monastery added on the southwest side of this church was given to the Canons of the Holy Sepulcher.

Under the direction of (Crusader) Queen Melisande, the site was converted (1138-1144) into an abbey for Benedictine nuns. Her younger sister, Iveta, became the abbess in 1157. The abbey was fortified with a tower and a cistern to provide refuge for the nuns in case of an attack by the Muslims.

In 1187, with the fall of Jerusalem to Saladin, the site was abandoned. A mosque was constructed in the sixteenth century on the east side of the tomb of Lazarus, with masonry blocking the original entrance to the tomb. Eventually, with some difficulty, the Franciscans obtained permission in 1613 from the local authorities to carve a new access to the tomb. Today, on the north side of the tomb, 24 worn steps lead down a cramped stairwell to the vestibule of the tomb. Three more steps lead to the burial chamber of Lazarus.

The Church of St. Lazarus

Italian architect Antonio Barluzzi wanted to give pilgrims at the present Church of St. Lazarus the impression that they are inside a mausoleum. His windowless design achieves this remarkable effect. The only natural light that enters the church is through an oculus at the top of the dome. The contrast of the light flooding from above into the dark interior helps pilgrims recall that Lazarus lay in a dark tomb for four days before the Lord brought him back to life.

The modern church was built on the site where the previous three churches were constructed, incorporating some elements from the earlier churches. For example, the mosaic pavement under the grille just inside the entrance is from the fourth century church. In the courtyard in front of the church, masonry and mosaics from all three previous churches can be seen.

Consecrated in 1954, the present-day church takes the form of a Greek cross. It has an architectural simplicity that is enhanced by richly adorned mosaics by renowned Italian mosaicist Cesare Vagarini. Images of Lazarus and his sisters Martha and Mary appear on the façade of the church. Inside, there are mosaic lunettes on the four upper walls to enliven the church's gray interior, illustrating the Gospel stories set in Bethany. Above the altar, Jesus stands next to Martha with the words, *"I am the Resurrection and the Life,"* in Latin at the base of the mosaic. On the left, Jesus is shown visiting Martha and Mary. The right panel shows Jesus raising Lazarus from the dead. Above the entrance, the lunette depicts Jesus dining with his disciples while Mary anoints his head. In Mark's Gospel, *a woman* pours ointment of pure nard on the head of Jesus (Mk 14:3).

To the left of the church entrance is a small bust of Pope Paul VI in memory of his visit here on Jan. 4, 1964.

BETHPHAGE
Jesus Rides the Colt to Jerusalem

All four evangelists record Jesus riding a colt into Jerusalem, but only John gives a timeline. In his narrative, Jesus travels from Bethany to Jerusalem five days before the Passover, which would have been a Sunday since Passover fell on a Friday that year. As Jesus was leaving Bethany, *the great crowd of Jews* went out to meet him.

So they took branches of palm trees and went out to meet him, crying, "Hosanna! Blessed is he who comes in the name of the Lord, even the King of Israel!" And Jesus found a young ass and sat upon it; as it is written, "Fear not, daughter of Zion; behold, your king is coming, sitting on an ass's colt!" His disciples did not understand this at first; but when Jesus was glorified, then they remembered that this had been written of him and had been done to him (Jn 12:9-16).

This narrative is the biblical basis for the liturgical practice of carrying palms in procession while singing hymns on the Sunday, Palm Sunday, before Easter. The crowd greeted Jesus by waving palm branches, which recalls the joyful celebration of Tabernacles when the Jews are commanded to *"take on the first day the fruit of goodly trees, branches of palm trees … you shall rejoice before the Lord your God for seven days"* (Lev 23:40).

Both John and Matthew (see Mt 21:1-11) cite Zechariah's

Entry into Jerusalem, Giotto di Bondone (14th century)

prophecy (see Zech 9:9) concerning a future triumphant and victorious king who is humble and rides a colt into Jerusalem. The disciples understood that Jesus was the fulfillment of this messianic prophecy: *they remembered that this had been written of him* (Jn 12:16).

In Matthew's narrative, Jesus mounted the colt in the village of Beth-phage, while Mark (Mk 11:1-11) and Luke (Lk 19:29-40) sets this event near *Bethphage and Bethany*. John does not give a name for the place where Jesus sat upon the colt. Jesus, accompanied by his disciples and the excited crowd, then rides the colt over the summit of the Mount of Olives, across the Kidron Valley and into Jerusalem. Every year on Palm Sunday, pilgrims gather at the Church of Palms in Bethphage and then walk in procession waving palm branches. The route they follow is likely not far from the hallowed path on which Jesus, the humble king, rode his colt.

History

It has been an abiding desire for pilgrims down through the centuries to retrace the steps of Jesus during his final days in Jerusalem. Since ancient times, one of the events recorded in the Gospels which pilgrims have wanted to recall is Jesus' triumphal entry into Jerusalem on the first Palm Sunday.

The historical record gives us an early witness, Egeria in about 384, to the liturgical observance of the Palm Sunday procession: "The Sunday that opens the pascal week," she writes in her pilgrimage journal, "all the people climb up the Mount of Olives ... When the eleventh hour [five o'clock in the afternoon] arrives, the Gospel passage that talks about the children who went before the Lord carrying branches and palms is read ... The bishop rises to his feet, and all the people with him. From there, that is, from the top of the mountain, we continue on foot; the bishop constantly sings hymns and antiphons; 'Blessed is he who comes in the name of the Lord' ... From the top of the mountain we continue to the city and then, after crossing the city, to the Anastasis [Church of the Resurrection]."

Sixth-century pilgrim and archdeacon Theodosius, writing in 530, found in Bethphage a church "which marked the place where the ass was brought on which Jesus sat to make his entrance into Jerusalem." Another witness, the monk Epiphanus, who saw the Palm Sunday procession in the ninth century reveals that it began farther to the east than in Egeria's time, perhaps at the present location of Bethphage: "About a mile away [from the site of the Ascension] is the place where

Jesus sat upon the foal of an ass. There is an olive tree there from which every year, after paying the price, one cuts a branch; in this way, one enters Jerusalem in procession on the Day of Palms."

In 1172, the German monk and pilgrim Theodoric of Wurzburg wrote, "Bethphage ... is on the road half way between Bethany and the Mt. of Olives; a small chapel was built there in honor of Jesus ... standing on the large rock that is exposed in this chapel, Jesus mounted the ass and then rode it to Jerusalem over the Mt. of Olives." The "large rock" mentioned by Theodoric can be seen today in the present-day Church of the Palms.

After the Crusaders left Jerusalem in 1187, the Palm Sunday procession ceased. Around 1480, the Franciscans revived the tradition, starting at Bethany and ending in the Kidron Valley. In 1552, the Franciscans began leading a new route, from Bethphage to Mount Zion. By 1648, it was forbidden by the Turkish authorities. After the Holy Land came under Christian rule as part of the British Mandate, the procession was reestablished by Latin Patriarch Barlassina in 1933. This marks its current route: from the Church of Palms in Bethphage to St. Anne's Church inside the Old City of Jerusalem. The faithful walk ahead of the Latin Patriarch and when he arrives at St. Anne's, he delivers a homily, and blesses the faithful with the Blessed Sacrament.

The Church of Palms

In 1876, ruins of the Crusader church were uncovered. The ancient stone cube on which tradition holds that Jesus stepped to mount the foal was discovered in 1883. This is the "large rock" Theodoric saw in 1172. It had colored frescoes and inscriptions on its sides. A Franciscan tertiary, which is the lay affiliate of the Franciscans, named Don Francesco Forzari da Caprio purchased the site of the ruins for the Franciscan Custody of the Holy Land in 1888.

Not long after the Franciscans acquired the site, a small chapel was built around the stone block. A few courses of stone from the apse of the Crusader church were incorporated into the modern church. The frescoes on the block were damaged and fading, so in 1950 Italian artist Cesare Vagarini was invited to restore the frescoes. On the north side of the block is an image of a castle, and the disciples collecting the colt

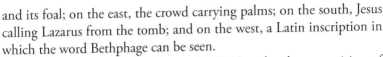
and its foal; on the east, the crowd carrying palms; on the south, Jesus calling Lazarus from the tomb; and on the west, a Latin inscription in which the word Bethphage can be seen.

Restoration of the church began in 1954 under the supervision of Italian architect Antonio Barluzzi. In 1955, a tower was built above the main door, and Vagarini painted frescoes illustrating the Palm Sunday story. The fresco above the altar shows Jesus riding the foal and receiving the acclaim of the crowd. In this scene, one person wears a cloak, thus concealing their identity. The artist invites each one of us to imagine that we could be that person in the procession, rejoicing in the presence of the Lord.

DOMINUS FLEVIT
Jesus Weeps over Jerusalem

As Jesus rode the colt over the Mount of Olives and began the descent down the west side of the mount, *the whole multitude of the disciples began to rejoice and praise God with a loud voice for all the mighty works that they had seen, saying "Blessed is the King who comes in the name of the Lord! Peace in heaven and glory in the highest!"* (Lk 19:37-38).

Many in the crowd had witnessed Jesus' *mighty works* and were convinced that he was now going to reveal himself as the Messiah King. They believed their redemption was at hand. But Jesus' heart was heavy, as he knew what lay ahead: *"For he will be delivered to the Gentiles, and will be mocked and shamefully treated and spit upon; they will scourge him and kill him, and on the third day he will rise"* (Lk 18:32-33). The city of Jerusalem and its sacred Temple in all its splendor was now in view.

And when he drew near and saw the city he wept over it, saying, "Would that even today you knew the things that make for peace! But now they are hid from your eyes. For the days shall come upon you, when your enemies will cast up a bank about you and surround you, and hem you in on every side, and dash you to the ground, you and your children within you, and they will not leave one stone upon another in you; because you did not know the time of your visitation" (Lk 19:41-44).

He Wept Over It, Enrique Simonet (1892)

History

There is no record in pilgrim literature of a site commemorating Jesus' lament over Jerusalem until the medieval period. However, it is known that there was a small chapel built by the Crusaders to recall this event in the twelfth century. The chapel was located next to a rock on the western slope of the Mount of Olives which tradition holds to be the place where Jesus wept. When the Crusaders left Jerusalem, the Islamic victors converted the church into a mosque and called it Al Mansurieh, in Arabic, The Triumphant. Over time it fell into disrepair, but has been restored in recent years.

The Franciscans tried without success to purchase the mosque in the late nineteenth century while it was still in ruins. Instead, with the assistance of Pio Alonzo, they were able to purchase land just south in 1886. A few years later, a small oratorio was built near the rock. More property was purchased from the Benedictine nuns in 1940, which expanded the Franciscan-held property. In 1953, tombs were discovered during the construction of a boundary wall marking the new property lines.

The discovery led to a complete excavation of the site by Franciscan archaeologist Fr. Bellarmino Bagatti and J. T. Milik from 1953-54. Tombs from the Canaanite period, sixteenth-fourteenth centuries BC, were uncovered. Jewish tombs were also found, dating from the first century BC to the first century AD, and from the second and third centuries AD. In the Jewish tombs, excavators found coins, sarcophagi and ossuaries, stone

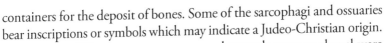

containers for the deposit of bones. Some of the sarcophagi and ossuaries bear inscriptions or symbols which may indicate a Judeo-Christian origin.

Ruins of a fifth-century monastery and seventh-century chapel were uncovered on this site as well. It is not known if this small sanctuary commemorated the weeping of Jesus. Among the remains the archaeologists uncovered was a stone slab inscribed with a Byzantine cross, which can be seen inside the modern church. It marked where the altar stood. To the east of the stone slab, some of the courses of stone which formed the apse can be seen. The foundations of the chancel are visible to the west of the altar space. Notice the Byzantine's church's orientation was to the east, which was standard practice in the early centuries of the Christian era. Antonio Barluzzi, architect of the present-day church, decided to turn the orientation to the west so that during Mass the faithful would face Jerusalem, the same view that Jesus and his disciples had of the Holy City.

There is also a remnant of the mosaic pavement that was part of the Byzantine monastery. It can be seen on the north side of the present church.

The Church of Dominus Flevit

Today a small, charming sanctuary called Dominus Flevit rests on the remains of the Byzantine ruins. Consecrated in 1955, its teardrop-shaped dome is meant to help pilgrims recall that Jesus wept here in his lament over Jerusalem. There are stone reproductions of jar-shaped tear vessels on the four corners of the dome. It was a common practice in antiquity, on the occasion of a funeral, for loved ones to collect their tears in small vessels, which were buried with the deceased as a sign of affection. The name, Dominus Flevit (Latin for "The Lord Wept") recalls one of only two times the Gospels record Jesus weeping. Only a few days earlier, while in Bethany, Jesus wept at the tomb of his friend, Lazarus (see Jn 11:35).

The impressive view from the inside of the church through the window facing Jerusalem is worth savoring. The window beautifully frames the city, and it has an etching of a chalice with a host pointing to the Basilica of the Holy Sepulcher, the site of the death and Resurrection of our divine Savior. Over the window is ornamentation that includes a depiction of the crown of thorns. Here is a special place where pilgrims can enter into the heart of Jesus as he faced those places where he would soon undergo the suffering and agony of death for the salvation of the world.

Just below the dome are four panels of images in plaster relief, three of which show Jesus riding the colt to the acclaim of the crowd. The east panel shows Roman soldiers setting fire to Jerusalem in 70 AD, fulfilling Jesus' prophecy: *"they will not leave one stone upon another in you."* On the face of the altar is a small mosaic that depicts a mother hen gathering her chicks: *"O Jerusalem, Jerusalem, killing the prophets and stoning those who are sent to you! How often would I have gathered your children together as a hen gathers her brood under her wings, and you would not!"* (Mt 23:37).

THE PATER NOSTER CHURCH
Jesus Teaches His Disciples How To Pray

In Luke's Gospel, Jesus *was praying in a certain place and when he ceased one of his disciples said to him, "Lord teach us to pray, as John taught his disciples"* (Lk 11:1). Without hesitation, Jesus gives them the holy words that Christians have prayed for nearly two thousand years:

"Father, hallowed be thy name. Thy kingdom come. Give us each day our daily bread; and forgive us our sins, for we ourselves forgive every one who is indebted to us; and lead us not into temptation" (Lk 11:2-4).

The setting for this teaching is not given, but it occurs immediately after Jesus' visit to Martha and Mary in Bethany, located about a mile west of the Mount of Olives. The cave on the Mount of Olives where tradition holds that Jesus taught his disciples the Our Father prayer is on a site that today is known as Pater Noster (Latin for "Our Father").

This same grotto was also associated with Jesus' teachings on the end times and the Last Judgment: *As he sat on the Mount of Olives, the disciples came to him privately, saying "Tell us, when will this be, and what will be the sign of your coming and of the close of the age?"* (Mt 24:3-25).

Could this cave also be the place Luke mentions when describing Jesus' activities just before suffering his Passion: *And every day he was teaching in the temple, but at night he went out and lodged on the mount called Olivet* (Lk 21:37)? For the early Christian community, this was indeed where Jesus would lodge while in Jerusalem. Here, according to accepted tradition, Jesus revealed to his disciples the mysteries of the kingdom of God. This gave rise to the name "Grotto of the Teachings" for the sacred cave. It is believed that the Grotto of the Teachings was

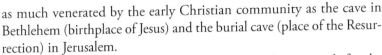
as much venerated by the early Christian community as the cave in Bethlehem (birthplace of Jesus) and the burial cave (place of the Resurrection) in Jerusalem.

Jesus' final visit to this cave occurs after the Last Supper just before he goes to pray in the Garden of Gethsemane where he was subsequently arrested. According to an early tradition, Jesus delivered the second part of his Farewell Discourse (see Jn 15-16) in the venerated cave. Egeria writes in her pilgrimage journal (c. 384) that on Holy Thursday the bishop of Jerusalem read Jesus' Farewell Discourse, "which on the same day, seated in the grotto, Jesus had addressed to his disciples." She goes on to note: "Each day in the afternoon during the octave of Easter he [the bishop of Jerusalem] brought the newly baptized children and his faithful ... to the grotto where the Lord had given his teachings to his followers."

History

According to the Church historian Bishop Eusebius (265-340), the Roman emperor Constantine ordered the construction of the first churches in the Holy Land: "the three places that gloried in the possession of a mystical grotto were endowed by the emperor [Constantine] with magnificent edifices." Three basilicas were built to commemorate the three principal mysteries in the life of Christ: his birth (Bethlehem); his death and Resurrection (Jerusalem); and his Ascension (Mount of Olives). Apparently, in the first centuries of the Christian era Christians commemorated the Ascension of our Lord in the Grotto of the Teachings.

Eusebius' history of the early church of the Holy Land records that Constantine built a basilica (326-334) over the sacred cave to commemorate the place where Jesus revealed the mysteries of the kingdom to his disciples and where he ascended into heaven: "And farther, the mother of the emperor [St. Helena] raised a stately structure on the Mount of Olives also, in memory of his ascent to heaven who is Savior of mankind, erecting a sacred church and temple on the very summit of the mount. And indeed authentic history informs us that in this very cave the Savior imparted his secret revelations to his disciples." According to Eusebius, St. Helena was in Jerusalem to oversee the basilica's construction: "It was St. Helena who on her arrival in the Holy Land [326] had a church built over the mystical grotto of the Mount of Olives, the very place where, according to accurate history, the Savior had stayed and had revealed the sacred mysteries to his disciples." The basilica was named the Church of the Disciples in honor of those who received Jesus' teachings in the venerated cave.

This is the church the anonymous pilgrim of Bordeaux saw in 333: "On the Mount of Olives, where the Lord taught before his passion, a basilica has been built by command of Constantine." By the end of the fourth century the place where the Ascension was commemorated had moved farther north by about sixty yards to a place Egeria (c. 384) called the Imbomon (Greek for "on the summit"): "then they go up to the Imbomon with hymns." Egeria is the first witness we have to the name Eleona given to the sacred grotto: "and on Tuesday [of Holy Week] a further service was added on the Eleona cave to read Christ's apocalyptic teaching [Mt 24-25] in the place where traditionally it had been uttered." Eleona, a word derived from the Greek language, is translated as "of olives" or perhaps "olive grove."

Constantine's basilica was probably destroyed by the Persians in 614. After the expulsion of the Persians in 628, the church was rebuilt, probably by the Patriarch Modestus. The pilgrim Arculf saw a church on the site in 670: "On the Mount of Olives, where the Lord taught before his passion, a basilica has been built by command of Constantine." During the destructive reign of Caliph al-Hakim, the seventh-century church was destroyed (1009).

When the Crusaders arrived in 1099, they found only ruins. A small sanctuary later was built on the site in 1102. Later, two brothers gave alms for the construction of a larger church, which was still under construction when both died in 1152. The two brothers, Admiral Eskill Sveinsson and Bishop of Viborg, Sveins Sveinsson, were both buried near the Grotto of Teachings. By then, the tradition of Jesus teaching the Our Father prayer to the disciples at this site was well established. For this reason, the newly constructed sanctuary was named the Church of the Pater Noster. After the Crusaders were forced out of Jerusalem (1187), the land was given to Moslem families by the Islamic conqueror Saladin. Over time, the twelfth-century church fell into ruins.

In 1857, Aurelia de Bossi, Princess de la Tour d'Auvergne (1809 – 1889), the Italian widow of a French prince, arrived in Jerusalem. She was disheartened to learn that no sanctuary commemorated the teaching of the Our Father prayer – her favorite prayer, to which she had special devotion – and that the location of the venerated cave had been lost. She made it her mission to locate the grotto and to restore its honor. Using her own personal fortune, she managed to purchase land where it was thought the sacred grotto was located. Over a period of eleven years (1857-1868), she bought, piece by piece, fifteen acres on the summit of the Mount of Olives. She even came to live on the site for several years in a wooden chalet brought from her native France.

For two years the princess, aided by Clermont-Ganneau, conducted excavations of the site. Their efforts paid off as the venerated cave was discovered in 1870, but not fully excavated at that time. They also uncovered the two large flagstones that covered the tombs of the two Sveinsson brothers, one with a crudely carved episcopal cross.

Next, the princess had a rectangular cloister (thirty yards by twenty yards) constructed (1870-1872) to enclose the grotto. The cloister, designed by renowned French architect André Lecomte, was a replica of the Campo Santo, a famous cloister located in a cemetery in Pisa, Italy. To ensure a constant presence of prayer at this venerated site, the princess had a Carmelite convent and chapel constructed (1872-1874) and then invited Carmelite nuns from Carpentras, France to come and take up residence. The Carmelite convent is today known as the Carmel of the Pater Noster. Ownership of the property was then transferred in 1868 and 1874 to the Republic of France, which explains why the flag of France is displayed at the entrance.

More comprehensive excavations (1910-1911) were conducted by the Missionaries of Africa (White Fathers). The foundations of the Constantinian basilica were uncovered. His basilica measured seventy yards by thirty-one and consisted of an apse (under which was located the sacred grotto), a central nave, an atrium, and a narthex. Small sections of the mosaic floor of the basilica can be seen today. Little of the twelfth-century church was uncovered. A complete excavation revealed some of the Constantinian masonry and several tombs in the west end of the cave. Because the site was not properly secured, local children would often play games in the cave and over time, there was pilfering of the Constantinian masonry. The forces of nature also contributed to the deterioration of the cave, resulting in the collapse of the natural-rock vaulted roof. Later, a concrete structure was installed over the exposed grotto to protect it and which also helps to give it the appearance of a cave.

During World War I, in 1917, a proposal was made by the Comité du Voeu de l'Univers Catholique to construct a basilica, dedicated to the Sacred Heart of Jesus, on the site of the Pater Noster. Archbishop Jean-Augustin Germaine, archbishop of Toulouse (1899-1928), took a personal interest in this project and gave it his enthusiastic support. The first stone for the basilica was laid on Jan. 20, 1920. Sadly, the western covered walk of the cloister was torn down to make way for the apse of the basilica, resulting in the loss of its original character. Exterior walls were constructed to a height of about ten feet when the work ceased. The church was never finished due to a lack of funding.

Pilgrims that visit the site today will find ceramic tile plaques depicting the Our Father prayer attached to these unfinished walls, to the walls of the cloister and the Carmelite's chapel. The Our Father prayer is now represented by nearly 200 languages, contributed by benefactors from all over the world. Pilgrims can search for the plaque with the prayer rendered in the native tongue, and the sight of these colorful ceramics along the walls form a beautiful symbol of the universality of the Church.

Just before entering the Carmelite's chapel on the right side is a small mausoleum containing the sarcophagus of the Princess de la Tour d'Auvergne. Before her death in 1889, the princess posed for the French sculptor, Jean-Auguste Barre, who created the effigy of her lying in repose. Her remains were transferred from Europe to this site in 1957. She had passed from this world with the knowledge that she had laid the foundations for the restoration of the venerated Pater Noster grotto. Now her mortal remains rest near to the site where our divine Savior had taught the prayer she held so dear to her heart.

THE UPPER ROOM
Jesus Celebrates the Passover Meal with His Disciples

Local tradition holds that Jesus chose the site known today as the Upper Room for his Passover meal (Last Supper) with his disciples. The term "Upper Room" comes from Luke's account of the celebration of the Passover meal:

Then came the day of Unleavened Bread, on which the passover lamb had to be sacrificed. So Jesus sent Peter and John, saying, "Go and prepare the *passover for us, that we may eat it." They said to him, "Where will you have us prepare it?" He said to them, "Behold, when you have entered the city, a man carrying a jar of water will meet you; follow him into the house which he enters, and tell the householder, 'The Teacher says to you, Where is the guest room, where I am to eat the passover with my disciples?' And he will show you a large **upper room** furnished; there make ready." And they went, and found it as he had told them; and they prepared the passover.*

And when the hour came, he sat at table, and the apostles with him. And he said to them, "I have earnestly desired to eat this passover with you before I suffer; for I tell you I shall not eat it until it is fulfilled in the kingdom of God." And he took a cup, and when he had given thanks he said, "Take this, and divide it among yourselves; for I tell you that from now on I shall not drink of the fruit of the vine until the kingdom of God comes." And he took bread, and when he had given thanks he broke it and gave it to them, saying, "This is my body which is given for you. Do this in remembrance of me." And likewise the cup after supper, saying, "This cup which is poured out for you is the new covenant in my blood" (Lk 22:7-20).

In this celebration of the Passover meal, known as the Seder in the Jewish tradition, Jesus transforms the Old Covenant Passover into the

The Last Supper, Juan de Juanes (c.1562)

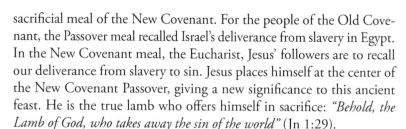
sacrificial meal of the New Covenant. For the people of the Old Covenant, the Passover meal recalled Israel's deliverance from slavery in Egypt. In the New Covenant meal, the Eucharist, Jesus' followers are to recall our deliverance from slavery to sin. Jesus places himself at the center of the New Covenant Passover, giving a new significance to this ancient feast. He is the true lamb who offers himself in sacrifice: *"Behold, the Lamb of God, who takes away the sin of the world"* (Jn 1:29).

After Jesus had taken the bread and *given thanks,* he broke it and gave it to the disciples. Likewise, with the cup of wine, after he had *given thanks,* he gave it to his disciples to drink. It is from the Greek word for *thanks* (*eucharisteō*) that the Sacrament of the Eucharist derives its name. He *broke* the bread and gave it to his disciples. This action (*broke*) gave rise to a name for the celebration of the Eucharist in the early Christian community: "the breaking of the bread" (see Lk 24:35; Acts 2:42; 20:7).

Jesus consecrates the unleavened bread with the words, *"This is my body,"* transforming the meaning of the bread as a symbol of the Passover event (*day of Unleavened Bread*) into the very substance of the New Covenant meal: Christ himself. In saying the words, *"Do this in remembrance of me,"* Jesus instructs his disciples and their successors (bishops) to imitate his actions. In this way the memorial of his sacrifice is perpetuated through the priestly ministry: the visible signs of bread and wine become the body and blood of Christ.

In the Old Covenant, the priest would pour out the sacrificial animal blood at the base of the altar to make atonement (see Ex 29:12; Lev 4:7, 18). On Calvary, Jesus' blood is *poured out,* establishing *the new covenant in my blood.*

History

After King David captured the city of Jebus around 1000 BC, he moved his capital from Hebron to the newly conquered city and changed the name to Jerusalem. The city was also known as Zion: *The inhabitants of Jebus said to David, "You will not come in here." Nevertheless David took the stronghold of Zion, that is, the city of David* (1 Chr 11:5). The name Zion became synonymous with Jerusalem. Many references to Zion, also called Mount Zion, can be found in the Hebrew Bible.

The *stronghold of Zion* was built on a narrow mountain ridge running north and south, bordered on the east side by the Valley of Jehoshaphat (also called the Kidron Valley) and on the west side by a shallower valley, the Tyropoeon Valley. The northern part of the ridge was not developed when David conquered the city. Later, David purchased a threshing floor on the northern ridge from a Jebusite: *So David paid Ornan six hundred shekels of gold for the site* (1 Chr 21:25). This is the place David chose to build a temple to house the Ark of the Covenant. However, that task would be given to his son, Solomon, as David was told by the prophet Nathan there was too much blood on his hands from his many battles.

Over time Jerusalem's population outgrew Zion, and so the higher mountain ridge to the west began to develop. This mountain ridge, also running north and south, was bordered on the east side by the Tyropoeon Valley and by the Valley of Ben Hinnom (Gehenna Valley in the New Testament) on the west and south sides. It was well populated by the time Jesus walked the streets of Jerusalem.

Around the time of the destruction of Jerusalem by the Romans in 70 AD, it was already commonplace to identify the western ridge with Zion. It made sense that David's palace could not have been situated on the lower eastern hill. His *stronghold of Zion,* which he captured from the Jebusites, must have occupied a more prominent site - on the highest point of the western ridge. This was the opinion of Flavius Josephus, the first-century Jewish historian who identified the western ridge as being the site of the City of David (*Antiquities of the Jews*). The "migration" of the name "Zion," from the eastern hill to the western hill had become fixed in the minds of the first-century residents of Jerusalem, and so it remains today.

It is believed that the first Christian community in Jerusalem lived at the southern end of the western ridge near the site of the Upper Room, the place of the Last Supper and the Pentecost event. Ancient tradition holds that Mary, the Mother of Jesus, lived (and "fell asleep") among these early Christians. For these early Christians, Zion would have been an entirely appropriate name for the place where the center of the early church was located on the western hill.

Today the term Mount Zion refers to the southern end of the western ridge. It is located just outside the western end of the southern wall of the Old City of Jerusalem. At the place on Mount Zion where tradition holds Mary "fell asleep," there is a sanctuary to honor this sacred event. Here Christians recall the moment her soul left her body to be welcomed by her Son into heaven. The name of the church is the Basilica of the Dormition of the Blessed Virgin Mary. Dormition comes from the Latin "dormitio," which means "falling asleep."

The earliest witness we have to a church on Zion is from Bishop Epiphanius of Salamis (315-403). Citing an unknown ancient source, he wrote that when the Roman emperor Hadrian visited the city in 131 he "found the city destroyed and the Temple of God raised to the ground and desecrated, except for some houses and a certain small church of the Christians, which had been built on the place where the disciples had gathered after the Lord had ascended into heaven from the Mount of Olives." According to scholars, the "certain small church" was a synagogue constructed by Jewish Christians who returned to Jerusalem after its destruction in 70. It was built as a memorial for the Pentecost event sometime between 73 and 130. In time the "certain small church" became known as the Church of the Apostles.

An octagonal-shaped memorial church was constructed next to the Church of the Apostles by the Byzantine emperor Theodosius I, who ruled from 379 to 395. This church was known in pilgrim literature as Mater Omnium Ecclesiarum, Latin for "Mother of All Churches." This title was meant to honor the place where the Church was born on the day the Holy Spirit descended on the apostles and Mary. It is also known from pilgrim journals that, beginning in the fifth century, the Last Supper, the post-Resurrection appearances of Jesus, and the outpouring of the Holy Spirit were consistently linked with the site where the Church of the Apostles and the Theodosius' Mother of All Churches were located. In the second half of the sixth century a large rectangular church was built near the Church of the Apostles and named "Hagia Sion" (Holy Zion). This church can be seen on the Madaba Mosaic Map and was described by the pilgrim Arculf who visited Jerusalem in the late seventh century.

It's likely that the Persians destroyed all the churches on Mount Zion in 614. Later, in the seventh century, Patriarch Modestus rebuilt the Holy Zion basilica. From this time, another pious tradition linked Zion with the place where Mary lived and where she ended her earthly journey.

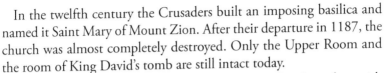

In the twelfth century the Crusaders built an imposing basilica and named it Saint Mary of Mount Zion. After their departure in 1187, the church was almost completely destroyed. Only the Upper Room and the room of King David's tomb are still intact today.

In 1333, Franciscan Father Roger Guerin arrived in Jerusalem with plans to purchase the Upper Room and the Tomb of David. He had the financial backing of the sovereigns of Naples, King Robert of Anjou and his wife, Queen Sancha of Majorca. After lengthy negotiations and, with a large payment, the Franciscans were able to take possession of the two sites in 1335. A friary, a residence for Franciscan friars, was built on the south side of the Upper Room. The cloister of the friary can be seen today.

Pope Clement VI issued two papal bulls in 1342, *Gratias agimus* and *Nuper carrissime*, in which the Franciscans were declared the custodians of the holy sites on behalf of the Holy See. This marked the birth of the Franciscan Custody of the Holy Land. The superior of the Cenacle friary (Upper Room friary) was given the title Guardian of Mount Saint Zion. However, the Franciscans' presence at the site was contested by both the Jews and the Muslims. In 1551, after many difficulties, the Franciscans were expelled from the site by the Muslim authorities. The two chapels were converted into mosques. During Israel's War of Independence of 1948, the Muslims abandoned the site due to intense fighting in the area. The newly established State of Israel seized the property and today administers the two rooms. David's tomb has become a synagogue, one of the most sacred sites for Jews.

The Franciscans are permitted to hold two official prayer services each year in the Upper Room: Washing of the Feet on Holy Thursday, and evening prayer and hymns on Pentecost. Today pilgrims are permitted to visit both sites. In the Upper Room, they are invited to take a moment to recall Jesus' most precious gift to the Church: his Body and Blood. In a corner of the Upper Room are steps leading to the Chapel of the Holy Spirit. The Crusaders had a chapel here dedicated to the Descent of the Holy Spirit. It was destroyed but then later rebuilt by the Turks. It is not generally open to the public.

Standing in the Upper Room looking towards the Chapel of the Holy Spirit pilgrims are invited to recall the mystery of the Holy Spirit's descent upon Mary and the apostles. Pope Paul VI visited the Upper Room in 1964, the first reigning pope to visit the Holy Land. Both St. John Paul II (2000) and Pope Francis (2014) celebrated Mass at this site where the Eucharist was instituted by Christ. In 2009, Pope Benedict led a prayer service in the Upper Room during his visit to the Holy Land.

The Tomb of King David

In Peter's Pentecost sermon (see Acts 2:14-36) he makes reference to Psalm 16: *"that he was not abandoned to hades, nor did his flesh see corruption"* (Acts 2:27). Peter wanted the crowd to understand that this is a reference not to the psalmist David (it is traditional Jewish belief that David authored the Psalms) but to Jesus Christ. To make his point clear, Peter makes reference to David's tomb: *"Brethren, I may say to you confidently of the patriarch David that he both died and was buried, and his tomb is with us to this day. Being therefore a prophet, and knowing that God had sworn with an oath to him that he would set one of his descendants upon his throne, he foresaw and spoke of the resurrection of the Christ, that he was not abandoned to hades, nor did his flesh see corruption"* (Acts 2:29-31).

In other words, David died and was buried in a tomb where his flesh experienced corruption. In contrast, the Christ's flesh did not experience corruption; and, three days after his death, he rose from the dead. Peter's reference to the tomb of David during his sermon at the site of the Upper Room has led to the erroneous association of this site with David's tomb. The Scriptures are clear as to the place of David's burial: *Then David slept with his fathers, and was buried in the city of David* (1 Kgs 2:10). The *city of David* is located on the eastern ridge, several hundred yards to the southeast of the Upper Room. In David's time, the western ridge (site of the Upper Room) was an undeveloped area outside the city wall. It would have been unwise for the city's inhabitants to bury their king at a site where grave robbers would have had easy access to the king's tomb.

Nevertheless, the tradition of David's tomb being next to the Upper Room became entrenched and is still held by both the Jews and Muslims. The early Christians may be the ones partly responsible for this misidentification. Because the western ridge assumed the name Zion (where the city of David was located) in the early Christian era, it seemed logical that this must be the place where David was buried. The earliest witness

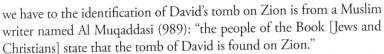
we have to the identification of David's tomb on Zion is from a Muslim writer named Al Muqaddasi (989): "the people of the Book [Jews and Christians] state that the tomb of David is found on Zion."

The Crusaders built a small chapel in their monumental basilica of St. Mary of Mount Zion to house the cenotaph, a solid stone coffin-shaped monument to King David. After their departure the site was taken by the Muslims who destroyed nearly all of the basilica, sparing only the Upper Room and the Tomb of David. The Muslims accepted the tradition that David was buried at this site. After many difficulties the Franciscans acquired the site of the Upper Room and Tomb of David in 1335.

Later, when the land came under Turkish rule, Sultan Suleiman learned that so-called "infidels" possessed the room above the Tomb of King David and that, in his words, they "cross the earth which covers the tomb of the Prophet David – may peace be upon him. It is neither just nor appropriate that this most noble place remain in the hands of the infidels and that, in obedience to their impious customs, their feet foul the places sanctified by the prophets who have a right to our complete veneration (Sultan Suleiman the Magnificent on March 18, 1523)." The Muslims expelled the Franciscans from the two sites in 1551. Both chapels were then converted into mosques with access given only to Muslims. A mihrab, or prayer niche, was attached to the south wall of the Upper Room to show the Muslims which direction to pray – towards Mecca.

Israel's War of Independence in 1948 opened a new page in the history of the two sites. Due to the fighting on Mount Zion, the Muslims abandoned the property; it was then seized by the newly formed State of Israel, the current administrator of the two sites. As mentioned above, the Tomb of David was eventually converted into a synagogue. Thus, King David's tomb has a rather unique history: its worship space was, in different periods, a chapel for Catholic Christians (Crusader and Franciscan), a mosque for Muslim prayer, and today it is a synagogue for Jewish prayer!

THE GARDEN OF GETHSEMANE
Gethsemane in the Gospels

Jesus' celebration of the Passover meal takes on an ominous tone when he tells his disciples that one of them will betray him: *And as they were at table eating, Jesus said, "Truly, I say to you, one of you will betray me, one who is eating with me.*" *They began to be sorrowful, and to say to him one after another, "Is it I?"* (Mk 14:18-19). Aware that his Passion was at hand, Jesus, too, was troubled with sorrow. After the meal they sang a hymn and then made their way to a garden called Gethsemane at the foot of the Mount of Olives. Upon arriving at the *garden* (Jn 18:1) of Gethsemane Jesus told his disciples that, *"You will all fall away because of me this night; for it is written, 'I will strike the shepherd, and the sheep of the flock will be scattered'"* (Mt 26:31).

And he came out, and went, as was his custom, to the Mount of Olives; and the disciples followed him. And when he came to the place he said to them, "Pray that you may not enter into temptation." And he withdrew from them about a stone's throw, and knelt down and prayed, "Father, if thou art willing, remove this cup from me; nevertheless not my will, but thine, be done" (Lk 22:36). Judas then arrived with a crowd and kisses Jesus on the cheek. This was the sign for the officers of the temple to arrest him. Jesus was then taken to the high priest Caiaphas *where the scribes and the elders had gathered* (Mt 26:57).

Christ in Gethsemane, Heinrich Hofmann (1886)

History

The pilgrim lady Egeria (381-384) mentions seeing an "elegant" church marking the site of the Agony of our Lord. It was built by the Byzantine Emperor Theodosius I in 380 to enclose the Rock of Agony, the site where tradition holds that Jesus knelt to pray for strength to accept his cup of suffering and where he sweat drops of blood. During the Persian occupation of the Holy Land (614-628) the church was destroyed. The Crusaders built another on the site and gave it the name Church of the Savior. This was also destroyed sometime after the Crusaders left Jerusalem in 1187.

When the foundation for the present church was being laid, remnants of the mosaic floor of the Theodosian church were uncovered. The architect of the present church, Antonio Barluzzi, decided to copy the pattern of the fourth-century church's mosaic floor. Small segments of the Theodosian mosaic floor can be seen through glass panels in the modern mosaic floor. There are no remains of the twelfth-century Crusader church inside the present church. However, some remains of this church can be seen outside, on the south side of the present church.

Eight ancient olive trees (the name "Gethsemane" comes from the Hebrew words for "oil press") can be seen on the north side of the present church. Pilgrims sometimes ask if these same trees were witnesses to Jesus' prayer in Gethsemane. A study was made by scientists from Italy in 2009. Their research indicated that the trees are about 900 years old, dating to the Crusader period. It's likely the Crusaders planted the trees to recreate the Garden of Gethsemane setting for pilgrims nearly a millennium ago.

Croatians Paul, Anthony and James, Christians from Sarajevo and Knights of the Holy Sepulcher of Jerusalem, bought the Garden of Gethsemane in 1681 and donated it to the Franciscans. The Franciscans continue to serve as caretakers of the site today.

The Basilica of the Agony of Our Lord Jesus Christ (Church of All Nations)

During excavations of the Garden in 1891, the ruins of the twelfth-century Crusader Church of the Savior were uncovered. Later excavations uncovered the ruins of the fourth-century church built by Theodosius I. Inspired by the piety of the Christians of these two eras to commemorate Jesus' Agony in the Garden with sanctuaries to enclose the sacred Rock of Agony, the Custody of the Holy Land Franciscans decided to do the same.

In 1919, the first stone for the new basilica was laid by Cardinal Fillipo Giustini, papal legate in Palestine. Roman architect Antonio Barluzzi was chosen to design the new church, which called for a style that would evoke the mystery of Christ's agony, when, as Mark's Gospel tells us, his soul was *sorrowful even to death* (Mk 14:34) as he contemplated the prospect of death on the cross.

Barluzzi proved himself up to the task. His daring and inspired design was influenced by the Byzantine style and it incorporated fragments of the mosaic floor from the fourth-century Byzantine church. The modern mosaic floor, by renowned mosaicist Pietro D'Achiardi, copies the Byzantine mosaic floor fragments that were found in place. The remainder of the floor is based on designs of other mosaics known from the Byzantine era.

Two rows of monolithic columns form three aisles and support the twelve cupolas in the ceiling, adorned with olive branches and stars in the night sky, symbols of the twelve apostles who were with Jesus in the garden. Pale, natural light passes through alabaster and violet-tinted windows, the liturgical color of mourning and penance. The muted visual effect creates a somber atmosphere for the pilgrims as they contemplate Jesus' hour of Agony in the Garden.

Benefactors from countries around the world contributed to the construction of the basilica, which gave rise to the popular name for the church today: Church of All Nations. Symbols of those nations that donated are included in the decorative art of the basilica in recognition of their generosity. The Basilica of the Agony was dedicated in 1924 with a Mass presided by Fr. Ferdinando Diotallevi, Franciscan Custos of the Holy Land.

The Rock of Agony, a large, bare, limestone outcrop, lies in front of the altar enclosed by a metal wreath shaped like a crown of thorns (a donation from the people of Australia). Jesus' innocence and helplessness as a sacrificial victim is symbolized by a dove caught on the spikes. A pair of thorn birds on each side of a chalice represent souls who wish to share the cup of Christ's Passion.

"The Kiss of Judas" mosaic panel (Ireland) to the left of the altar shows the betrayer Judas kissing Jesus on the cheek. The center panel of "Christ in Agony" (Hungary) above the altar depicts Jesus praying on the Rock of Agony, consoled by an angel. The *"I am"* panel (Poland) to the right of the altar depicts the band of soldiers who came to arrest Jesus, fallen on the ground, having heard the *"I am"* of Christ's majestic declaration (Jn 18:6). Embedded in the mosaics, predominantly in blues and greens, on the twelve cupolas in the ceiling are more national symbols. The national symbols for the first row on the south aisle are: United States, Germany, Canada, and Belgium; the center aisle: England, Spain, France, and Italy; the north aisle: Mexico, Chile, Brazil and Argentina.

The tympanum on the façade of the basilica, in sight of Jerusalem's Golden Gate, features a glorious mosaic panel created by Professor Giulio Bargellini. It depicts Jesus as a mediator between man and God, offering his suffering to his Father on behalf of all humanity. The Latin text from the Letter to the Hebrews inscribed at the base of the panel reads: *He offered prayers and supplications with loud cries and tears and he was heard because of his reverence* (Heb 5:7). Statues of the four evangelists stand above Corinthian columns supporting the façade.

At the top of the façade, a pair of bronze stags raise their heads to the cross above, an image that recalls the words of confidence amidst near despair of the psalmist: *As a hart [deer]longs for flowing streams, so longs my soul for thee, O God* (Ps 42:1).

The Grotto of the Betrayal

About a *stone's throw* (Lk 22:41) northeast of the Rock of Agony is a cave which tradition links with the betrayal of Jesus by one of his disciples, Judas:

While he was still speaking, Judas came, one of the twelve, and with him a great crowd with swords and clubs, from the chief priests and the elders of the people. Now the betrayer had given them a sign, saying, "The one I shall kiss is the man; seize him." And he came up to Jesus at once and said, "Hail Master!" And he kissed him (Mt 26:47-49).

History

The pilgrim Egeria, who travelled through the Holy Land in the late fourth century, was an eyewitness to the ancient liturgy in Jerusalem on Holy Thursday. She wrote in her diary that the bishop led the congregation "to the same place where, the Lord had prayed, as is written in the Gospel: and *he withdrew away from them a stone's cast and prayed*, etc. Here there is an elegant church [today on this site is the Basilica of the Agony] into which enter the Bishop and the congregation. A prayer and a hymn appropriate to the circumstances are recited, then the passage of the Gospel which runs: *you should be awake and praying not to be put to the test*, is read. Then all reciting psalms go down with the Bishop to Gethsemane [to the Grotto of the Betrayal]. Arriving here a prayer is said, then a hymn, finally is read the passage of the Gospel relating the arrest of Jesus."

At the time of Jesus, the grotto was likely used for agricultural purposes. It had a cistern and perhaps an olive oil press. The Byzantine Christians used the cistern as a burial chamber. In the Crusader era, frescoes illustrating Gospel stories were painted on the walls of the grotto. On the ceiling of the cave, images of stars were painted, some of which can be seen today.

In 1361, the Franciscans took possession of the grotto. Between 1956 and 1959, the sacred cave was restored. Three frescoes were installed by Italian artist Umberto Noni of Trieste. Above the altar Jesus is shown praying with his disciples. A smaller fresco on the left depicts the Assumption of Mary (her burial cave is next door). On the wall to the right of the altar is a depiction of the kiss of Judas.

THE CHURCH OF ST. PETER IN GALLICANTU
Peter Denies Knowing Jesus Three Times

During the Passover meal, Jesus turns to Peter and says *"Simon, Simon, behold, Satan demanded to have you, that he might sift you like wheat, but I have prayed for you that your faith may not fail."* Peter responds with great confidence, *"Lord, I am ready to go with you to prison and to death."* Jesus then makes this prediction: *"I tell you, Peter, the cock will not crow this day, until you three times deny that you know me"* (Lk 22:31-34).

Jesus knows that Peter will fall away, even to the point of denying him three times. But by assuring Peter that he has prayed for him, he prepares him for the deep shame he will experience in denying having known Jesus. After finishing the Passover meal, Jesus and the disciples went to the Mount of Olives. There Jesus was betrayed by Judas, arrested, and then taken to the house of the high priest (identified as Caiaphas in Matthew's Gospel, Mt 26:57), while *Peter followed at a distance* (Lk 22:54). After arriving at the house of the high priest, Peter sat next to a fire that had been kindled in the courtyard. As he warmed himself a maid saw him and said,

"This man also was with him." But he denied it, saying, "Woman, I do not know him." And a little later some one else saw him and said, "You also are one of them." But Peter said, "Man, I am not." And after an interval of about an hour still another insisted, saying, "Certainly this man also was with him; for he is a Galilean." But Peter said, "Man, I do not know

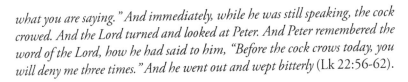
what you are saying." And immediately, while he was still speaking, the cock crowed. And the Lord turned and looked at Peter. And Peter remembered the word of the Lord, how he had said to him, "Before the cock crows today, you will deny me three times." And he went out and wept bitterly (Lk 22:56-62).

History

The earliest witness we have to the veneration of the place of Jesus' trial before the high priest Caiaphas is from the journal of an unknown pilgrim who visited Jerusalem in 333, referred to as the pilgrim of Bordeaux. In the journal of the pilgrim of Bordeaux, we find this passage: "One climbs the Mount Zion and one sees where the palace of the priest Caiaphas was and there still remains a column against which Christ was beaten." It's not clear from this description where on Mount Zion "one sees the palace." This has led to different opinions by scholars as to its actual location.

During excavations begun in 1888 by the Augustinians of the Assumption (Assumptionist Fathers), the current caretakers of the site, ruins of several churches were found. It is believed that the earliest church was built by the Empress Eudoxia, wife of Theodosius II, sometime between 443 and 460. According to the testimony of Archdeacon Theodosius in 530, the church went by the name Church of Saint Peter: "From holy Zion to the house of Caiaphas, which is now the Church of Saint Peter, it is more or less 50 steps." It's not clear when this church was destroyed.

A pilgrim named Saewulf, who visited Jerusalem in 1102, named the Crusader church he saw on this site St. Peter in Gallicantu (Gallicantu is Latin for "cockcrow"). After the Crusaders left Jerusalem, the church was destroyed.

Count Amédée of Piellat came on pilgrimage with the French Assumptionist Fathers to the Holy Land in 1882. After visiting the site of Caiaphas' palace, he decided to purchase it. In 1887, he sold the land to the Assumptionist Fathers. Excavations began the next year. A number of rock-cut structures, such as cisterns, cellars, and stables, can be seen on the east side of the present-day church. These ruins date to the Herodian and Roman periods. A few mosaic floor fragments dating from the Byzantine-era church can be seen in different parts of the compound outside the modern church.

The Church of St. Peter in Gallicantu

The modern church commemorating St. Peter's denial of Jesus and his subsequent remorse is a striking hillside shrine on the eastern slope of Mount Zion. French architect, Rev. Etienne Boubet, supervised the construction of the neo-Byzantine-style church between 1924 and 1931. His Beatitude Luigi Barlassina, Latin Patriarch of Jerusalem, presided over the consecration Mass in 1931. After a restoration project carried out in the 1990s the church was rededicated in 1997 by His Beatitude Michel Sabbah, Latin Patriarch of Jerusalem. It is known for its wealth of mosaics and icons to help pilgrims reflect on St. Peter and his relationship with Christ.

A dramatic scene depicting Jesus' prophecy of Peter's denial can be seen in bronze relief panels on the main doors leading to the upper church. Inside, the visitor is greeted with an array of mosaic panels which treat various themes related to the Gospel events recalled here, and which also reveal how God's mercy heals the wounds of sin and inspires holiness of life.

Above the main altar, a mosaic panel shows Jesus being interrogated by the Sanhedrin, which condemns him for proclaiming he is the Son of God, *the son of the Blessed One* (Mk 14:62) as angels lower the cross which Jesus will take up on the following day. On the left in the small apse are depicted three sinners who became saints: St. Dismas (the Good Thief) in the center, St. William the Hermit on the left, and St. Dositheus on the right. The apse on the right shows St. Mary Magdalene in the center, St. Pelagia on the left and St. Mary of Egypt on the right. All these saints are known for having experienced a conversion, and for renouncing a sinful past.

The lower chapel is adorned with icons depicting the events related to Peter's denial and to his reconciliation with the risen Christ by the Sea of Galilee. On the left, Jesus looks at Peter after his third denial. Behind the altar, Peter is shown weeping bitterly over his denial of Jesus. And on the right, Peter is handed the shepherd's rod and his mission to feed his flock after he has affirmed his love for Jesus three times (see Jn 21:15-17).

Below the lower chapel is the Sacred Pit, which the Assumptionist Fathers claim was used as a prison for Jesus before he was put on trial by the Sanhedrin. Here in this dark and lonely place, Jesus would have spent the long night before his court appearance in limbo between heaven and earth and in the most total abandonment. The outline of a kneeling figure in prayer, with arms outstretched, can be seen on the limestone wall. Notice the Byzantine crosses inscribed in the circular opening at the top. Here pilgrims can meditate on the words of Psalm 88 and reflect on Jesus in his moment of great distress: *Friend and neighbor you have taken away; my one companion is darkness* (Ps 88:19).

Outside on the north side of the church, ancient worn steps lead down to the pool of Siloam. Tradition holds that Jesus descended these steps after the Passover meal with his disciples. A short time later, he was dragged up these same steps under arrest as he was being brought to the house of the high priest. On this remnant of the ancient stairway that once connected the Holy City with the Kidron Valley, pilgrims can truly walk in the footsteps of Our Savior.

THE BASILICA OF ST. ANNE

Jesus Heals the Paralytic at the Pools of Bethesda

John's Gospel depicts Jesus in Jerusalem more frequently than the Synoptic Gospels. In the Fourth Gospel, Jesus makes his way from the Galilee to Jerusalem on several different occasions to celebrate a Jewish feast. The narrative in chapter five tells us that Jesus was in Jerusalem for *a feast of the Jews*, but the feast is not named. This was the setting for one of Jesus' greatest miracles.

Now there is in Jerusalem by the Sheep Gate a pool, in Hebrew called Bethzatha, which has five porticoes. In these lay a multitude of invalids, blind, lame, paralyzed. One man was there, who had been ill for thirty-eight years. When Jesus saw him and knew that he had been lying there a long time, he said to him, "Do you want to be healed?" The sick man answered him, "Sir, I have no man to put me into the pool when the water is troubled, and while I am going another steps down before me." Jesus said to him, "Rise, take up your pallet, and walk." And at once the man was healed, and he took up his pallet and walked" (Jn 5:1-9).

Note that the name of the pool in John's narrative is Bethzatha, but it's more commonly known as Bethesda. According to scholars, Bethesda is Hebrew for "House of Mercy." This site was at a higher altitude and just north of the nearby Temple. Water was one of the daily needs of the priests serving at the Temple. It was needed for ablutions, and to clean the area where the animal sacrifices were prepared. Fortunately, a shallow valley sloped in the direction of the Temple at the site.

Around the eighth century BC, city leaders built a dam across it to create a reservoir. The winter rain would fill the reservoir, providing the much-needed water for the Temple throughout the year. An open conduit brought the water to the Temple from the reservoir. This is likely the *upper pool* mentioned in the Hebrew Scriptures (see 2 Kgs 18:17; Isa 7:3). In the third century BC, a second pool was constructed south of the dam which required that the open air channel be covered and converted into a tunnel. This project likely was carried out during the time of the high priest Simon (see Sir 50:3).

At the time of Jesus, the site had two pools with porticoes on the four sides and another running between the pools. The two pools combined were 300-330 feet long, 180-240 feet wide and 21-24 feet deep. Apparently, these pools also served as ritual baths (in Hebrew, mikve'ot) for Jewish pilgrims making their way to the Temple. Excavations at the site revealed steps leading down to the western edge of the northern pool. One step was wider than the others. It is believed that the pilgrims would leave their clothes on this step before dipping into the pool. Jewish pilgrims were required to immerse themselves in a ritual bath before entering the Temple compound to pray.

The porticoes served as an ideal location for the *multitude of invalids, blind, lame, paralyzed* (Jn 5:3) to beg for alms. Jewish pilgrims who came to the pools for their purification rites would likely be in a generous and charitable frame of mind to assist the less fortunate.

Natural caves located to the east of the pool were adapted for use as medicinal baths for pagan rituals. Roman soldiers from the Jerusalem garrison housed in the Antonia Fortress may have founded these baths. Here prayers were offered to Asclepius, the god of medicine. Several pagan ritual objects (ex votos, offerings left in gratitude for a healing) were found in the area of the baths. The pagan ritual baths continued to serve the needs of the pagan population after the two disastrous Jewish wars (66-70 AD and 132-135 AD) against Roman rule. After the second rebellion, Roman Emperor Hadrian forbade Jews to live in Jerusalem. He rebuilt the city, named it after himself (Aelia Capitolina), and thoroughly paganized it. A temple to Asclepius was erected next to the medicinal pools around this time.

During the early part of the fifth century, a basilica was built on the ruins of the Pool of Bethesda. Named the Church of St. Mary, it was probably meant to honor the birth of Mary. By the fifth century it was already a well-established tradition that Mary was born in a nearby cave. Badly damaged during the Persian occupation of the land (614-628) it was later restored by the Patriarch Modestus. The restored church likely was destroyed on Caliph al-Hakim's order in 1009. When the Crusaders arrived, they found the site mostly in ruins.

A small chapel was built on the ruins of the Byzantine basilica by the Crusaders to commemorate the miracle. A small remnant of that chapel – part of the apse and façade – can be seen today. Nearby the Crusaders built a basilica (1131-1138) above the grotto which tradition holds to be the birthplace of Mary. It was named in honor of Mary's mother, St. Anne. St. Anne's name does not appear in the four canonical Gospels, but it does appear in the Proto-Gospel of St. James, an apocryphal work which circulated among the Christian communities in the early Christian era. It tells of the childhood of Mary, born of infertile parents blessed by the Lord in their old age. During the Crusader period the basilica served as a chapel for Benedictine nuns who took up residence in an abbey adjoining the chapel.

After the Crusaders abandoned Jerusalem, the Basilica of St. Anne was converted into a Muslim theological school by Saladin in 1192. The Arabic inscription above the main doors of the church describes this transformation. In the centuries which followed, the site was neglected and fell into disrepair. Despite the run-down conditions, pilgrims continued to visit the nativity grotto, usually upon payment to the Muslim authorities.

In an act of gratitude for France's alliance with the Ottoman Turks in the Crimean War, the basilica was offered to the French republic in 1856. The French government accepted the offer from Ottoman Sultan Abdul Mejid and began restoration work in 1863. When the restoration work was finished in 1878 the basilica was given to the Missionaries

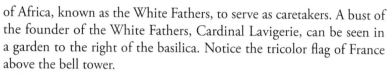
of Africa, known as the White Fathers, to serve as caretakers. A bust of the founder of the White Fathers, Cardinal Lavigerie, can be seen in a garden to the right of the basilica. Notice the tricolor flag of France above the bell tower.

The simple, elegant lines of the Romanesque-styled basilica make it one of the most beautiful of the Crusader-era churches in the Holy Land. The thick walls of bare stone and arches and vaults, lend it an austere fortress-like appearance. Its marvelous acoustics inspire pilgrimage groups from around the world to sing popular hymns and canticles to Mary in their native languages, and then listen to their voices echo throughout the church. Hearing the songs of praise from so many different nations, pilgrims can truly appreciate the universal dimension of the Church.

Against the north wall in the back of the church is a white marble statue of St. Anne seated and holding a scroll with the inscription (in Latin) *you shall love the Lord your God* (Dt 6:4). Mary, depicted as a little girl, stands next to her mother. With the spiritual guidance of the Torah, Anne teaches her daughter about her Jewish faith.

Pilate Orders Jesus to be Scourged and Crucified

After Jesus had been condemned by the high priest for blasphemy, he was taken to Pontius Pilate, the governor of Judea. Pilate interrogated him briefly about the charge that the crowd had made that Jesus claimed to be their king: *"Are you the King of the Jews?"* (Jn 18:33). Jesus told Pilate that he was indeed a king but not in the way Pilate expected:

Jesus answered, "My kingship is not of this world; if my kingship were of this world, my servants would fight, that I might not be handed over to the Jews; but my kingship is not from the world." Pilate said to him, "So you are a king?" Jesus answered, "You say that I am a king. For this I was born, and for this I have come into the world, to bear witness to the truth. Everyone who is of the truth hears my voice." Pilate said to him, "What is truth?" (Jn 18:36-38).

Then Pilate took Jesus and scourged him. And the soldiers plaited a crown of thorns, and put it on his head, arrayed him in a purple robe; they came up to him, saying, "Hail, King of the Jew!" and struck him with their hands (Jn 19:1-3).

Pilate was reluctant to condemn Jesus, but the crowd insisted crying out: *"If you release this man, you are not Caesar's friend; everyone who makes himself king sets himself against Caesar."* In the end Pilate felt he had no other option: *Then he handed him over to be crucified* (Jn 19:12, 16).

The Church of Flagellation

In the Crusader era (twelfth century) a chapel was constructed on the site and named the Church of the Flagellation. After the departure of the Crusaders in 1187, it fell into ruins. By the 1600s, pilgrims reported the building was being used as a stable by a scion of the Ottoman ruling class, Musta-fay Bey. According to an account by Fr. Roger in 1632, Bey had a room for his harem constructed on a second floor above, which collapsed. In

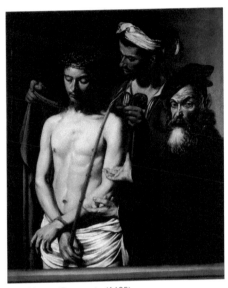

Ecce Homo, Caravaggio (1605)

1719, the run-down building was being used by a Turkish weaver, but pilgrims were admitted on payment of a candle.

In 1838, the Franciscans acquired the site and began the work of restoring the sanctuary. A financial gift from the Duke of Bavaria, Maximillian, made it possible to bring the restoration to a completion in 1839. There was another restoration of the church between 1927 and 1929, supervised by Roman architect Antonio Barluzzi.

Barluzzi kept the medieval style in his design. He brought artists from Italy to create and install the stained glass windows and mosaics. The stained glass panel behind the altar shows Jesus being scourged. On the left, Pilate washes his hands, and on the right Barabbas is freed from prison on Pilate's order. In the dome above the altar is a mosaic in the form of a crown of thorns, studded with radiant stars, symbolizing the victory of Jesus' resurrection over sin and death. The tabernacle door and the sanctuary lamp are the work of Aurelio Mistruzzi.

The Church of the Condemnation

Shortly before the present Church of the Condemnation was constructed in 1904, ruins of a previously unknown medieval church were uncovered on the site. The name of this church is not known.

The construction of the present church was supervised by a Franciscan architect, Br. Wendelin Hinterkeuser, who retained the Byzantine design. It was given the name Church of the Condemnation after large striated flagstones were uncovered. In the early twentieth century, it was believed that these flagstones formed part of *The Pavement, and in Hebrew, Gabbatha,* the place where Pilate had his judgement seat (Jn 19:13). Subsequent studies have shown that these flagstones were put in place when Emperor Hadrian rebuilt Jerusalem after the second Jewish revolt (132-135 AD) and formed part of the eastern forum of Aelia Capitolina.

To the left of the altar a diorama shows John trying to shield Mary's eyes from seeing her son take up the cross. The diorama above the altar depicts Jesus walking down the steps of the Antonia Fortress to accept his cross. In the windows of the dome, angels are shown holding the cruel instruments of the Passion, flanked by a depiction of Pilate washing his hands and the Imposition of the Cross. Notice the striated flagstones in the back of the church.

Adjacent buildings house the Studium Biblicum Franciscanum, Faculty of Biblical Science and Christian Biblical Archaeology. Also in this compound, there is a Sound and Light show on the history of Jerusalem and the Via Dolorosa. At the east end of the compound is the Archaeological Museum.

The Praetorium

Over the centuries pilgrims and scholars have held various opinions regarding the location of Jesus' trial before Pontius Pilate. Some hold that Pilate's praetorium was located at Herod's palace in the southwest part of the city, next to present-day Jaffa Gate. It is interesting to note that Mark does refer to the place of the praetorium as a palace: *And the soldiers led him away inside the palace (that is, the praetorium)* (Mk 15:16). Herod's palace would have been a comfortable residence for Pilate during his stay in Jerusalem for the Passover feast.

Literary sources from the Byzantine era place Pilate's praetorium on the site of the Hasmonean palace, located in the southeastern part of the Jewish Quarter of the Old City. A church built on this site was initially called the Church of Pilate. The name was later changed to the Church of St. Sophia (Greek for "Wisdom") because it was at the praetorium that Divine Wisdom was judged by a pagan judge. Near this church a large basilica was built in honor of the Holy Virgin named the New Church of Mary Mother of God. Sometimes referred to as the Nea (Greek for "New") Church, both of these churches can be seen represented on the famous sixth-century Madaba Mosaic Map in Jordan. The sixth-century Italian pilgrim from Piacenza made reference to these churches in his journal: "the basilica of St. Mary [the Nea Church] at St. Sophia which was the Praetorium."

Another possible location for the praetorium is the Antonia Fortress. This fortress, located in the northwest corner of the Temple compound, was built by Herod the Great to house Roman soldiers. Josephus, the Jewish historian, wrote that a cohort of soldiers (360-800) were assigned to the fortress: "a Roman cohort was permanently quartered there, and at the festivals took up positions in arms around the porticoes to watch the people and repress any insurrectionary movement." He describes the fortress as having one tower almost 100 feet high, giving Pilate and his soldiers a clear view of the entire Temple compound. Pilate had come to Jerusalem from his capital at Caesarea to oversee the security of the city during the feast of Passover, a time when tensions ran high between the Jews and their Roman occupiers. What better place for Pilate to stay than in a fortress with his soldiers, and which offered a commanding view of Temple activities?

Another argument in favor of the Antonia Fortress comes from a small detail given by two of the evangelists. After Pilate had Jesus scourged and delivered him to be crucified, *the soldiers of the governor took Jesus into the praetorium, and they gathered the whole battalion [cohort?] before him* (Mt 27:26-27). Mark records a similar scene. After Jesus was delivered to be crucified, *the soldiers led him away inside the palace (that is, the praetorium); and they called together the whole cohort* (Mk 15:15-16). According to Josephus, a cohort was housed in the Antonia Fortress.

Today, across the street from the Church of Condemnation, is an elementary school for Muslim boys. In the time of Jesus, a large fortification housing Roman soldiers lay on this site called the Antonia Fortress.

The Franciscans accepted the tradition that Pilate's praetorium was located in the Antonia Fortress. For over a hundred years they have been leading the faithful in a devotional prayer called the Via Dolorosa (Latin for "Sorrowful Way") which retraces the path Jesus followed from the moment of his condemnation to his burial near Golgotha. Every Friday afternoon at 3:00 in the courtyard of the El-Omariya School (formerly the location of the Antonia Fortress), the Franciscans begin the prayer with the first station, Jesus is Condemned to Death. The second station, Jesus Takes up His Cross, is prayed on the street next to the Church of the Condemnation.

The Crucifixion, Death, Burial and Resurrection of Our Lord Jesus Christ

After Pilate pronounced the unjust sentence of death, Jesus was led out of the gates of the praetorium. Exhausted from his two trials and suffering terribly from the scourging, he was dressed in his rough tunic, now encrusted with blood. He was taken to the designated execution ground, which was a former rock quarry *a place called Golgotha (which means the place of the skull)* and *they offered him wine to drink, mingled with gall; but when he tasted it, he would not drink it* (Mt 27:33-34). Gall, a mixture of herbs and myrrh, is a form of a narcotic offered to Jesus to help alleviate some of the pain he would experience during his Crucifixion. His refusal to accept the gall is a sign of his desire to offer himself fully in an act of total sacrificial love.

Crucifixion was a method of execution used by the Romans to deter rebellion and criminal activity. It was not the punishment for citizens or aristocrats but for the lowest classes: servants and slaves; peasants and bandits and foreigners. Carrying out crucifixions was the work of specialists known as "immunes." First they stripped Jesus of his garments, and bound his arms to the crossbeam, known as a "patibulum," with rope. Then they drove six-inch nails through a spot just above the wrist of both forearms and lifted the crossbeam, and slammed it into an open notch of the tall vertical stake. They squeezed Jesus' feet onto a small wooden block and nailed his heels and the block to the stake.

In this posture, suspended by the arms, it becomes very difficult and painful to breathe. The condemned must struggle to lift himself up, thereby putting more strain on his nailed arms and feet and bringing fresh waves of agony. It results in a slow and torturous death from a combination of blood loss and asphyxiation.

Typically the Romans affixed a sign on the cross above the crucified indicating the charge against him: *And over his head they put the charge against him, which read, "This is Jesus the King of the Jews"* (Mt 27:37). In John's Gospel the title written by Pilate read, *"Jesus of Nazareth, the King of the Jews." Many of the Jews read this title, for the place where Jesus was crucified was near the city; and it was written in Hebrew, in Latin, and in Greek.* Though literacy was not yet widespread, many who passed by the site were able to read the title, such as Jews trained in reading the Hebrew Scriptures; or members of the Roman ruling class, as Latin was the language of the Roman occupiers; or merchants or travelers, as Greek was the commercial language of the region. The chief priests objected to this title saying, *"Do not write, 'The King of the Jews,' but, 'This man said, I am King of the Jews.'" Pilate answered, "What I have written I have written"* (Jn 19:19-22).

And when they had crucified him, they divided his garments among them by casting lots; then they sat down and kept watch over him there (Mt 27:35-36). The division of Jesus' seamless robe among the soldiers is an allusion to Psalm 22: *they divide my garments among them, and for my raiment they cast lots* (Ps 22:18). John makes an explicit reference to this messianic prophecy: *This was to fulfill the scripture, "They parted my garments among them, and for my clothing they cast lots"* (Jn 19:24). This is also the Psalm Jesus quotes just before he *yielded up his spirit: Eli, Eli, lama sabachthani?" that is, "My God, my God, why have you forsaken me?"* (Ps 22:1; Mt 27:50).

Psalm 22 was often invoked by Jews in moments of great despair. In this Psalm, we encounter a righteous man who has been abused and mocked for his faith by his ungodly enemies. He turns to God for help in his suffering and is ultimately vindicated. Like the innocent one who undergoes humiliation and mistreatment in the Psalm, Jesus' suffering will also end in a total victory.

Mark records the time of the Crucifixion: *And it was the third hour, when they crucified him,* that is, at nine o'clock in the morning on Friday of Passion Week (Mk 15:25). Jesus was crucified between two *robbers* (Mt 27:38; Mk 15:27) or *criminals* (Lk 23:32), one on the right and one on the left. Typically, the crucified would spew curses and blasphemies as they hung on the cross. Jesus instead offered words of mercy and kindness and he prayed for his executioners: *"Father, forgive them; for they know not what they do."* It was not enough for Jesus to pray for his persecutors, he also wanted to make excuses for them. One of the criminals declared that, *"this man has done nothing wrong." And he said, Jesus, remember me when you come into your kingdom." And [Jesus] said to him, "Truly, I say to you, today you will be with me in Paradise"* (Lk 23:34; 41-43).

Hour after hour, Jesus hung on the cross, enduring the agony of breathing at the cost of tearing his flesh against the Roman nails. He was mocked and struck by the soldiers and he was taunted by the jeering crowds. Even worse than the physical suffering of the crucifixion was the mental agony which Jesus took on himself: humiliation, abandonment and loneliness.

The three Synoptic evangelists record that there was darkness from the sixth hour (12:00 noon) until the ninth hour (3:00 pm). At the ninth hour, *Jesus cried again with a*

Christ on the Cross, Rembrandt van Rijin (1631)

loud voice and yielded up his spirit. And behold, the curtain of the temple was torn in two, from top to bottom; and the earth shook, and the rocks were split (Mt 27:50-51). When the Roman centurion and others with him saw the earthquake they *were filled with awe, and said, "Truly this was the Son of God!"* (Mt 27:54). Doubtless this soldier of Caesar had crucified many before, but he felt something mysterious in Jesus and the supernatural event that followed his final breath, and he publicly proclaimed the divinity of Christ.

In the Jewish Temple, beyond the court of entrance was a place that was called "Holy," and beyond it, a place called the "Holy of Holies." A curtain separated it from the other chambers of the Temple. Only the high priest was permitted into this most sacred chamber once a year to perform rituals: *but into the second [Holy of Holies] only the high priest goes, and but once a year, and not without taking blood which he offers for himself and for the errors of the people* (Heb 9:7).

The tearing of the Temple curtain signaled the establishment of the New Covenant (New Testament) through Jesus' sacrificial death on Golgotha: *But when Christ appeared as a high priest of the good things that have come, then through the greater and more perfect tent (not made with hands, that is not of this creation) he entered once for all into the Holy Place, taking not the blood of goats and calves but his own blood, thus securing an eternal redemption* (Heb 9:11-12).

All of the evangelists mention the presence of women at the place of Jesus' Crucifixion. Matthew records that there were *many women, among whom were Mary Magdalene, and Mary the mother of James and Joseph, and the mother of the sons of Zebedee* (Mt 27:55-56). In John's narrative, the Mother of Jesus was also present, in addition to the other women. *When Jesus saw his mother, and the disciple whom he loved standing near, he said to his mother, "Woman, behold, your son!" Then he said to the disciple, "Behold, your mother!" And from that hour the disciple took her to his own home* (Jn 19:26-27).

The term *"Woman"* was a polite form of address in biblical antiquity and not in any way impersonal. Jesus' use of the word *"Woman"* is probably a reference to the Genesis account of the curse of the serpent in which the Mother of the Messiah is referred to as *woman*: *"I will put enmity between you and the woman, and between your seed and her seed; he shall bruise your head, and you will shall bruise his heel"* (Gen 3:15).

Jesus' last earthly act was providing a home for his Mother. He entrusts the care of his Mother Mary to the apostle John, the beloved disciple. Here John represents all of Jesus' beloved disciples to whom he gives his Mother. And his Mother, in turn, offers her maternal care for all the

disciples whom Jesus loves.

When Jesus said *"I thirst,"* the soldiers *put a sponge full of vinegar on hyssop and held it to his mouth.* At the original Passover, the Israelites used hyssop branches to smear the blood of the lamb on their doorposts to protect their homes from the destroying angel (see Ex 12:21-23). *When Jesus had received the vinegar, he said, "It is finished": and he bowed his head and gave up his spirit* (Jn 19:28-30).

The Sabbath was approaching and Jewish law did not allow the bodies of the crucified to remain on the crosses during this sacred day of rest. So the Jews asked Pilate if their legs might be broken, thus hastening death. Their bodies could then be taken away for burial. The soldiers first broke the legs of the two criminals, but when they came to Jesus they found that he was already dead. *For these things took place that the scripture might be fulfilled, "Not a bone of him shall be broken"* (Jn 19:36). According to the *ordinance of the passover*, the Passover lamb was to have no broken bones (Ex 12:43; 46).

Instead, one of the soldiers pierced his side with a spear to ensure that he was dead, *and at once there came out blood and water* (Jn 19:34). The *water* streaming from Jesus' side is a symbol of the new life given to those who receive Baptism; the *blood* is the nourishment offered in the Eucharist. Jesus, the new Adam, gives birth to his bride, the Church, constituted by these sacraments of Baptism and Eucharist, just as Adam's bride, Eve, came forth from his side (see Gen 2:21-23).

All four of the Gospels record Joseph of Arimathea's request to Pilate to remove Jesus' body from the cross, so as not to deny him the dignity of a proper burial. Joseph was a wealthy and respected member of the Sanhedrin who had a family tomb nearby. Pilate granted Joseph's request after learning from the centurion that Jesus was truly dead (see Mk 15:45). In John's narrative, Nicodemus brought a mixture of myrrh and aloes weighing about a hundred pounds to assist Joseph in preparing Jesus' body for burial. They wrapped his body with the spices in a linen shroud and place it the tomb which was *close at hand* (Jn 19: 42). Matthew is the only evangelist to mention that the Jesus was laid *in his own [Joseph's] new tomb, which he had hewn in the rock.* Joseph then *rolled a great stone to the door of the tomb and departed* (Mt 27:60).

Mary Magdalene and the other Mary came to the tomb around

dawn on the Sunday after the Sabbath and witnessed a great earthquake and an angel of the Lord descend from heaven. The angel rolled back the stone covering the entrance to the tomb and sat upon it.

The Entombment of Christ, Caravaggio (1602-1603)

His appearance was like light-ning, and his raiment white as snow. And for fear of him the guards trembled and became like dead men. But the angel said to the women, "Do not be afraid; for I know that you seek Jesus who was crucified. He is not here; for he has risen, as he said. Come and see the place where he lay. Then go quickly and tell his disciples that he has risen from the dead, and behold, he is going before you to Galilee; there you will see him. Lo, I have told you so" (Mt 28:1-7).

As the two women were making their way to tell the disciples what they had seen, they encounter the Risen Jesus and *took hold of his feet and worshiped him* (Mt 28:9). The Resurrection of Jesus is the climax of his earthly mission and the greatest miracle in all history.

"It is an extraordinary grace to be gathered here in prayer. The empty tomb, that new garden grave where Joseph of Arimathea had reverently placed Jesus' body, is the place from which the proclamation of the resurrection begins: "Do not be afraid; I know that you are looking for Jesus who was crucified. He is not here, for he has been raised, as he said.

Come, see the place where he lay. Then go quickly and tell his disciples, 'He has been raised from the dead'" (Mt 28:5-7). This proclamation, confirmed by the testimony of those to whom the risen Lord appeared, is the heart of the Christian message, faithfully passed down from generation to generation...

Let us receive the special grace of this moment. We pause in reverent silence before this empty tomb in order to rediscover the grandeur of our Christian vocation: we are men and women of resurrection, and not of death.

From this place we learn how to live our lives, the trials of our Churches and of the whole world, in the light of Easter morning. Every injury, every one of our pains and sorrows, has been borne on the shoulders of the Good Shepherd who offered himself in sacrifice and thereby opened the way to eternal life. His open wounds are the cleft through which the torrent of his mercy is poured out upon the world.

Let us not allow ourselves to be robbed of the basis of our hope! Let us not deprive the world of the joyful message of the resurrection! And let us not be deaf to the powerful summons to unity which rings out from this very place, in the words of the One who, risen from the dead, calls all of us 'my brothers'" (see Mt 28:10; Jn 20:17). From A Speech by Pope Francis during his Holy Land Pilgrimage at The Holy Sepulcher Ecumenical Celebration Jerusalem. May 25, 2014

History

At the time of Jesus' Crucifixion, *the place of the skull* or *Golgotha* (derived from the Aramaic word for skull) was a rock mound which may have resembled a skull. This would explain how the site got its name. A more recognizable name for Golgotha is Calvary, derived from the Latin word for skull – "calvaria." Archaeological research has revealed that Calvary was an abandoned quarry, probably due to the poor quality of the rock. Its location just outside the city walls along a well-travelled road was an ideal place for the Roman executors to display the bodies of the crucified as a deterrent to anyone who might consider defying Roman authority.

John tells us the site of the crucifixion had a garden: *Now in the place where he was crucified there was a garden, and in the garden a new tomb where no one had ever been laid* (Jn 19:41). He also mentions that *the tomb was close at hand*, about 140 feet from Calvary. The presence of another first-century tomb adjacent to the Sryriac Orthodox chapel, and very near to Jesus' burial cave, in the present-day church points to the fact that this area was also used as a cemetery.

It is believed that the early Christian community came to this site in the years following Jesus' Resurrection to pray and to recall the central mysteries of their faith. When it became clear to these early Christians that Jesus may not be returning in their lifetime, knowledge of the location of the death, burial and Resurrection of Jesus was passed down to the next generation in a practice known as "oral tradition." An unbroken succession of bishops of Jerusalem in the following centuries helped to ensure that the location of these sacred events would not be forgotten.

From 41-44 AD, Herod Agrippa constructed the so-called Third Wall north of Calvary, bringing the site inside the city limits for the first time. It doesn't seem likely that the sacred site would have been developed at this time due to the fact that it was a cemetery.

A widespread Jewish rebellion against Roman rule ended in 70 AD with the total destruction of the city of Jerusalem. An eyewitness, first-century historian Flavius Josephus, describes the devastation: "It was so thoroughly laid even with the ground … that there was left nothing to make those that came thither believe it had ever been inhabited." Over time, those who had fled Jerusalem before the siege, including the Christians, returned and the city gradually recovered.

About 50 years later, another war known as the Bar Kochba revolt, erupted between the Jews and the Romans which brought more devastation to Jerusalem. The Roman emperor at that time, Hadrian, decided to punish the Jews for their insurrection by banning them from living in, or even visiting, the city of Jerusalem under penalty of death. After the war ended in 135 AD Hadrian rebuilt Jerusalem on a Roman model and named the new city after himself: Aelia Capitolina, which referred to his hereditary surname, Aelius. He also decided to thoroughly paganize the city. A temple to Jupiter was constructed on the site where the Jewish Temple previously stood. Hadrian's Capitoline temple was constructed on the site of Calvary and included a temple to the goddess Aphrodite (Venus).

According to St. Jerome, Hadrian placed the temple of Aphrodite here to discourage Christians from praying there, and to assert the dominance of the Roman state religion at the site Christians venerated. As he wrote in 395: "From the time of Hadrian to the reign of Constantine, a period of about one hundred and eighty years, a statue of Jupiter stood on the site of the Resurrection, while a marble statue of Venus was placed by the pagans on the rock of the Cross and became an object of worship. The authors of this persecution thought that by defiling the holy places with idols, they could take away our faith in the Resurrection and the Cross."

At the Council of Nicaea in 325, Bishop Macarius, bishop of Jerusalem, consulted with Emperor Constantine concerning the status of the sacred sites of Calvary and the Holy Tomb. Constantine then made the momentous decision to construct a splendid sanctuary of Christian worship for the first time on these sacred sites. In his *Life of Constantine*, early church historian Eusebius, bishop of Caesarea, tells of Constantine's motivation to commemorate these holy places at this "august location." According to Eusebius, Constantine "deemed it necessary to bring to life in Jerusalem the blessed place of the resurrection of the savior." He "commanded that here shall be erected round the Grotto of Salvation a sanctuary of magnificence..."

The first task was to raze the Capitoline temple from the site. When all the debris had been removed, Bishop Macarius, an eyewitness to this work, was overjoyed to lean that the rock of Calvary and the sacred burial cave were intact. Eusebius describes the dramatic scene, as "layer after layer of subsoil was stripped away, the most holy memorial of the savior's resurrection, beyond all hopes, came into view. The Holy of Holies, the cave was, like our savior, restored to life... And over the true memorial of salvation was built the New Jerusalem, facing the far-famed one [Jewish Temple] of old." The rock-cut Tomb, which included a vestibule for the preparation of the body, and the burial couch for the Divine Savior's body, were apparently found undisturbed.

Next, workers removed all the rock around the Holy Tomb and built an Edicule, from the Latin word "aedicule," meaning "small edifice," over the burial cave. A rotunda, called the Anastasis, Greek for "Resurrection," was constructed to enclose the Edicule, which consisted of a dome supported by columns forming a circle around the Edicule. To the east of the Anastasis, a courtyard, open to the sky and enclosed by a Triportico, with columns on three sides, was constructed. It was built to set apart the rock of Calvary, which was located in the southeast corner of the courtyard, left exposed and surmounted by a cross. Attached to the east side of the courtyard was an apsidal basilica consisting of five naves and four rows of columns. The apse of the basilica faced west toward the Holy Tomb, contrary to the usual practice of church apses facing east.

Capable of holding a large number of worshipers, the spacious basilica was called the Martyrium, in honor of the Divine Martyr who laid down his life here at this most sacred of all places. Beneath the basilica was a crypt and an ancient cistern, marking the site of the discovery of the True Cross. To the east of the Martyrium was an atrium followed by steps leading down to the main thoroughfare in Jerusalem, the Cardo Maximus. Construction of Constantine's church, to be named the Church of the Resurrection, began in 326 and was later consecrated on September 17, 335, even though work on the domed rotunda would not be finished for many more years due to the enormous effort required to free the Tomb from the surrounding rock.

Eusebius was the bishop appointed to preach the sermon at the dedication in 335 for the absentee emperor Constantine. Eusebius records that Constantine had hoped to be baptized in the Jordan River but he died in 337 before he was able to visit the Holy Land.

In 614, Persian invaders set fire to Constantine's church causing an unknown amount of damage. The destruction of many churches and the mass killings of Christians continued for nearly a decade, until an edict of 622 allowed Abbot Modestus of the monastery of St. Theodosius near Bethlehem to restore the church. With the support from the Armenians, Modestus completed his redesign but it lacked the grandeur of Constantine's basilica.

When the Islamic army of Caliph Omar arrived in Jerusalem in 638 to take possession of the city, the caliph was invited by the local patriarch to pray in the church. But he declined, saying, "If I had prayed in the church it would have been lost to you, for the Believers would have taken it saying: Omar prayed here."

As the new ruler of Jerusalem and Palestine, Omar guaranteed Christians the possession of their churches and freedom of worship, upon paying a certain "infidels" tax. Under successive Arab dynasties for several centuries, pilgrims from Europe and Byzantium were allowed safe passage to visit the holy sites.

This era of relative peace and goodwill ended in 1009, when the third

Fatimid Caliph al-Hakim initiated a violent, fanatical persecution of non-Muslims and ordered the destruction of all Christian churches. According to the Arab chronicler, Yahia, Hakim gave orders to destroy the church "until all traces of it have disappeared, and to endeavor to uproot its foundations." Constantine's grand basilica, which for nearly 700 years had so spectacularly affirmed to pilgrims the centrality of their Christian faith, now lay in ruins. So complete was the destruction that the rock of the holy burial cave was "broken by pickaxe, and indeed most of it was hewed out and carried off." Today only a small remnant of the burial cave remains, mostly covered in marble by the present-day Edicule.

After the death of Hakim in 1021, a treaty was signed between Hakim's son Ali az-Zahir and the Byzantine Emperor Romanus III, which granted permission for the construction of a new church on the site. Work began in 1042 with funds provided by the imperial court in Constantinople during the rule of Constantine IX Monomachus. However, the contributions weren't enough to rebuild the church on the scale of Constantine's grand basilica.

The atrium and the Martyrium were abandoned. Only the site of the courtyard, now called the Holy Garden, and the rotunda were kept. An apse was built into the west side of the Holy Garden adjacent to the rotunda, this time facing east. Three chapels were added to the east side of the Holy Garden, each one commemorating events connected with Jesus' Passion: the Chapel of the Insults, the Chapel of the Crowning with Thorns, and the Chapel of the Division of the Raiment. Next to the rock of Calvary, a chapel called the Chapel of the Nailing to the Cross was added. The new Church of the Resurrection was completed in 1048.

This was the church the Crusaders led by Godfrey of Bouillon entered on July 15, 1099, after a bloody battle with Jerusalem's Muslim defenders. A council was held July 22 in the Holy Sepulcher to decide what form of government would be established. Godfrey's followers wanted to make him the first Crusader king, but he refused the title, saying, "God forbid that I should wear a crown of gold where my master wore a crown of thorns." He was called instead "Advocatus Sancti Sepulchri," which means Defender of the Holy Sepulcher, and he became the first Latin ruler of Palestine as head of the Crusader Kingdom of Jerusalem until his death in 1100. Godfrey himself seems to have preferred the more ambiguous term "Princeps," Latin for the "foremost," or simply his title of "dux," or duke, from back home in Lower Lorraine.

The Crusaders laid plans for a total restoration of the church. In 1114, work began on a Western-style redesign, led by the finest crafts-men from all over Europe. For the first time, both the rotunda and the Holy Garden were brought under one roof. The crypt under the site where the Martyrium (basilica) stood was excavated and two chapels were constructed, one named the Chapel of St. Helena and the other the Chapel of the Finding of the Holy Cross. Above the Chapel of St. Helena a monastery was constructed for the Canons of the Holy Sepulcher who were responsible for the Latin liturgy in the church. The apse in the western wall of the Holy Garden was removed and a choir was constructed joining it to the rotunda. A new apse was added to the east part of the choir. Around the east wall of the choir a semicircular ambulatory was constructed which included three new chapels replacing those of Monomachus' church. The Chapel of Calvary was extended westward and a new entrance to Calvary was added on the south side of the church.

The Crusaders renamed the church, consecrated on July 15, 1149, the Church of the Holy Sepulcher. Marking the 50th anniversary of the First Crusade, the rededication of the church was a celebration of what had now become an important aspect of Christian devotion – pilgrimage. From this era onward, the Latin term "peregrinus," which had previ-ously simply meant a "traveler" of any kind, now referred exclusively to a "pilgrim." By 1128, the Crusaders had liberated all the Gospel sites from Muslim control (except Caesarea Philippi) and the faithful were once again able to see firsthand, "all the places where Christ our God had walked for our salvation," in the words of the pilgrim Daniel the Abbot. Most importantly, pilgrims to the Holy City could now commemorate all the events of Jesus' Passion, culminating in the Church of the Holy Sepulcher.

A bell tower was added to the west of the new entrance around 1170. The basic form of the church today is that of the twelfth-century Crusader basilica. However, damage from earthquakes (including one that destroyed the upper part of the bell tower), fires and the effects of time and weather, have required periodic repairs. The Franciscans carried out two important restorations in 1555 and 1719.

In 1808, a massive fire almost wholly gutted the rotunda and Edicule. While the Franciscans appealed in vain to the West for funds to repair the damage, the Russians, on behalf of the Orthodox Church, obtained permission from the Ottoman Turkish sultan to replace the Edicule. Designed by the Greek architect Nikolaos Komnenos, the new Edicule featuring a Muscovite cupola was dedicated in 1810. During this extensive redesign, the sarcophagi of the Crusader kings of Jerusalem, located beneath Calvary and on the north side of the Stone of the Anointing were removed to make way for the construction of two staircases to Calvary and for other alterations to the church. The Greek-led restoration has had many critics who believe that much of the basilica's beauty was lost. The restoration also enclosed the Crusader choir (Katholicon) with walls, giving the building a dark and dismal appearance. It had the unfortunate effect of making it more difficult for the visitor to visualize the physical relationship between Calvary and the Holy Tomb.

An earthquake in 1927 caused major damage to the church. Both the dome of the rotunda and the Edicule were so badly damaged they were in danger of collapsing. The British Mandate authorities had scaffolding installed to support the dome and steel beams were fastened around the outside of the Edicule to prevent it from collapsing. After an agreement was reached among the three communities, Greeks, Franciscans and Armenians that hold rights in the church, work began in 1961 to restore the dome and Edicule as much as possible to their original splendor. New columns were added in the rotunda and the damaged pillars and walls were repaired.

On January 2, 1997, the new dome was dedicated. The modern design of the rotunda above the edicule represents the glory of God enveloping the Risen Christ. Restoration of the Edicule was completed on March 22, 2017, at a cost of nearly $4 million which included a large donation by King Abdullah II of Jordan.

The Basilica of the Holy Sepulcher

The reconstructions and additions that have shaped the Church of the Holy Sepulcher over the centuries make it a complex building to

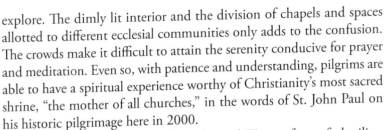

explore. The dimly lit interior and the division of chapels and spaces allotted to different ecclesial communities only adds to the confusion. The crowds make it difficult to attain the serenity conducive for prayer and meditation. Even so, with patience and understanding, pilgrims are able to have a spiritual experience worthy of Christianity's most sacred shrine, "the mother of all churches," in the words of St. John Paul on his historic pilgrimage here in 2000.

The church is not laid out in the traditional Western form of a basilica. The entrance is from the courtyard on the south side through a door framed by decorated masonry dating to the Crusader period. Originally there were two doors, but the one on the right side was closed and filled in on the orders of Saladin after the Crusaders were expelled from Jerusalem in 1187. Just before entering the church, look to the right in the pavement where you will find a wooden cover above the tomb of the English knight, Philip d'Aubigny, tutor to Henry III. In 1810, when all the other Crusader tombs were desecrated, it was spared because it was hidden behind the doorkeeper's bench.

To the right of his tomb steps lead up to the Chapel of Our Lady of Sorrows, also called the Chapel of the Franks, which is under the care of the Franciscans. During the Crusader era, exclusive access to Calvary was possible through this chapel but the entrance has been blocked since the Middle Ages. Underneath is the small Greek Orthodox chapel named in honor of St. Mary of Egypt, a prostitute who experienced a conversion during her visit to the Constantinian church in the fourth century.

Nearby, a door leads to two Ethiopian Orthodox chapels on two different levels. On the ground level, upon passing through the door, is the Chapel of St. Michael, dedicated to the Archangel. Stairs to the left lead to the upper level Chapel of the Four Beasts, alluding to the four beasts mentioned in the Book of Revelation. The exit of the upper chapel leads to the Ethiopian monastery of Deir es-Sultan. Here, pilgrims can see the Crusader ruins of the monastery of the Canons Regular of the Holy Sepulcher.

The main doors to the basilica are opened each morning by members of two Muslim families, Nusseibeh and Judah, whose ancestors were entrusted with this responsibility by Saladin in the twelfth century as a way of keeping the peace between the three main custodians of the

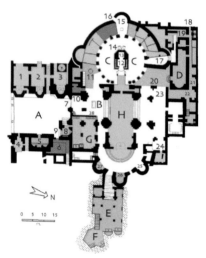

CHURCH OF THE HOLY SEPULCHRE (ACTUAL PLAN):
A. Forecourt. B. Stone of Unction. C. Rotunda or Anastasis. D. Chapel of the Apparition. E. Chapel of St. Helena. F. Chapel of the Discovery of the Cross. G. Calvary. H. Greek Choir. 1-6. Chapels of St. James, St. John the Baptist, Forty Martyrs, St. Abraham, St. John the Evangelist, St. Michael. 7. Entrance. 8. Chapel of the Franks (upper floor). 9. Chapel of St. Mary the Egyptian. 10. Muslim Doorkeepers. 11. Altar of the 3 Marys. 12. Chapel of the Angel. 13. Sepulchre of Jesus. 14. Chapel of the Copts. 15. Chapel of the Syrian Jacobites. 16. Jewish tombs: "Sepulchre of Joseph of Arimathea". 17. Passageway. 18. Crusader Chapel. 19. Cistern. 20. Altar of St. Mary Magdalen. 21. Franciscan Convent. 22. Franciscan Sacristy. 23. Arches of the Virgin. 24. Prison of Christ. 25-27. Chapels of St. Longinus, Division of the Raiment, Mocking. 28. Chapel of Adam (beneath Calvary).

basilica: the Greek Orthodox Church, the Franciscans (Latin-rite Catholic Church) and the Armenian Apostolic Church. One family holds possession of the key, the other uses the key to unlock the door. Representatives of the three custodians wait inside the church, then open the door once it has been unlocked. The same ritual is performed in reverse in the evening when it is time to lock the doors.

Upon entering the basilica, a large mosaic panel by an Italian artist in the Greek style installed in 1991 comes into view directly ahead. It depicts the deposition of Christ's body from the cross, and its preparation for burial by Joseph of Arimathea and Nicodemus. Below the panel, a rectangular slab of marble marks the place where Jesus' body was anointed with *myrrh and aloes* and then bound *in linen cloths with the spices, as is the burial custom* of the Jews (Jn 19:39-40). Devout

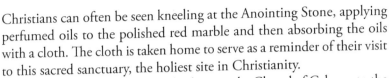

Christians can often be seen kneeling at the Anointing Stone, applying perfumed oils to the polished red marble and then absorbing the oils with a cloth. The cloth is taken home to serve as a reminder of their visit to this sacred sanctuary, the holiest site in Christianity.

On the right, a steep stairway leads up to the Chapel of Calvary, to the southern nave (Franciscan) of the chapel. This floor is on level with the top of the rocky outcrop where Jesus was crucified. Here, in the center of the nave, the tenth station of the Via Dolorosa is prayed: Jesus is Stripped of His Garments. At the east end of the nave is the Altar of the Crucifixion (Franciscan), before which is prayed the eleventh station of the Via Dolorosa: Jesus is Nailed to the Cross. The silver-plated bronze altar was a gift of Ferdinand de Medici in 1588. A mosaic above the altar shows Jesus being nailed to the cross. On the southern wall, the story of the Binding of Isaac (see Gen 22:1-19) is depicted. Christians see in this story a foreshadowing of Jesus' sacrifice on Calvary. The three half-circle mosaics on the eastern and southern walls are the work of Italian artist Luigi Trifoglio. Renowned Italian mosaicist Pietro D'Achiardi created the mosaics for the ceiling and arches. Antonio Barluzzi supervised the work of the artists whose work was finished in 1937. In the center of the ceiling, there is a mosaic depicting the Ascension of Christ, the only mosaic remaining from the Crusader period.

The northern nave of the chapel is under the care of the Greek Orthodox Church, and includes the Altar of the Cross of Jesus. It marks the place where tradition holds that the cross of Jesus stood and where he suffered his agonizing death. Before this altar the twelfth station of the Via Dolorosa is prayed: Jesus Dies on the Cross. A large silver icon above the altar lit by lamps and candles in the Greek style shows the crucifixion of Jesus with Mary and John standing at the cross. Glass panels on either side of the altar allow pilgrims to see the ancient rock of Calvary. Pilgrims can touch the rock of Calvary by kneeling beneath the altar and reaching through an opening in the silver disc directly above the rock.

To the right of the Greek altar is the Altar of Our Lady of Sorrows (Franciscan). Above the altar is a bust of the sorrowful Mother of Jesus, the thirteenth station of the Via Dolorosa: Jesus is Taken Down from the Cross. This commemorates the place where Mary received the body of her Son. The bust of Mary shows a sword piercing her heart, fulfilling

Simeon's prophecy: and a sword will pierce through your own soul (Lk 2:35). A gift of Queen Maria I Braganza of Portugal, the statue was brought from Lisbon in 1778.

Leave the Greek chapel using the stairs at the west end and turn left at the bottom, walking past the Anointing Stone. On the left, a floor-mounted marble disk surmounted by a cupola marks the place where the three Marys stood while watching Jesus in agony on the cross: *But standing by the cross of Jesus were his mother, and his mother's sister, Mary the wife of Clopas, and Mary Magdalene* (Jn 19:25). On the wall behind the cupola is a large Armenian mosaic installed in 1970 depicting the crucifixion of Jesus. This area belongs exclusively to the Armenians, and a sacristy and residence for Armenian clergy are located up the steps to the left of this wall.

Turn right and you will find yourself under the great dome of the rotunda, built in the classical Roman style. In the center of the rotunda lies the Edicule, the shrine containing Christ's tomb that marks the site of Christianity's greatest mystery: the Resurrection of Jesus Christ. Here pilgrims pray the fourteenth station of the Via Dolorosa: Jesus is Buried in the Tomb.

The Edicule, installed by the Greek Orthodox Church in 1810, encloses the scant remains of the original rock-cut tomb in which Jesus was buried. Pilgrims enter the two-chamber Edicule through a vestibule called the Chapel of the Angel in which can be found a pedestal, said to contain part of the original rolling stone which covered the entrance to the rock-cut tomb and upon which the angel sat after it had been rolled away. Entrance to the burial chamber requires most pilgrims to bend down as the opening is quite low. The marble slab on the right covers the rock where tradition says that Jesus' body was laid to rest. The slab was installed in 1555 and was purposefully cracked to deter Ottoman looters.

Above the slab are three images of the Resurrection of Jesus, each belonging to one of the principal communities of the Holy Sepulcher: On the left is an oil painting (Franciscan); in the center the image is in marble relief (Greek); and on the right is another oil painting (Armenian). On the opposite wall is a glass panel installed in 2017 to allow pilgrims a glimpse of the original rock of the burial cave.

"Here, at the Holy Sepulcher, I kneel before the place of His burial: 'Behold the place where they laid him.' The tomb is empty. It is a silent witness to the central event of human history: the Resurrection of our Lord Jesus Christ. For nearly two thousand years, the empty tomb has borne witness to the victory of Life over death. With the Apostles and Evangelists, with the Church of every time and place, we too bear witness and proclaim: 'Christ rose from the dead, he will never die again; death no longer has dominion over Him.'" (St. John Paul II on March 26, 2000 during his visit to the Basilica of the Holy Sepulcher)

Above the Edicule is the great dome which shows twelve golden rays representing the twelve apostles. Each of the twelve rays divide into three streams of light symbolizing the Holy Trinity. Stars radiating on a mother-of-pearl backdrop, symbolize the luminous cloud, a sign of God's presence: *Then Moses went up on the mountain, and the cloud covered the mountain. The glory of the Lord settled on Mount Sinai* (Ex 24:15-16).

Directly opposite the Edicule is the Greek Orthodox cathedral, called the Katholicon. Notice the small, navel-shaped marble pedestal near the center. The "omphalos," Greek for navel, is meant to mark this holy site as the center of the world.

Attached to the west side of the Edicule is the Coptic Orthodox Chapel of the Holy Virgin. Pilgrims are invited to touch part of the original tomb of Jesus located beneath the altar, the virgin rock blackened by centuries of votive candle smoke.

Pass through the doorway to the west to reach the Syriac Orthodox Chapel of St. Nicodemus. Its curved back wall is actually one of the original apses of the fourth-century Constantinian rotunda. Note the dilapidated condition of the chapel. Syriac Orthodox clergy celebrate their liturgy here each Sunday morning and on feast days but are not permitted to make any changes to the appearance of the space. This is due to the fact that the Armenian Apostolic Church is the owner of the chapel, and does not want to risk losing ownership of the chapel by allowing the Syriac Church to make improvements. On the south wall, is a low entrance leading to first-century tombs. Their traditional names are the tombs of Joseph of Arimathea and Nicodemus. As noted above, it was Joseph of Arimathea who offered his own tomb for Jesus' burial. Nicodemus assisted Joseph in preparing Jesus' body for burial.

After exiting the Syriac chapel, turn left to reach the Franciscan section of the basilica. Here, an altar dedicated to St. Mary Magdalene can be seen attached to a pillar. The bronze relief panel above the altar, created by Fr. Andrea Martini, OFM, depicts Mary Magdalene's encounter with the Risen Christ on the morning of the Resurrection: Jesus said to her, "Mary" (Jn 20:16).

To the left, bronze doors lead to the Chapel of the Apparition. It commemorates the tradition, though not found in the Gospels, of Jesus' encounter with his Mother on the morning of the Resurrection. The splendid bronze doors were donated by the people of Australia in 1982. Inside, on the right, a small niche holds a truncated, reddish remnant of the Column of Flagellation, the column to which Jesus was tied when he was scourged by the soldiers. A daily procession led by the Franciscans visits the principal holy places within the church and concludes here with Benediction of the Most Blessed Sacrament.

Pass through the large pillars to reach the Arches of the Virgin where there are more pillars, columns and walls from previous basilicas. At the far end of the transept is the small Greek Chapel of the Prison of Christ. Although not recorded in the Gospels, tradition holds that Jesus was temporarily imprisoned here before his crucifixion.

After exiting the Prison of Christ, turn left to enter the ambulatory which includes three small chapels commemorating different events related to Jesus' Passion. The first is a Greek chapel dedicated to St. Longinus, the Roman soldier, recalling the moment the soldier pieces Jesus side with a spear: But one of the soldiers pierced his side with a spear, and at once there came out blood and water (Jn 19:34). Next is the Armenian Chapel of the Division of the Raiment: When the soldiers had crucified Jesus they took his garments and made four parts, one for each soldier; also his tunic (Jn 19:23). Finally, the Greek Chapel of Mocking recalls the soldiers' mistreatment of Jesus: And the soldiers plaited a crown of thorns, and put it on his head, and arrayed him in a purple robe; they came up to him, saying, "Hail, King of the Jews!" and struck him with their hands (Jn 19:2-3). The column beneath the altar is said to be the column Jesus sat on when he was crowned with thorns and mocked by the soldiers.

Between the second and third chapels in the ambulatory, steps lead down to the Armenian Chapel of St. Helena. There are a multitude of crosses carved by pilgrims through the centuries etched into the walls on both sides of the steps leading down to the chapel. Notice the images in the mosaic floor of major churches of Armenia. The oil paintings on the walls depict martyrs and important events in the history of the Armenian Apostolic Church. The Armenians are especially proud of the fact that their nation was the first to officially embrace Christianity in the early fourth century.

Continue down the steps to the right to reach the Franciscan Chapel of the Finding of the Cross. A small marble slab in the corner of the austere cave chapel, formerly an abandoned cistern, marks the place where tradition holds that St. Helena discovered the cross of Jesus in 327. Above the altar on a rough-hewn rock pedestal is a statue of St. Helena holding the True Cross. On the walls are a few remnants of frescoes painted in the Crusader period.

Return to the ambulatory and turn left past the Chapel of Mocking to reach the Chapel of Adam, located beneath the Chapel of Calvary. A glass panel above the altar allows pilgrims to view the rock of Calvary which has a crack running down the center. It is said that this fissure in the rock appeared at the moment of Jesus' death due to the earthquake: and the earth shook, and rocks were split (Mt 27:51).

Before the restoration work of 1808, the tombs of Crusader kings Godfrey de Bouillon (d. 1100) and Baldwin I (d. 1118) could be found here. On the south side of their tombs were the tombs of Baldwin II (d. 1131) and Fulk of Anjou (d. 1143). On the north side of the Anointing Stone were the tombs of Baldwin III (d. 1163), Amaury I (d. 1174), Baldwin IV (d. 1185) and Baldwin V (d. 1186). Unfortunately, these tombs were removed to make way for the reconfiguration of the Chapel of Calvary and the Greek Katholicon.

An ancient tradition holds that Adam was buried here at the base of the rock of Calvary. His mortal remains, the so-called "first guilty head" of humanity, were the first to receive the redeeming blood of Jesus as it flowed down from Calvary above. So it was that Jesus' sacrifice on Calvary reversed the consequences of Adam's disobedience in the Garden of Eden.

Consequently, in many depictions of the Crucifixion, a skull representing Adam's (and all of humanity's) original sin appears at the foot of the cross. St. Paul puts it in a more positive and properly spiritual manner in his First Letter to the Corinthians, a fitting reflection for pilgrims to ponder as they conclude their visit of the Church of the Holy Sepulcher:

For as by a man came death, by a man has come also the resurrection of the dead. For as in Adam all die, so also in Christ all shall be made alive (1 Cor 15:21-22).

Status Quo

Fierce disputes lasting centuries between Christian creeds over ownership of the church were for the most part resolved by an Ottoman decree in the eighteenth century. The Status Quo is an arrangement according to which liturgical and property rights were granted to six different ecclesial communities in the Basilica of the Holy Sepulcher: the Greek Orthodox Church, Franciscan, Armenian Apostolic Church, Coptic Orthodox Church, Syriac Orthodox Church and the Ethiopian Orthodox Church. According to the Status Quo, most of these ecclesial communities have exclusive property rights in, or near, the basilica. For example, the Greeks have exclusive ownership of the large choir chapel, called the Katholicon, located in front of the Holy Tomb (Edicule).

The principal rights holders, the Greeks, Franciscans and Armenians, also have residential rights in the basilica. Some of the property in the basilica is held in common by the three communities. An exam-ple of commonly held property would be the Edicule, a small edifice enclosing the remains of the rock-cut tomb of Jesus. Around midnight each night, except Sundays, the Greeks take exclusive possession of the Edicule for about two hours to celebrate their liturgy. Next, the Armenians take possession of the Edicule for about two hours. Finally, after the Armenians have finished their liturgy, the Franciscans have possession from about 5:00 am until 7:45 am. After the Franciscans have finished their liturgies, the Edicule is open to the public for visitation. A description of other property rights can be found below.

The present arrangement of the Status Quo was made by a firman from Turkish Sultan Osman III in 1757. Additional firmans were issued in 1852 and 1853 which decreed that no changes could be made without the approval of the relevant church authorities. Article 9 of the Treaty of Paris (1856) gave international recognition to these firmans.

Chapter Seven

The Good News Goes Out from Jerusalem

EMMAUS

Emmaus in the Gospel of Luke

n Luke's account of the Resurrection, Mary Magdalene was not the first to witness the risen Lord. She had gone to the tomb with Joanna, Mary the mother of James and other women, but they found it empty. While they stood, perplexed, next to the empty tomb, two figures in dazzling apparel appeared to them and announced, *"He is not here, but has risen"* (Lk 24:5). After the women reported to the disciples what they had seen, the narrative shifts to the appearance of Jesus to two men on their way to the nearby village of Emmaus.

The pair were leaving Jerusalem after Passover. They were heavy of heart and confused by the dreadful event they had witnessed. The *prophet mighty in deed and word* who they hoped to be the Messiah had been crucified and buried. Now, the risen Christ walked by their side, but they took him for a stranger. As they did not recognize him, Jesus engaged them in conversation. Then, he undertook a long catechesis so they would understand what had been foretold in Scripture.

That very day two of them were going to a village named Emmaus, about seven miles from Jerusalem, and talking with each other about all these things that had happened. While they were talking and discussing together, Jesus himself drew near and went with them. But their eyes were kept from recognizing him. And he said to them, "What is this conversation which you are holding with each other as you walk?" And they stood still, looking sad. Then one of them, named Cleopas, answered him, "Are you the only visitor to Jerusalem who does not know the things that have happened there in these days?" And he said to them, "What things?" And they said to him, "Concerning Jesus of Nazareth, who was a prophet mighty in deed and word before God and all the people, and how our chief priests and rulers delivered him up to be condemned to death, and crucified him. But we had hoped that he was the one to redeem Israel. Yes, and besides all this, it is now the third day since this happened. Moreover, some women of our company amazed us. They were at the tomb early in the morning and did not find his body; and they came back saying that they had even seen a vision of angels, who said that he was alive. Some of those who were with us went to the tomb, and found it just as the women had said; but him they did not see." And he said to them, "O foolish men, and slow of heart to believe all that the prophets have spoken! Was it not necessary that the Christ should suffer these things and enter into his glory?" And beginning with Moses and all the prophets, he interpreted to them in all the scriptures the things concerning himself.

So they drew near to the village to which they were going. He appeared to be going further, but they constrained him, saying, "Stay with us, for it is toward evening and the day is now far spent." So he went in to stay with them. When he was at table with them, he took the bread and blessed, and broke it, and gave it to them. And their eyes were opened and they recognized him; and he vanished out of their sight. They said to each other, "Did not our hearts burn within us while he talked to us on the road, while he opened to us the scriptures?" And they rose that same hour and returned to Jerusalem; and they found the eleven gathered together and those who were with them, who said, "The Lord has risen indeed, and has appeared to Simon!" Then they told what had happened on the road, and how he was known to them in the breaking of the bread (Lk 24:13-35).

Supper at Emmaus, Caravaggio (1601)

As Luke makes clear in his account, this is a Eucharistic story. Jesus' preaching has opened their eyes and they recognize the risen Christ present in the breaking of the bread. Luke names one of the pair as Cleopas, but does not tell us the name of the second person, who represents every one of us. We are all called to recognize Jesus in the breaking of the bread of the Eucharist each Sunday so that we can have a personal encounter with the risen Christ.

History

There are three sites that claim the name of Emmaus from Luke's Gospel. Emmaus-Nicopolis is the earliest site and is honored by the Church Fathers of East and West. Abu Ghosh is the Emmaus of the Crusaders. El Qubeibeh is the shrine run by the Franciscans. A fourth site, Motza, is the Emmaus mentioned in Josephus' history, *The Jewish War*. None of them has definite proof that would disqualify the other sites.

For most of the last two millennia, Christians have debated the location of Emmaus, which is somehow fitting for a Gospel story so filled with mystery. The controversy is partly due to the fact that Luke offers few details regarding its location, instead focusing on the encounter itself. He does mention that the village was *about seven miles from Jerusalem*. In Greek, the language in which Luke wrote, the text reads that Emmaus was *about 60 stadia* (one stadium = about 606 feet) from Jerusalem. But some ancient Gospel manuscripts read *about 160 stadia*. The confusion between these two numbers and the lack of details from the text have given rise to competing propositions for just where Emmaus was located.

Emmaus-Nicopolis (Amwas/Latroun)

The earliest site, found in the historical record from the Byzantine era and usually referred to as Emmaus-Nicopolis, is located about 18 miles from Jerusalem (about 176 stadia). It was known as Emmaus in the biblical period (see 1 Macc 3:40, 57; 4:3; 9:50). According to Jewish historian Josephus, after the death of Herod in 4 BC, the city was the center of a rebellion, which was suppressed by Varus and led to the burning of the city. In 221 AD, Julius Africanus, a soldier-diplomat turned scholar, led a delegation to request permission from Emperor Elagabalus to rebuild Emmaus and grant it the status of a Roman city. His request was honored, and the city was renamed Nicopolis, "City of Victory."

Early Church Fathers and ancient scholars agree this is where Cleopas and his companion shared a meal with Jesus. Eusebius the historian locates the Gospel story here in this city in his *Onomasticon*, his compendium of ancient place names in the Scriptures. St. Jerome and Origen of Alexandria also placed the Gospel story at this site. In 639, a plague wiped out the town's population and it seems to have been forgotten with the passing of time.

L. H. Vincent and F.M. Abel, two Dominican priests from the Ecole Biblique in Jerusalem, excavated the site from 1924 to 1927. Their work uncovered the ruins of a Byzantine triapsidal basilica which very likely dates to the fifth century. Unfortunately, no inscriptions or mosaics were discovered from the ruins of this church to confirm this site as the setting for Luke's Emmaus narrative. But earlier testimonials mentioned above make it probable that the church was constructed to commemorate the Emmaus story. A smaller basilica was also constructed about this time north of the large basilica, constructed in front of the baptistery which had water flowing into it from a well to the north. The Byzantine churches were likely destroyed during the Persian invasion of 614.

In the twelfth century, the Crusaders built a Romanesque-style church on the site of the large Byzantine basilica, reusing the central apse.

The site was in ruins when, in the late nineteenth century, a Carmelite nun, Sister Mariam Baouardy, O.C.D. (her name in religious life was Sister Mariam of Jesus Crucified, 1846-1878) passed through the area and experienced a mystical revelation telling her that this was the true site of the Emmaus story. Her Carmelite community in Bethlehem, moved by her testimonial, purchased the property in 1878. St. Mariam of Jesus Crucified was canonized May 17, 2015, in St. Peter's Square by Pope Francis. Her reliquary can be seen today in the Carmelite monastery in Bethlehem.

Up the hill from the ruins is a former monastery, built by the Fathers of Betharram in the 1930s, which was named the "House of Peace." It now is a museum displaying artifacts discovered on the site. Nearby, one can find the chapel of the Community of the Beatitudes, which has served as the site's caretakers since 1993.

Abu Ghosh

The second site with a claim as the Emmaus of the Gospel is in Abu Ghosh. This village, located about nine miles (83 stadia) from Jerusalem, was known as Kiriath-jearim (see Josh 9:17) in the biblical period. The Philistines returned the *ark of the Lord* (Ark of the Covenant) to the villagers of Kiriath-jearim, where it was kept in the house of Abinadab for 20 years. Abinadab's son, Eleazar, was consecrated to have charge of the ark (see 1 Sam 6:21-7:2). After capturing Jerusalem from the Jebusites, King David brought the *ark of God* from Kiriath-jearim in a procession to the *city of David* (Jerusalem) with great rejoicing, *And David danced before the Lord with all his might* (2 Sam 6:14).

Overlooking the Arab-Israeli town of Abu Ghosh today, the site of the biblical village of Kiriath-jearim, is a church built on the summit to honor the Virgin Mary and named Our Lady of the Ark of the Covenant (1924). Crowned by a white statue of the Madonna and Child, this church stands on top of the ruins of a fifth-century church. Apparently, the Byzantines believed this was the site of Abinadab's house, the resting place of the *ark of the Lord* for 20 years.

In the second century AD, a detachment of the Tenth Roman Legion became stationed in the village. The legionaries built a reservoir over the spring in the valley below the hill. An inscription of the Tenth Legion can be seen on a block of stone next to the door frame leading to the lower crypt of the present-day church. In the ninth century, the reservoir was incorporated into a caravanserai - an inn surrounding a court where caravans rest at night. The Arabs named the village which grew up around the spring Qaryet el-Enab, and is simply the Arabic version of Kiriath-jearim.

It's not clear why the Crusaders decided to locate the Emmaus story in the village of Qaryet el-Enab. Perhaps they believed that Emmaus-Nicopolis was too far from Jerusalem, relying on Gospel manuscripts which stated that Emmaus was *about seven miles from Jerusalem.* The existence of a caravanserai with an abundance of fresh water available to drink may have convinced the Crusaders that this was the setting for the Emmaus story. Its location on a main road connecting Jerusalem with the coastal plain offered further evidence in its favor. The Knights Hospitallers of St. John - today known as the Knights of Malta - identified this site with the Emmaus of the Gospel. In 1143, they built their Romanesque-style church over the spring to commemorate the place where Jesus broke bread with Cleopas and his companion.

After the Crusaders abandoned the village in 1187, it eventually lost its importance as travelers began to journey to Jerusalem on a different route. The Arabs residents of the village turned the church into a mosque in the fourteenth century. The frescoes in the church were likely defaced at this time. Later, a mosque was built next door and the church was used as a stable for farm animals.

In 1873, the Ottoman Turkish Sublime Porte gave the church and property to the Republic of France. Benedictine monks built a monastery next door in 1900. The former stable was rededicated as a church in 1907. Today, Benedictine monks from the Bec-Hellouin Abbey (in Normandy, France), together with oblate nuns, serve as custodians of the Crusader church and greet the pilgrims who come to recall the mystery of Christ's presence to us in the Eucharist, the place where he was made known in the breaking of the bread.

The present-day name, Abu Ghosh, recalls a sixteenth century Arab sheikh and infamous brigand who imposed tolls on pilgrims and other travelers making their way to Jerusalem. Known as "the Rob Roy of the hills" in homage to Walter Scott's fictional hero, he exacted fifteen piasters (about 63 cents) from every traveler. [cf. *Youthful Explorers of the Holy Land*, by Robert Morris] He and other members of the Ghosh clan down through time would periodically hold Franciscans for a ransom, knowing that the Franciscan Custody of the Holy Land would pay the ransom. The Custody has in its archives some of these ransom notes.

El Qubeibeh

The third site that bills itself the Emmaus of Luke is El Qubeibeh, an Arab village about 7.5 miles (about 65 stadia) from Jerusalem. The earliest documentation identifying El Qubeibeh with Emmaus is from a text written by the Franciscan superior (Custos) Father Francesco Suriano in 1485: "The castle of Emmaus became known by the name Kubeibeh, where there was a church similar to the one of Al Bireh." It is thought that the Franciscans conducted pilgrimages to the site from the fifteenth century until 1687 when they were suspended due to a lack of safety in travelling the roads. The pilgrimages resumed in 1852, the same year the Franciscans discovered extensive Crusader remains on the site.

In 1859, a pious French noblewoman, Marquise Paulina de Nicolay came to the Holy Land on one of these pilgrimages. She had a special devotion to Emmaus and when she saw how the site was neglected, she decided to purchase the land in 1861. She believed that on this site was an "ancient room" in some way connected to the Gospel story. She built several structures among the Crusader ruins, and in 1863, she ceded the property to the Franciscans. After her death in 1868, her remains were taken back to her beloved Emmaus.

Excavations by the Franciscans (1873-75, 1881-89, and 1940-45) revealed evidence of occupation of the site in the Hellenistic, Roman and Crusader periods. A section of an ancient Roman road was discovered, alongside ruins of Crusader-era housing. The road connected the coastal plain with the hills of Judea. Some claimed this as evidence of the road that Luke tells us Cleopas and his companion walked with the risen Jesus. Ruins of a Crusader castle with a small chapel inside, mentioned by Fr. Suriano above, were on the site, as well as remains of a large triapsidal church from the Crusader era.

A Romanesque-style church, designed by Franciscan scholars Wendelin Hinterkeuser and Barnabas Meistermann, was built on the site of the Crusader church. Graced by somber, elegant architecture evoking the time period of Roman Palestine, it is known today as the Basilica of the Manifestation. It was consecrated by Cardinal Andrea Carlo Ferrari, archbishop of Milan, in 1902. A triptych of colorful majolica, added above the door in 1958, depicts the Gospel scene.

In the north aisle of the church, a glass panel in the floor allows visitors to see the remains of "the house of Cleopas," who hosted our Divine Redeemer at the mystical supper of Emmaus. The two side altars, on either side of the main altar, honor St. Cleopas and his son St. Simon, by tradition, the companion of Cleopas in the Gospel story, who was the second bishop of Jerusalem. Both were said, by ancient tradition, to have suffered martyrdom. In the northwest corner of the church, the remains of Marquise Paulina de Nicolay's are interred, according to her wishes.

The Franciscan identification of Qubeibeh with Emmaus relies mainly on its distance from Jerusalem (about 7.5 miles), which is very close to the distance mentioned in Luke (*about seven miles*). The village's location alongside a Roman road leading down to the coastal plain from the hills of Judea also lends support to this claim. However, the ruins from the Hellenistic, Roman and Crusader eras do not convincingly point to their identification of this site with the Emmaus of the Gospel. The historical record shows that it is only in the post-Crusader era that a tradition develops, eventually adopted by the Franciscans, identifying El-Qubeibeh with the Emmaus story.

Motza (Qalunya)

Motza is the last of the four sites that scholars propose as the Emmaus of Luke. Its distance of 3.5 miles from Jerusalem would fit Luke's account, if it is understood that the description *about seven miles from Jerusalem* refers to a round-trip journey. Josephus, in his work *The Jewish War*, mentions this other "Emmaous" as a refuge for 800 veterans of the Roman army after the First Jewish Revolt from 66-70 AD. These legionaries were settled by Vespasian in a Roman "colonia," a distance of 30 stadia, about 3.5 miles, from Jerusalem.

This is the village known as Motza, or Moza, in the biblical period (see Josh 18:26). The name Colonia eventually replaced the earlier name of Emmaus. In the Arab period, the name becomes Qalunya.

Luke relates that Cleopas and his companion walked to Emmaus from Jerusalem and then returned in the same day. Motza has the advantage of being within an easy walking distance (about 7 miles round trip) of Jerusalem. Abu Ghosh and Qubeibeh, at 18 miles and 15 miles round trip respectively, would also be a reasonable distance to cover in one day. However, travelling 36 miles (18 miles in each direction) from Jerusalem to Emmaus-Nicopolis and back in one day would be challenging, but not impossible.

THE UPPER ROOM
Jesus' Appearances in the Upper Room

On the evening of the day of the Resurrection, the disciples were gathered together. Only three days ago Jesus had joined with them for the

Passover meal. But now they were in hiding behind bolted doors for *fear of the Jews*, the authorities [of the Sanhedrin] who had pressured Pilate to condemn Jesus to death. Mary Magdalene, who in John's account was the first to see the risen Lord, had already told the disciples that she had seen the Lord when she visited his empty tomb earlier that morning. Would they be the next victims of the persecution; would they be put under arrest on the false charge of stealing the body? They were full of confusion and doubt. In their time of darkness, little did they know that they too would now experience the overwhelming joy of seeing their risen Lord.

On the evening of that day, the first day of the week, the doors being shut where the disciples were, for fear of the Jews, Jesus came and stood among them and said to them, "Peace be with you." When he had said this, he showed them his hands and his side. Then the disciples were glad when they saw the Lord. Jesus said to them again, "Peace be with you. As the Father has sent me, even so I send you." And when he had said this, he breathed on them, and said to them, "Receive the Holy Spirit. If you forgive sins of any, they are forgiven; if you retain the sins of any, they are retained."

Now Thomas, one of the twelve, called the Twin, was not with them when Jesus came. So the other disciples told him, "We have seen the Lord." But he said to them, "Unless I see in his hands the print of the nails, and place my finger in the mark of the nails, and place my hand in his side, I will not believe."

Eight days later, his disciples were again in the house, and Thomas was with them. The doors were shut, but Jesus came and stood among them, and said, "Peace be with you." Then he said to Thomas, "Put your finger here, and see my hands; and put out your hand, and place it in my side; do not be faith-less, but believing." Thomas answered him, "My Lord and my God." Jesus said to him, "Have you believed because you have seen me? Blessed are those who have not seen and yet believe" (Jn 20:19-29).

By showing the wounds in his hands and feet, which had been pierced by

The Incredulity of Saint Thomas, Caravaggio (1601-1602)

nails on the cross, and the wound of the lance in his side, Jesus wants his disciples to know that his wounded body is the same one which endured the Crucifixion three days earlier. This is the wounded, now glorified, body he will take with him to heaven.

In an allusion to the creation account, John records that Jesus *breathed on them, and said to them, "Receive the Holy Spirit."* We find similar wording that Greek translators of the Old Testament Hebrew used to describe in God's creation of man: *then the Lord God formed man of dust from the ground, and breathed into his nostrils the breath of life; and man became a living being* (Gen 2:7). It is the only time this Greek wording to express Jesus *breathed on them* appears in the New Testament. This act of breathing on the disciples is an anticipation of the coming of the Holy Spirit on Pentecost 50 days later (see Acts 2:1-4).

To ensure that his ministry of mercy and reconciliation will continue after his return to the Father, Jesus grants to the disciples the authority to forgive and retain sins: *"If you forgive sins of any, they are forgiven; if you retain the sins of any, they are retained."* Through the apostles and their successors (bishops), and their assistants in the presbyterate (priests), Christ's divine mercy will continue to be administered to the world.

The term "Upper Room" used in the title of this section is a reference to the place where Jesus celebrated the Passover meal (Last Supper) with his disciples (see Mk 14:15; Lk 22:12). It is also where Mary, the disciples and others gathered to pray after Jesus' Ascension to heaven (see Acts 1:13). John does not explicitly state that the disciples were staying in the *upper room* when Jesus appeared to them twice after his Resurrection; he simply refers to the place where they were gathered behind a shut door as *the house*. Local Christian tradition holds that *the house* and the *upper room* were the same.

The history of the Upper Room is covered in the previous chapter.

THE PRIMACY OF PETER
The Primacy of Peter in the Gospel of John

In Matthew's resurrection narrative, Mary Magdalene and the other Mary rush to tell the disciples that Jesus had risen from the dead. They run from the empty tomb with *fear and great joy*. On the way, Jesus appears to them and says, *"Do not be afraid; go and tell my brethren to go to Galilee, and there they will see me"* (Mt 28:10).

In Mark's account, Mary Magdalene, Mary the mother of James, and Salome go to the tomb with spices to complete the anointing ritual. They look into the empty tomb and see *a young man sitting on the right side, dressed in a white robe; and they were amazed.* He explains to them that Jesus has risen and says, *"But go, tell his disciples and Peter that he is going before you to Galilee; there you will see him, as he told you"* (Mk 16:7). John does not record Jesus instructing his disciples to meet him in Galilee; but he is the only one to record Jesus' post-Resurrection encounter there with the disciples by the lakeshore.

It is not explained why Jesus should have the disciples make a long journey of nearly 90 miles to Galilee. But the Gospels make it clear that Jesus wanted to meet them there. Biblical scholars point out that it was here where the disciples were fishing when the Lord had first called them to be *fishers of men*, so there is a sense of events coming full circle. Likewise it was here in Galilee where Jesus worked wonders to inspire his disciples to have faith in him, including his first miracle, when he turned the water into wine at Cana. Now it would be the scene of his last miracle.

With confidence in their Master's plans, the disciples dutifully followed his instructions. After their meeting with the risen Jesus by the lakeshore in Galilee, they return to Jerusalem, as Scripture records their presence at Jesus' Ascension (see Acts 1:6-11). This round trip journey of roughly 180 miles will need to be completed in forty days!

Upon arriving in Galilee at the Sea of Tiberias, the disciples returned to their former livelihood - fishing. Though they labored all that night, they caught nothing. *Just as day was breaking, Jesus stood on the beach; yet the disciples did not know that it was Jesus.* After learning they had not caught any fish, Jesus called to his *children* to cast the net over the right side of the boat. They did as he instructed them. The net, now filled with a bountiful catch, could not be hauled into the boat due to its size. John, the *disciple whom Jesus loved* recognized it was the risen Jesus on the beach and told Peter, who then jumped into the water and swam to the shore (Jn 21:1-8).

The other disciples dragged their bulging net to the shore with their miraculous catch of fish, which added up to a hundred fifty three. They found Jesus next to a charcoal fire preparing a meal of fish and bread. Jesus invited them to bring some of their recently caught fish and to share breakfast with him. They would later understand that this great catch symbolized the faithful who would be brought to the bark [boat] of the Church led by Peter. John explains that this was the third time Jesus had revealed himself to the disciples after being raised from the dead.

When they had finished breakfast, Jesus said to Simon Peter, "Simon, son of John, do you love me more than these?" He said to him, "Yes, Lord; you know that I love you." He said to him, "Feed my lambs." A second time he said to him, "Simon, son of John, do you love me?" He said to him, "Yes, Lord; you know that I love you." He said to him, "Tend my sheep." He said to him the third time, "Simon, son of John, do you love me?" Peter was grieved because he said to him, "Do you love me?" And he said to him, "Lord you know everything; you know that I love you." Jesus said to him, "Feed my sheep" (Jn 21:15-17).

In this exchange of words between Jesus and Peter, we learn that Jesus

The Miraculous Draught of Fishes, Raphael (1515)

gives Peter the opportunity to express his love for him, not once but three times. Peter's affirmative response to Jesus' question *"do you love me?"* is followed each time by a mandate to govern his flock. Jesus makes it clear that love, both for him and his flock, precedes pastoral authority. After Peter assures Jesus of his love for him, Jesus, the Good Shepherd, confers on Peter the authority to govern his flock: *"Feed my sheep."*

Peter is selected to be the first (primacy) among the apostles in pastoral authority. Jesus has not only given Peter the primacy; he has also given the First Apostle another precious gift: a public opportunity to be forgiven in the sight of the other disciples.

"Rightly then did the Lord after his resurrection entrust Peter with the feeding of his sheep. Yet he was not the only disciple to merit the feeding of the Lord's sheep; but Christ in speaking only to one suggests the unity of all; and so he speaks to Peter, because Peter is first among the apostles. Therefore do not be disheartened, Peter; reply once, reply twice, reply a third time. The triple confession of your love is to regain what was lost three times by your fear [recall Peter's denial of Jesus three times at the house of Caiaphas]. You must loose three times what you bound three times; untie by love that which your fear bound. Once, and again, and a third time did the Lord entrust his sheep to Peter" (From a sermon by St. Augustine).

History

In the diary of the pilgrim lady Egeria from the late fourth century, we read: "Not far away [from Capernaum] the stone steps on which the Lord stood can be seen." There are ancient stone steps on the lake side of the modern chapel that commemorates the site where tradition has it that the risen Lord stood on the sandy beach and called to his disciples as they fished on the Sea of Tiberias. It is believed that these worn stone steps, cut into the south face of the rock close to the water's edge, are the same ones that Egeria mentions in her diary.

Archaeological excavations conducted by Franciscan Father Stanislao Loffreda in 1968 revealed that the bedrock on which the present church rests and the adjacent stone steps had been a quarry in the early Christian era. Two metal wedges, used by quarrymen to separate the block of stone from the bedrock, were found in the area.

Excavations also revealed the presence of a small church in the fourth century enclosing the rock on which, according to local tradition, Jesus had the *charcoal fire there, with some fish lying on it, and bread.* A fifth century church replaced the earlier one, remnants of which can be seen in the lower courses of stone supporting the back three walls of the present church.

A ninth-century document mentions a church on the site called the Twelve Thrones, which could explain the presence of six heart-shaped stones, two lobes on each stone totaling 12 lobes, lying in the beach gravel next to Egeria's "stone steps." They are double-column blocks designed for the angle of a colonnade, probably bought here from an abandoned building in the area. The Twelve Thrones reference can be linked to Jesus' words to his twelve disciples: *"Truly I say to you, in the new world, when the Son of man shall sit on his glorious throne, you who have followed me will also sit on twelve thrones, judging the twelve tribes of Israel"* (Mt 19:28).

In the twelfth century, a Russian monk named Daniel visited the site and recorded: "a church built on this site is consecrated to the Holy Apostles." This may have been the church from the Crusader era. The Crusaders erected a small structure, perhaps a fortress of sorts, to the north of the present church. Today, the sacristy rests on top of the ruins of that Crusader building. After the Crusaders withdrew from the region in 1187, the church was destroyed. Later in the thirteenth century, it was rebuilt but was soon after razed by the Sultan Baybars in 1265.

The Franciscan Custody of the Holy Land acquired the site in 1889 and built the present Church of the Primacy of Peter in 1933. Built of black basalt rock and white limestone native to the area, it sits on the foundations of the fifth-century church. Inside, there is a large cream-colored rock elevated a couple of feet off the floor in front of the altar. It is called "Mensa Christi," Latin for "Table of Christ." Tradition holds that it was on this rock that Jesus prepared a meal of fish and bread for his disciples, and it has been venerated by pilgrims since the early Byzantine era.

The bronze doors, depicting images of two modern popes and Gospel scenes that happened here, are gifts from a family from Krakow, Poland. In

1965, Pope Paul VI, now St. Paul VI, visited this sanctuary and, in 2000, Pope John Paul II, now St. John Paul II, also came to this shrine where the first pope was given his mandate by the risen Lord to *"Feed my sheep."*

Next to the church is a prayer area enclosed in an amphitheater, for the celebration of Mass and other worship services. It is a peaceful spot with views of the water and lends itself to reflection and prayer. Nearby, a bronze sculpture depicts Jesus handing Peter the shepherd's rod, Jesus' transferal of pastoral authority to Peter. The modern sculpture is the work of Italian Franciscan Father Andrea Martini.

Near the entrance gate of the site is a circular water tower, one of many in the area from the Byzantine period. It was likely constructed in the third to fourth century AD to raise the level of the spring water from the ground in the center of the tower. This gushing spring water was then sent through irrigation channels to water the crops in adjacent fields. After entering the site and walking about thirty yards, one can view on the left a perennial spring. Its water can be seen flowing in an open channel under the walking path.

Wildlife enthusiasts take note: Throughout the site of the shrine, especially in the area of the garden path and along the outcropping of rocks on the shoreline, rock hyraxes often make their presence known. These sociable mammals, which resemble badgers and are native to the Middle East, are sometimes hard to spot if the weather is overcast or cold. But on clear days, they can be seen on the rocks in large numbers basking in the sun.

THE ASCENSION OF OUR LORD JESUS CHRIST
The Ascension in the Scriptures

Mark and Luke are the only evangelists to record Jesus' Ascension, when he was *taken up into heaven.* Mark's account is brief: *So then the Lord Jesus, after he had spoken to them, was taken up into heaven, and sat down at the right hand of God* (Mk 16:19). Luke is also brief but he gives a small but precious detail regarding the location: *Then he led them out as far as Bethany, and lifting up his hands he blessed them. While he blessed them, he parted from them, and was carried up into heaven* (Lk 24:50-51).

The account of Jesus' Ascension in the first chapter of the Acts of the Apostles gives more details. Most scholars agree that Luke, the evangelist, is also the author of Acts. In both the beginning of Luke's Gospel and of Acts, the author addresses Theophilus. Furthermore, the first line in Acts reads in part: *In the first book, O Theophilus* (Acts 1:1). The *first book* is a reference to Luke's Gospel.

From Luke's point of view, his account of the Ascension was a way to clearly draw the line between the earthly mission of Jesus and the evangelical mission of the Apostles, which would begin with the descent of the Holy Spirit at Pentecost (see Acts 2:1-4). Before describing the Ascension, Luke reveals that Jesus appeared to his apostles over a period of forty days after his Passion, and instructed them to remain in Jerusalem *"for the promise of the Father"* when they will be *"baptized with the Holy Spirit"* (Acts 1:4-5).

So when they had come together, they asked him, "Lord, will you at this time restore the kingdom to Israel?" He said to them, "It is not for you to know times or seasons which the Father has fixed by his own authority. But you shall receive power when the Holy Spirit has come upon you; and you shall be my witnesses in Jerusalem and in all Judea and Samaria and to the end of the earth." And when he had said this, as they were looking on, he was lifted up, and a cloud took him out of their sight. And while they were gazing into heaven as he went, behold, two men stood by them in white robes, and said, "Men of Galilee, why do you stand looking into heaven? This Jesus, who was taken up from you into heaven, will come in the same way as you saw him go into heaven."

Then they returned to Jerusalem from the mount called Olivet, which is near Jerusalem, a sabbath day's journey away; and when they had entered, they went up to the upper room, where they were staying (Acts 1:6-13).

The Ascension of Christ, Benvenuto Tisi da Garofalo (1520)

In Luke's narrative, we learn that Jesus was *carried up to heaven* at a place described as being *as far as Bethany.* In the Acts' account, the apostles were on the *mount called Olivet* (Mount of Olives). The village of Bethany is located on the eastern slope of the Mount of Olives, which suggests that Luke places the event at nearly the same site in both stories.

Notice that Luke states that after the Ascension, the apostles returned to Jerusalem and went *up to the upper room, where they were staying.* The words *where they were staying* suggests the apostles were there for some time, perhaps since the time of the Passover meal (Luke places the Last Supper in the *upper room,* Lk 22:12) through the Passion, Death and Resurrection of Jesus, and the following forty days, excluding the time spent on their journey to Galilee and back. It is in this same *upper room* that we find the apostles, Mary, and others gathered on the day of Pentecost, ten days after the Ascension..

History

In his *Life of Constantine* written in the fourth century, early Church historian Eusebius of Caesarea records that the emperor Constantine ordered the construction of "sumptuous" churches over three caves, to honor the principal mysteries of Jesus' life: the cave of Jesus' birth in Bethlehem; the rock-cut burial cave of Jesus near Golgotha; and the cave of teachings on the Mount of Olives. Our interest here is in the cave of teachings, where Eusebius tells us, "the Lord entrusted to his disciples the mysteries of the end of ages."

On the western slope of the Mount of Olives, there is a cave where Jesus would gather his disciples to give them instruction. Among the teachings of Jesus in this cave was his description of the end times: *As he sat on the Mount of Olives, the disciples came to him privately, saying, "Tell us, when will this be, and what will be the sign of your coming and of the close of the age?"* (Mt 24:3). Here Christ unfolded before his apostles the vision of Jerusalem laid waste and the world coming to an end, when all the people of the earth will be aroused by the trumpets of angels and gather around the throne of Christ, who will descend in triumph from heaven to pronounce on the just and faithful.

It was above this cave of teachings that Constantine built a basilica to commemorate the Ascension. The initial work was supervised by the emperor's mother, St. Helena, who had come on pilgrimage (326-328) to pray at the holy sites. Before the construction of Constantine's church, local Christians gathered in this cave to recall Jesus' Ascension into heaven. The actual site of Jesus' Ascension is about 100 yards north of the cave on the crest of the mount. In the pre-Constantinian period of widespread persecution, Christians probably felt safer praying in the cave rather than in the open on the summit of the mount.

After Constantine legalized the Christian religion in 313, the focus of the remembrance of the Ascension moved to a place the pilgrim Egeria called the "Imbomon," from Greek meaning "on the hill." In 384 she was present for the liturgies celebrated at the Imbomon and in the cave of teachings during Holy Week and the Easter season. There is no mention in her writings of a church on the site of the Ascension. Later, sometime before 392, a circular church was built on the site by a pious Roman noble woman, Poimenia, who was a member of the imperial family. It was open to the sky and at the center of the enclosed court was the sacred stone with the imprint of Jesus' feet, marking the place where he stood before ascending into heaven.

The Persian invasion and occupation of the land (614-628) resulted in the destruction of Poimenia's church and other religious buildings on the mount. When the Gallic pilgrim, Bishop Arculf visited Jerusalem around 670, he reported a circular church with its center open to the sky. It seems that Modestus, the Patriarch of Jerusalem, restored the round church and rebuilt some of the monasteries and convents after the Persians were driven out of the land. The round church disappeared sometime before the arrival of the Crusaders in 1099. It was probably destroyed by Caliph al-Hakim in 1009.

The Crusaders built an octagonal-shaped wall around the elegant open court containing the sacred stone. A small octagonal-shaped edicule, still present today, was built around the stone with the imprint of Jesus' feet. A church was built next to the wall, as well as a monastery for Canons of St. Augustine, who were charged with celebrating the liturgies on the site. It is reported that eight lamps shone brightly through the windows so they could be seen from the Holy City.

When the Crusaders were forced out of Jerusalem in 1187, the site was seized by Saladin, the leader of the Muslim army, and given to two of his followers. The edicule was converted into a mosque. A dome was added to the octagonal wall of the edicule and the arches were filled in with blocks of stone. A mihrab, a niche giving the direction of Mecca for Muslim prayer, was installed in the south wall.

Muslims revere Jesus as a prophet. Even though it is not mentioned explicitly in the Quran, Muslims hold that Jesus was "raised up" in body to God. Likewise, they believe Jesus will raise Mohammad on Resurrection day. They accepted the local tradition that the Ascension of Jesus happened here. Today, the site is held by the Waqf, an Islamic Trust.

The site is redolent with mystery and holiness, especially on the feast of the Ascension for Latin-rite Catholics. Every year on the feast of the Ascension, the Franciscans are allowed to celebrate liturgies in the enclosure. They set up a portable altar inside the edicule for the celebration of Mass, which are said, hour by hour, from the middle of the night to the evening of the following day. They also set up tents to serve as a sacristy just inside the entrance of the courtyard, making use of the embedded hooks and rings in the wall for support. On the feast of the Ascension for the Orthodox churches (Greek, Armenian, Syrian and Coptic), the clergy make use of altars on the east side of the enclosure outside of the edicule. They are also permitted to set up tents.

PENTECOST
The Descent of the Holy Spirit

St. Leo the Great (400-461) gives us an eloquent description of how the apostles felt after they had witnessed the Ascension of Jesus:

"The blessed apostles together with all others had been intimidated by the catastrophe of the cross, and their faith in the resurrection had been uncertain; but now they were so strengthened by the evident truth that when their Lord ascended into heaven, far from feeling any sadness, they were filled with great joy. Indeed that blessed company had a great and inexpressible cause for joy when it saw man's nature rising above the dignity of the whole heavenly creation, above the ranks of angels, above the exalted status of archangels." (From an Ascension sermon by St. Pope Leo the Great)

And so the apostles, emboldened and strengthened in faith by the Ascension, *returned to Jerusalem from the mount called Olivet, which is near Jerusalem, a sabbath day's journey away; and when they had entered, they went up to the upper room, where they were staying.* Ten days later, *When the day of Pentecost had come, they were all together in one place [the upper room]* (Acts 1:12-13; 2:1).

The word Pentecost comes from Greek meaning "fiftieth." It indicates that 50 days have passed from the second day of Passover, a way of reckoning the date of the *feast of the harvest* or the *feast of weeks* (Ex 23:16; 34:22) in the Jewish calendar. Later, theological significance was attached to this agricultural feast, which was also known as the Festival of First-Fruits. It became a commemoration of the gift of the Torah, the Law of Moses, to the children of Israel at Mount Sinai.

In the Christian calendar, Pentecost indicates the fiftieth day since Jesus' Resurrection. The *day of Pentecost* witnesses the fulfillment of Jesus' promise to his apostles that, *"you shall be baptized with the Holy Spirit"* (Acts 1:5). It is the day the Church celebrates the coming of the Holy Spirit and the birth of its missionary role to gather the "first-fruits" of the faithful in the world Gospel harvest.

And suddenly a sound came from Heaven like the rush of a mighty wind, and it filled all the house where they were sitting. And there appeared to them tongues as of fire, distributed and resting on each one of them.

Pentecost, Duccio di Buoninsegna (1308-1311)

And they were all filled with the Holy Spirit and began to speak in other tongues, as the Spirit gave them utterance (Acts 2:2-4).

The sound from heaven *like the rush of a mighty wind* and the image of fire evokes the dramatic scene at Mount Sinai just before Moses presented the sacred stone tablets of the Law to Israel: *a very loud trumpet blast* could be heard and *the Lord descended upon it [Mount Sinai] in fire*

(Ex 19:16-18; 31:18). At the Day of Pentecost comes the miraculous manifestation of the Holy Spirit, with *tongues as of fire* parting asunder upon each of the apostles, Mary and the others gathered in the *upper room*. Now the new law of the Spirit is written, not on stone tablets, but on the hearts of believers. *And they were all filled with the Holy Spirit.* The gift of the Holy Spirit is the foundational gift to the community of believers establishing the New Covenant.

There were devout Jews *from every nation under heaven* in Jerusalem for the *feast of the harvest,* one of the three pilgrim feasts which obliges adult males to travel to Jerusalem (see Dt 16:16). These important feasts, which include Passover and Tabernacles, were designed to keep God in the minds of the people and to promote national unity. The crowd would have included Jewish converts and God-fearing Gentiles on pilgrimage from throughout the known world. At the sound of *the rush of a mighty wind* the *multitude came together* to listen to what the apostles had to say.

The apostles, full of zeal and empowered by the Holy Spirit, began to *speak in other tongues* to the Jews gathered before them about *the mighty works of God.* They were heard speaking in the native tongues of those who were present and the crowd was *amazed* (Acts 2:5-12). The scene of a multitude speaking different tongues recalls the tragedy of the tower of Babel in which the Lord *confuse[d] their language, that they may not understand one another's speech,* and they were scattered *abroad over the face of the earth* (Gen 11:7-9). At the coming of the Holy Spirit, there is no confusion. The Gospel message is heard and understood by each in his own tongue, bringing together those who were scattered to form the family of God.

At the site of the *upper room* the apostles, *filled with the Holy Spirit,* have begun to fulfill Jesus' mandate to give witness to him and his Gospel message in Jerusalem. Later, their call to give witness will bring them to *Judea and Samaria and to the end of the earth* (Acts 1:8). This is the birth of the Church's missionary role to evangelize. Most of the apostles, tradition tells us, would later die as martyrs in distant lands, sacrificing their lives to spread the Gospel of Jesus Christ.

Today, the cross-ribbed vaults of the high ceiling in the Upper Room resound with the prayers and chants to the Holy Spirit by Christian pilgrims of all denominations and nations. They often sing the universal call to the Holy Spirit heard the world over in the Gospel acclamation during Mass on the Feast of Pentecost: "Come, Holy Spirit, fill the hearts of your faithful and kindle in them the fire of your love. Send forth your Spirit and they will be created and you shall renew the face of the earth."

Local Christian tradition tells us that the Last Supper and the Pentecost event both happened in the *upper room*. The history of the Upper Room is covered in chapter six.

JAFFA
Jaffa in the Scriptures

With a recorded history of more than 3,000 years, Jaffa is one of the ancient Mediterranean world's most storied port towns and it had dramatic roles in both the Old and New Testaments. At the time of the division of the land of Canaan among the tribes of Israel, territory given to the tribe of Dan included Jaffa, Yafo in Hebrew, which means "the beautiful." *When the territory of the Danites was lost to them, the Danites went up and fought against Leshem.* They captured and took possession of Leshem and renamed it Dan, *after the name of Dan their ancestor* (Josh 19:40-48).

Under King Solomon, Jaffa, which in Greek is called Joppa, became Jerusalem's seaport. After succeeding his father, David, to the throne, Solomon made plans to build the first Jewish Temple. Such an undertaking would require a multitude of laborers and a wide array of materials. He requested timber of cedar, cypress and algum from Huram, king of Tyre, who replied: *"and we will cut whatever timber you need from Lebanon, and bring it to you in rafts by sea to Joppa, so that you may take it up to Jerusalem"* (2 Chr 2:16). About five hundred years later, when the second Jewish Temple was being rebuilt under the supervision of the governor of Judah, Zerubbabel, timber was once again imported from Lebanon through the port here: *So they gave money to the masons and the carpenters, and food, drink, and oil to the Sidonians and the Tyrians to bring cedar trees from Lebanon to the sea, to Joppa* (Ezra 3:7).

Joppa also played a role in the story of the reluctant prophet, Jonah. The word of the Lord came to Jonah that he should go preach repentance to the people of Nineveh *for their wickedness has come up before me.* Jonah fled from the mission the Lord had given him and *went down to Joppa and found a ship going to Tarshish; so he paid the fare and went on board, to go with them to Tarshish, away from the presence of the Lord* (Jon 1:1-3).

During the Maccabean revolt against Greek rule, Simon conquered the city (1 Macc 12:34). Later, the men of Joppa carried out an *ungodly* deed against the Jews of the city by inviting them to board boats in the port, *And when they accepted, because they wished to live peaceably and suspected nothing, the men of Joppa took them out to sea and drowned them, not less than two hundred* (2 Macc 12:3-4).

But it played a crucial part in spreading the Gospel and making new converts as recorded in the Acts of the Apostles. Faithful to his commission to bear witness *in all Judea,* Peter, as the first of the apostles, went down from Jerusalem to Lydda (Lod in Hebrew) to visit the saints, a term for the followers of Jesus. There he found a paralytic named Aeneas who had been bedridden for eight years. Peter said to him, *"Aeneas, Jesus Christ heals you."* Immediately Aeneas rose from the bed. The people of the region turned to the Lord and were converted to Christ because of the miracle they witnessed (Acts 1:8; 9:32-35).

At that time, a pious woman known for her great charity named Tabitha (Dorcas in Greek) suddenly died in the city of Joppa. Because it was not far from Lydda, two men were sent to bring Peter to the room where Tabitha's body had been laid. Peter entered the room and said to the lifeless body, *"Tabitha, rise."* Peter then presented her alive and well to the saints and widows. This was made known throughout the city and *many believed in the Lord* (Acts 9:36-43).

Peter stayed for many days in Joppa, lodging as a guest in the home of a tanner named Simon. The work of a tanner required constant contact with animal skins and carcasses, rendering him in a perpetual state of uncleanness, since a Jew is rendered unclean when coming into contact with blood. Lodging with a person who is unclean anticipates the message Peter will receive from a vision he has while praying on the roof of Simon the tanner:

And he became hungry and desired something to eat; but while they were preparing it, he fell into a trance and saw the heaven opened, and some-

thing descending, like a great sheet, let down by four corners upon the earth. In it were all kinds of animals and reptiles and birds of the air. And there came a voice to him, "Rise, Peter; kill and eat." But Peter said, "No, Lord; for I have never eaten anything that is common or unclean." And the voice came to him again a second time, "What God has called cleansed, you must not call common." This happened three times, and the thing was taken up at once to heaven (Acts 10:9-16)

Peter's Vision of a Sheet with Animals, Domenico Fetti (c. 1619)

While Peter was pondering this vision, the Spirit told him to accompany three men sent by Cornelius, a Roman centurion, to the city of Caesarea.

History

Joppa lost importance as a seaport when Herod built Caesarea 30 miles north on the Mediterranean coast. But under the Crusaders, it regained prominence as the principal port for pilgrims to the Holy Land. Crusader Richard the Lion Hearted built a citadel here and St. Louis rebuilt the city wall in 1251, and it was fortified by Emperor Fredrick II. The town was captured by the Mameluke Sultan Baybars in 1267. It was razed by Napoleon in 1799 and rebuilt by the Ottoman Turks when Jaffa flourished as a gateway for pilgrims in the nineteenth century. In modern times, Jaffa was revived under the British Mandate but with the growth of neighboring Tel Aviv declined into today's sleepy but picturesque town.

The Church of St. Peter

The Franciscans took up residence in Jaffa in the late thirteenth century. Their friary was located next to a magnificent church built by King Louis IX in 1251. It was completely destroyed in 1267 by the Mameluke Sultan Baybars shortly after the Crusaders abandoned the site. In 1650, the Franciscans returned and built a residence and guest house for pilgrims. A church was built in 1654 to honor St. Peter who visited the city and had his perplexing vision. More destruction came to these structures in the following centuries.

Today, Jaffa's most notable building is the Church of St. Peter, a landmark which towers over the town square and crowns the skyline above the harbor. The church and monastery belongs to the Franciscans, and it commemorates Peter's Vision of the Great Sheet. Dedicated in 1894, St. Peter's was built with funding from Spain in the Latin American Baroque style, and has an impressive brick façade crowned by an imposing bell tower.

The church stands on a site by the seaside formerly occupied by previous buildings, including a Crusader citadel and guest house for pilgrims arriving to the Holy Land. Inside are high vaulted ceilings, marble walls, and stained-glass windows, created in Munich by German artist Franz Xaver Zettler. Panels depict major episodes from the life of St. Peter: the Miraculous Catch of Fishes; the Giving of the Keys; the Transfiguration of Christ; and the Washing of the Feet at the Last Supper. A wooden pulpit is carved in the form of a fruiting tree, and above the altar a depiction of Peter's Vision of the Great Sheet. There are also depictions of Tabitha, St. Francis of Assisi and the Immaculate Conception. The rest of the stained-glass windows feature an array of Spanish saints, in keeping with the fact that the Spanish royal family was the donor for the construction of the church.

CAESAREA
Caesarea in the Scriptures

The seaport city of Caesarea (Maritima), the administrative capital of Roman Palestine for nearly 600 years, witnessed some of the most important moments of the Church's earliest evangelization reported in the Acts of the Apostles. In this city, Peter baptized the first Gentile converts, Cornelius and his family. Here Philip the evangelist made his home and hosted Paul when the Apostle to the Gentiles passed through on his missionary journeys. Here Paul was imprisoned by authorities for two years before being transferred to Rome to stand in judgment before the emperor.

The apostles were faithful to their commission to *"be my witnesses in Jerusalem and in all Judea and Samaria and to the end of the earth"* (Acts 1:8). Now empowered by the Holy Spirit, they boldly ventured out of Jerusalem to bring the message of the Gospel to the neighboring regions.

After baptizing the Ethiopian eunuch *on the road that goes down from Jerusalem to Gaza*, Philip *preached the gospel to all the towns till he came to Caesarea* (Acts 8:26, 40).

Shortly after Paul was baptized in Damascus, he escaped a plan by the Jews of the city to kill him. He made his way to Jerusalem where *he attempted to join the disciples,* but they were afraid of him. While in Jerusalem, Paul preached *boldly in the name of Jesus* and aroused the anger of the Hellenists, who sought to kill him. So the brethren *brought him down to Caesarea and sent him off to Tarsus* (Acts 9:26, 29-30).

At Caesarea there was a man named Cornelius, a centurion of what was known as the Italian Cohort, a devout man who feared God with all his household, gave alms liberally to the people, and prayed constantly to God. It is important to note that Cornelius was a prominent Roman citizen, one of the best known and respected men of the region. Cornelius saw a vision of an angel of God instructing him to send men to fetch Peter, who was staying in Jaffa. Shortly before the arrival of the soldier and two servants sent by Cornelius, Peter had seen a vision of a canvas being lowered from the sky with *all kinds of animals and reptiles and birds of the air* placed on the canvas. And a voice came to him *"Rise, Peter, kill and eat."* But Peter said, *"No, Lord: for I have never eaten anything that is common or unclean."* The voice spoke to him again: *"What God has cleansed you must not call common."* *This happened three times, and the thing was taken up at once to heaven* (Acts 10:1-16).

Now Peter was inwardly perplexed as to what the vision which he had seen might mean when the Spirit instructed him to accompany the men sent by Cornelius to Caesarea. Peter entered Cornelius' house and began to tell him and all his household about the life and mission of Jesus Christ. *While Peter was still saying this, the Holy Spirit fell on all who heard the word.* Peter, and the circumcised believers who accompanied him from Jaffa, were amazed that *the gift of the Holy Spirit had been poured out even on the Gentiles.* Now, Peter could interpret the vision he had earlier: The life-giving grace of the Gospel was now being offered to the Gentiles. Peter went up to Jerusalem and explained to the circumcision party consisting of Jews who had accepted Jesus as the Messiah about what he had experienced. Their response was, *"Then to the Gentiles also God has granted repentance unto life"* (Acts 10:17-48; 11:1-18). These events, spurred by Peter's Vision of the Sheet (Canvas), mark an important turning point in the spread of Christianity. The Gospel message will now be brought to the Gentile world, opening new horizons to the new faith.

After King Herod had James, the brother of John, killed by the sword, he saw that this slaying of one of the three inner circle friends of Jesus, pleased the Jews. This James was the first of the twelve apostles to die by martyrdom. So Herod ordered the arrest of Peter. An angel sent by the Lord helped Peter to escape from the jail. Knowing that Herod was seeking him, Peter *went down from Judea to Caesarea, and remained there* (Acts 12:1-19).

Paul passed through Caesarea on his way up to Jerusalem toward the end of his second missionary journey (see Acts 18:22). Paul's third missionary journey ended in Caesarea, where he entered the house of *Philip the evangelist, who was one of the seven, and stayed with him.* A prophet named Agabus had come from Jerusalem to warn Paul not to go up to Jerusalem. But Paul could not be dissuaded: *"For I am ready not only to be imprisoned but even to die at Jerusalem for the name of the Lord Jesus"* (Acts 21:8-13).Paul's preaching in Jerusalem provoked anger among the Jews, who then made plans to kill him. The tribune Claudius Lysias decided to bring Paul to Caesarea for his own safety. Later, he was brought before the Roman governor Felix, who commanded that he be guarded in Herod's praetorium. After two years, Felix was replaced as governor by Porcius Festus. Paul was brought before Festus for questioning and to hear the charges against him by the Jews, who were still plotting to murder him. Festus was convinced of Paul's innocence but was disposed to turn him over to the Jews, which Paul knew would mean death. As a Roman citizen, Paul had the right to have his case heard by the emperor, a right to appeal that Festus had to honor. He declared to Festus: *"I appeal to Caesar."* Festus responded, *"You have appealed to Caesar; to Caesar you shall go."* Paul was then sent to Rome by ship where tradition holds he was later martyred. (Acts 21:17- 27:2)

History

At the height of his power in 29-22 BC, Herod the Great, ruler of the kingdom of Judea, decided to build a magnificent city over the site of an ancient Phoenician port and dedicate it to Augustus Caesar, the Roman emperor. Caesarea Maritima would feature an artificial harbor on the Mediterranean coast in order to strengthen Herod's ties with Rome. The harbor would provide ships the opportunity to transport passengers and goods to and from Herod's territorial kingdom from all across the Mediterranean Sea. The increase in trade and tax revenue would help fund the many ambitious building projects throughout his kingdom, for which he was famous in the ancient world. He chose the location of Strato's Tower, a former Phoenician naval station, for this massive project.

Spearheaded by Roman engineers and architects, the construction of the city and harbor began in 22 BC. The artificial harbor was the largest of its time, enclosing an area of about a third of a square mile. Along with the engineering feat of lowering huge stones 20 fathoms deep, this was the first use of underwater concrete used in this region to construct a break-water so the harbor was protected from the tumultuous waves of the sea.

Modeled on a Roman city, Caesarea Maritima boasted a theater, an amphitheater, wide streets, baths, a market place, and a luxurious palace for Herod on a promontory jutting out into the sea. On a hill overlooking the harbor, Herod erected a temple to honor both the goddess Roma and the Roman emperor, Caesar. At its inauguration in 10 BC, the city was named in honor of his patron, Caesar Augustus.

The splendor of the city was described in great detail by Josephus in his history, *The Jewish War*. He marveled at Herod's achievement, especially the size of the harbor and the ingenuity of the sewer system flushed daily by sea water, calling it a city "on a scale worthy of the name [Caesarea]." Until recent excavations, the lavish description of Josephus had been seen by many scholars as wild exaggeration. Beyond its grandeur, the city eclipsed Jerusalem as the most important civil and military center of Roman Palestine.

In 6 AD, following Rome's dismissal of Herod's son, Archelaus, Caesarea came under direct Roman rule and was named the capital of the province of Judea. Roman procurators likely took up residence in Herod's palace, including Pontius Pilate (26-36 AD). The First Jewish Revolt (66-70 AD) began in the city, triggered in part by the desecration of a synagogue. An earthquake destroyed the harbor in the early second century, but the city continued to flourish.

In the third century, renowned early Church scholar Origen founded his celebrated school of theology here. His famous scholarly work, *Hexapla*, six Hebrew and Greek biblical texts presented in parallel columns, would become the basis for future translations of the Bible. His pupil, Eusebius, bishop of Caesarea from 314 to 340, was one of the most learned Christians of his time. Eusebius was known as the first Church historian and the first biblical geographer. Without his work *Onomasticon*, a compendium of place names in Scripture, many biblical sites in the Holy Land would have never been identified.

Conquered by the Arabs in 640, the city began a long decline in population and wealth. Crusaders took the city in 1101 making some repairs to the city's harbor. Saladin expelled the Crusaders in 1187 and demolished the Crusader fortifications. Occupied once again by the Crusaders in 1228, the work of fortifying the city with defensive walls and a dry moat was completed by King Louis IX of France by 1252.

Even so, Caesarea was not able to withstand the assault in 1265 of Mameluke Sultan Baybars, who levelled the city after its inhabitants managed to escape by sea. Bosnian Muslim refugees were settled on the site in 1878 by the Turkish government. Their abandoned mosque can still be seen today near the harbor.

Caesarea is now one of Israel's major archaeological sites. The picturesque ruins include the walls of the ancient city and, by the harbor, the remnants of the Crusader citadel. Also in the area there are impressive ruins of a Roman hippodrome and aqueduct.

THE DORMITION OF THE BLESSED VIRGIN MARY
History

A brief history of Mount Zion can be found in the Upper Room section of the previous chapter.

In the late nineteenth century, the German Holy Land Association (GHLA) made numerous failed attempts to purchase land near the Last Supper site. The property on Mount Zion the GHLA wanted to acquire was, by tradition, associated with Mary's "falling asleep," formally known as the "Dormition of Mary," from the Latin, *dormitio*, "to fall asleep."

Wilhelm II, the German Kaiser who ruled 1888-1918, came to the aid of the GHLA. He acquired the land for 120,000 Reich marks, which was paid to the Turkish Sultan Abdul Hamid II, and entrusted it to the GHLA and German Benedictines. During his visit to Jerusalem on October 31, 1898, Wilhelm II took possession of the land and granted permission to the GHLA to develop the site.

The Basilica of the Dormition of the Blessed Virgin Mary

Crowned by its stately bell tower and conical roof, the church and abbey of the Dormition is one of the most distinctive landmarks on the Jerusalem skyline. German architect Heinrich Renard, master builder for the Diocese of Cologne, was commissioned to design both the church and monastery. When the neo-Romanesque-style monastery was completed in 1906, Benedictine monks from Beuron, Germany, took up residence.

Renard's design for the basilica followed the layout of the medieval Imperial Chapel in Aachen, one of Germany's oldest chapels and known as the "Royal Church of St. Mary" in the Middle Ages. He also included elements of St. Gereon's in Cologne. These architectural homages were meant to highlight the two birth places of the GHLA.

The Church of the Dormition was consecrated by the Latin Patriarch on April 10, 1910. Ownership of the land was transferred in 1924 to the GHLA, whose president is also the archbishop of Cologne.

The sculpture of a bronze pine cone at the entrance symbolizes the Resurrection. The lofty, spacious circular hall in the upper part of the church is often used for concerts. Above the main altar, the apse is dominated by a golden mosaic of Mary cradling the Christ child, who holds a book open to the words (in Greek) *"I am the light of the world"* (Jn 8:12). Just below Mary and Jesus are the words (in Latin) of the Prophet Isaiah: *Behold a virgin shall conceive and bear a son, and shall call his name Emmanuel* (Is 7:14). Below are depictions of the eight prophets who foretold the coming of the Messiah: Micah, Isaiah, Jeremiah, Ezekiel, Daniel, Haggai, Zechariah and Malachi.

The hall's floor mosaic dating from 1932 was designed by Fr. Mauritius Gisler, a monk of the Dormition Abbey. Its pattern of concentric circles represents the spreading of the Word through time and space. In the center are three intertwined gold rings with the words, "Holy, Holy, Holy," in Greek, symbolizing the Holy Trinity. Radiating out from the Holy Trinity are its wisdom and love through the ages, revealed through the writings of the four major prophets, and, the ten minor prophets, followed by the four evangelists, the twelve apostles, and, finally, into all the cosmos, symbolized by the signs of the zodiac.

Stairs lead down to the crypt chapel where a recumbent effigy of the Virgin Mary, carved from ivory and cherry wood, is lying in repose. The cupola above is adorned with a mosaic depicting Christ with open arms welcoming his Mother's soul into heaven and surrounded by images of prominent women of the Old Testament: Eve, Miriam, Yael, Judith, Ruth, and Ester. Above the side altar is an icon painting of the Dormition of Mary, depicted in the eastern Orthodox tradition. She lies on her death bed with the apostles gathered around her. Above her, Jesus takes her soul into heaven. Mary's soul is depicted as a small girl wrapped in a white shroud. The column, nearly three feet in diameter, supporting the altar comes from one of the early churches on Mount Zion, and bears the words: "Mater omnium ecclesiarum," Latin for "Mother of all churches." It was on Mount Zion on the day of Pentecost that the Church was born.

THE TOMB OF MARY
Assumption of the Blessed Virgin Mary

The New Testament says nothing about the death of Mary. According to both Catholic and Orthodox teachings, Mary was taken up by God, body and soul. This was a tradition held by ancient Christians, although not defined by the Catholic Church as dogma until 1950.

When Mary said to the angel Gabriel, *"Behold, I am the handmaid of the Lord; let it be to me according to your word,"* God's plan for the salvation of the world was set in motion. Later, in Bethlehem, Mary gave birth to Jesus in a humble cave on the outskirts of the city. In Cana, she prompted her Son to begin his public ministry. She was near him during

The Repose of the Virgin Mary, Theophanes the Greek (1392)

his Passion, even witnessing his Crucifixion, which fulfilled Simeon's prophecy, *"and a sword will pierce through your own soul"* (Lk 2:35). Jesus' Resurrection brought his divine mission to its perfect victory. Though subject to him, Mary was closely associated with her Son in his mission to conquer sin and death. Mary's participation in her Son's struggle against the enemy would end with the glorification of her virginal body.

St. John Damascene (676-749) eloquently summarizes the early Church's beliefs regarding Mary's glorification:

"It was necessary that she who had preserved her virginity inviolate in childbirth should also have her body kept free from all corruption after death. It was necessary that she who had carried the Creator as a child on her breast should dwell in the tabernacles of God. It was necessary that the bride espoused by the Father should make her home in the bridal chambers of heaven. It was necessary that she, who had gazed on her crucified Son and been pierced in the heart by the sword of sorrow which she had escaped in giving him birth, should contemplate him seated with the Father. It was necessary that the Mother of God should be venerated by every creature as the Mother and handmaid of God."

The glorification of Mary meant that her virginal body was kept free from all corruption following her Dormition, or "falling asleep." The Catholic Church has not taken a position on whether or not Mary died.

In one early apocryphal text of Mary's Dormition, the apostles are instructed by the Holy Spirit to carry her body to a rock-cut burial cave in the Kidron Valley (*Transitus Mariae*, an anonymous work whose origin dates to the second or third century). It is not known how long her body lay in the tomb before it was brought to heaven. Another apocryphal account states that her body lay in the tomb for three days (*Dormitio Virginis*). Typical artistic representations of Mary's Assumption show the apostles gathered around her tomb, some looking at her glorified body as it is assumed into heaven, while some looking at her empty tomb.

Both the eastern and the western Churches have upheld Mary's Assumption as an article of faith from the dawn of the Christian era. On November 1, 1950, Pope Pius XII proclaimed it a formal dogma of the Catholic Church:

"Hence, the august Mother of God, mysteriously united from all eternity with Jesus Christ in one and the same decree of predestination, immaculate in her conception, a virgin inviolate in her divine motherhood, the whole-hearted companion of the divine Redeemer who won complete victory over sin and its consequences, gained at last the supreme crown of her privileges – to be preserved immune from the corruption of the tomb, and, like her Son, when death had been conquered, to be carried up body and soul to the exalted glory of heaven, there to sit in splendor at the right hand of her Son, the immortal King of the ages" (From the apostolic constitution Munificentissimus Deus).

"All that concerns Mary concerns the Church in general," affirms St. Bernard of Clairvaux (1091-1153) often called the Marian Doctor of the Church, "God has wanted that we obtain nothing if not thorough the hands of Mary... With her for guide, you shall not go astray. While invoking her, you shall never lose heart."

History

It is known from the historical record that Christians, probably Judeo-Christians, had made Mary's tomb a place of veneration and a place of pilgrimage as early as the second century. Writers in the sixth century attest to the presence of a church situated above the tomb. It may have been built by the Patriarch Juvenal (422-458). The crypt area beneath the church was developed at this time as well.

The bedrock around the tomb of Mary was removed to make easy access to her tomb as a shrine for pilgrims. The fifth-century church was probably destroyed by the Persians in 614. By 670, it was rebuilt as Gallic pilgrim Arculf reports "a church built at two levels, and the lower part, which is beneath a stone vault, has a remarkable round shape." The widespread destruction of churches ordered by Caliph al-Hakim in 1009 left the site in ruins.

During the Crusader period, Benedictines rebuilt the church and also constructed an abbey next door. A marble edicule was constructed over the tomb, as well as a monumental stairway at the entrance, which was adorned with an ornate façade.

When the Crusaders left Jerusalem in 1187, the upper church was destroyed while the crypt church remained intact. The crypt church, where the Tomb of Mary is located, may have been spared because the Mother of Jesus is venerated in Islam. She is the only woman mentioned by name in the Muslims' holy book, the Koran. In fact, Mary is mentioned more in the Koran than in the New Testament. The site is holy to Muslims because, according to the teachings of Islam, Mohammed saw a light over the tomb of his "sister Mary" on his night journey to Jerusalem.

Franciscans acquired the site around 1363 but were forced out in 1757, when the Turkish sultan, under pressure from various Christian churches and governments, established a realignment of liturgical and property rights among the traditional Christian churches (Greek, Franciscan [Latin], Armenian, Coptic, Syriac and Ethiopian) in the Holy Land. This arrangement came to be known as the *status quo*, Latin for "state in which" or more plainly "the existing state of affairs."

Today, the shrine is shared by the Greeks and Armenians, with minor rights granted to the Coptic and Syriac communities.

The Tomb of Mary

Inside the Crusader-era façade, forty-seven steps lead down the monumental stairway to the crypt chapel in a deep underground chamber. About half way down the steps on the right, there is a chapel named in honor of St. Joachim and St. Ann, the parents of Mary. Behind the altar is the tomb of Queen Melisande (d. 1161), wife of Crusader King Fulk of Anjou and daughter of King Baldwin II. On the opposite side is another chapel, dedicated to St. Joseph. Here, Queen Mary, wife of King Baldwin III is buried. By tradition, Crusader queens were buried in the crypt of Mary's tomb and the Crusader kings who ruled Jerusalem were buried near Calvary in the Basilica of the Holy Sepulcher.

Near the bottom of the steps, the architectural style changes from the pointed arches of the Crusaders to the round vaults of the Byzantine era. The crypt is in part constructed with dressed stones while the remainder has been cut from the natural stone. On the left sits an Armenian chapel.

The alcove straight ahead, in the Crusader period, had a stairway leading to the Benedictine abbey, now filled in with masonry. On the right is the small edicule enclosing where tradition holds is the Tomb of Mary. The Armenian icon on the left above the entrance to the Tomb depicts the Dormition, or Mary lying in repose on her deathbed. The Armenian oil painting in the center shows the Assumption of Mary, and the Greek icon on the right is another depiction of the Dormition of Mary. Inside the edicule, the rock-cut bed where Mary was laid to rest can be seen behind glass panels.

Our journey in the footsteps of Jesus ends here before the empty tomb of his Mother. Mary's Assumption is a singular participation in her Son's Resurrection. She now waits in anticipation of the resurrection of all Christians who are faithful in living the Gospel message. Mary, Mother of the Church, pray for us.

Important Dates in the History of the Holy Land

18th century BC	Abraham settles in the land of Canaan.
13th century BC	Exodus from Egypt.
1000 BC	David captures Jerusalem.
960-928 BC	Solomon's reign and the construction of the first Temple.
928 BC	Death of Solomon and the split of the kingdom into the northern kingdom of Israel and the southern kingdom of Judah.
722 BC	Fall of the northern kingdom of Israel to the Assyrians. Inhabitants are assimilated into the Assyrian empire. Ten lost tribes of Israel.
586 BC	Fall of the southern kingdom of Judah to the Babylonians. Inhabitants are sent into exile to Babylon.
538 BC	Persian king, Cyrus, allows the Judeans to return to Jerusalem.
516 BC	Second Temple is built under the governorship of Zerubbabel.
332 BC	Alexander the Great conquers the Holy Land.
301-152 BC	Alexanders successors, the Ptolomies and the Seleucids, rule the Holy Land.
168 BC	Maccabean family organizes a rebellion against Seleucid rule.
165 BC	Temple Mount is captured from the Seleucids and the Temple is rededicated.
152-63 BC	Hasmoneans (Maccabean family) rule the Holy Land.
63 BC	The Holy Land comes under Roman rule after the capture of Jerusalem by Pompey.
40 BC	Roman senate appoints Herod the Great king of Judea.
20 BC	Herod rebuilds the Temple expanding the esplanade surrounding the Temple.
6 AD	Archelaus is deposed and Judea becomes a Roman province.
26	Pontius Pilate is appointed procurator of Judea.
27-30	Public ministry of Jesus.
66-73	First Jewish War against Rome.

132-135	Bar Kochba Revolt against Rome.
135	Emperor Hadrian rebuilds Jerusalem and changes name to Aelia Capitolina.
313	Emperor Constantine issues Edict of Milan granting Christianity a legal status.
335	Dedication of the Basilica of the Resurrection (Anastasis).
527-565	Reign of Emperor Justinian (he restored the Basilica of the Nativity).
614	Chosroes II's Persian army conquers the Holy Land resulting in the widespread destruction of churches.
638	Caliph Omar's Islamic army captures Jerusalem.
1009	Fatimid Caliph al-Hakim orders the destruction of churches, including the Basilica of the Resurrection.
1099	Crusaders capture Jerusalem and establish the Kingdom of Jerusalem.
1149	Dedication of the Crusader Church of the Holy Sepulcher.
1187	Saladin takes Jerusalem from the Crusaders.
1517-1917	Ottoman Turkish rule of the Holy Land.
1520-1566	Reign of Suleiman the Magnificent. He builds the walls of Jerusalem that can be seen today.
1917	The British take possession of Jerusalem.
1947	U.N. partitions British-mandated Palestine into a Jewish and an Arab state. Arabs reject the plan.
1948	State of Israel is established. Jerusalem is divided between Israel and Jordan. Jordan occupies the West Bank.
1967	Six Day War. Jerusalem is reunited. Jordan loses the West Bank to Israel.
1973	Yom Kippur War.
1993	Oslo Accords are signed by Israel and the Palestine Liberation Organization creating the Palestinian Authority.

Epilogue
Reflections to Carry Home

Our pilgrimage together is finished, but we can continue the journey we started in the Holy Land for the rest of our lives. Following in the footsteps of our Savior gave us many new insights, and hopefully, granted to us a firmer grasp and stronger love of our faith.

The Word of God can take on a deeper meaning for us now that we have seen the land where that Divine Word was revealed, the land where God revealed to his people the mysteries of his love. We can have a more in-depth perspective on the Gospel stories now that we have visited the settings where they happened.

And we've also been privileged to see firsthand how the Holy Land draws pilgrims from around the world. We have seen our fellow pilgrims from Russia and Nigeria and Italy and Argentina and Korea and Spain and Brazil. They have enlarged our concept of what the Church as the mystical Body of Christ really is and crystallized for us the universality of our Christian faith.

Like us, these pilgrims did not come here for touristic reasons, but for spiritual reasons. They came to learn more about their faith, which shows that they dearly value their faith, just as we value our faith, as a precious gift from God. As pilgrims, we have had the wonderful opportunity to nourish that faith in a special way.

It has been my privilege and pleasure to accompany you and to serve you on this journey of faith in the Holy Land. Know that you are in my prayers every day and in the prayers of the Franciscans who operate and care for the shrines here. We pray for the pilgrims daily. As custodians of the Holy Land shrines, we are here to help you on your journey of faith.

Who knows, maybe someday you will come back, or if not yourself, maybe your children or grandchildren. You may have started a family tradition that will bear spiritual fruit for generations to come.

Acknowledgements

I would like to give my sincere thanks to my brothers in our Holy Land province of Franciscans and former pilgrims who've kindly, and patiently, encouraged me to bring this project to completion. The book could not have been completed without your support and enthusiasm.

Special thanks go to Eddie Dean whose invaluable service as editor and contributor was instrumental in producing this book.

I would also like to express my deepest gratitude to my late parents, Melvin and Eleanor Wathen, for grounding me in the Catholic faith and anchoring that faith with their undying love.

The Author

Fr. David Wathen, OFM, is a member of a Franciscan community known as The Custody of Holy Land. This community of Franciscans serve as caretakers of most of the Christian shrines in the Holy Land.

Fr. Wathen has been guiding group pilgrimages to the Holy Land since 1990. For nine years he lived in the Holy Land (Bethlehem, Jerusalem and Tiberias) while guiding groups from many different English-speaking countries.

He is currently the Director of the Franciscan Monastery Pilgrimage Office located at the Franciscan Monastery of the Holy Land in Washington, D.C.

Image Credits

The publisher gratefully acknowledges the cooperation of those who provided works of art and photography which has been used to illustrate this book. Following is a list of the artwork and its location.

Cover, Path to Emmaus, Fritz von Uhde 1891, SKD Museum Germany

18, Goya Annunciation, Francisco Goya, Museum of Fine Art, Boston

21, Annunciation, Henry Ossawa Tanner (1898), Philadelphia Museum of Art: Purchased with the W. P. Wilstach Fund, 1899, W1899-1-1

29, The Grotto of the Annunciation, photo by the author

33, St. Jerome, painting by El Greco, The Met

34, St. Louis of France, Wexford Friary Window, Ireland

35, Mark Twain

36, The Visitation, Philippe de Champagne, Princeton Univ. Art Museum

40, The Visitation, Miguel Cabrera (18th century) Arocena Museum

42, Birth of St. John the Baptist, Luca Giordano www.hermitagemuseum.org, courtesy of The State Hermitage Museum, St. Petersburg, Russia

48, The birth place of St. John the Baptis, photo by the author

51, Portrait of Antonio Barluzzi

52, Nativity of Jesus, Sandro Botticelli (1473-1475) Columbia Museum of Art

57, The Adoration of the Magi, Giuseppe Bartolomeo Chiari (1654-1727)

65, The birthplace of Jesus, photo by the author

69, Annunciation to the Shepherds, The Master of the Houghton Miniatures (1470) Getty Museum

70, The Baptism of Christ, Francesco Albani, courtesy of The State Hermitage Museum, St. Petersburg, Russia

73, Joshua Passing the River Jordan with the Ark of the Covenant, Benjamin West (1800) The Art Gallery of New South Wales

76, The Baptism of Christ in the Jordan River, Karoly Marko (1840-1841) Hungarian National Gallery

78, The site of the baptism of Jesus, photo by the author

86, St. Mary of Egypt, Jusepe de Ribera (1651) Filangieri Museum, Italy

87, Battle of Cresson, Sebastien Mamerot, miniature redo by Jean Colombe 1474 French National Library

88, St. Peter Attempting to Walk on Water by François Boucher (1766) Versailles Cathedral collection

91, Jesus walking on the Sea of Galilee (1590s), Museum of John Paul II Collection

Index

A Pilgrim's Spiritual Handbook to the Holy Land by DAVID WATHEN, OFM, was designed and typeset using Adobe Indesign. The pages are set in Adobe Garamond Pro and Gill Sans Nova.
Cover painting is a 66x90 cm pastel on paper by German painter Fritz von Uhde painted in 1891 titled *Path to Emmaus*. Special gratitude to The Staatliche Kunstsammlungen Dresden (SKD) museum complex for their kind permission.

In spirituality lighthouses represent guidance, refuge and safety. The recognizable logo of Medinger Media Press signals readers that they are encountering a special book by a very special author. We have been delighted that David Wathen, OFM, entrusted us with the opportunity of producing this historic book for pilgrims to the Holy Land. His life's work of bringing to life the "Fifth Gospel" to those who are blessed to walk in the footsteps of Jesus or those who can only go there vicariously through this book is a cause for celebration and rejoicing. Medinger Media is proud to make this work available to readers today and in the future. To learn more about us, please check our website at ampsinc.net